ADVANCED CLINICAL SOCIAL WORK PRACTICE

ADVANCED CLINICAL SOCIAL WORK PRACTICE

RELATIONAL PRINCIPLES AND TECHNIQUES

Eda G. Goldstein, Dennis Miehls, and Shoshana Ringel

COLUMBIA UNIVERSITY PRESS   NEW YORK

KH

COLUMBIA UNIVERSITY PRESS
Publishers Since 1893
New York   Chichester, West Sussex
Copyright © 2009 Columbia University Press
All rights reserved

Library of Congress Cataloging-in-Publication Data
Goldstein, Eda G.
Advanced clinical social work practice : relational principles and techniques /
Eda G. Goldstein, Dennis Miehls, Shoshana Ringel.
p. cm.
Includes bibliographical references and index.
ISBN 978-0-231-14318-9 (cloth : alk. paper) — ISBN 978-0-231-14319-6 (pbk. : alk. paper) —
ISBN 978-0-231-52044-7 (ebook)
1. Social service. 2. Social case work.   I. Miehls, Dennis. II. Ringel, Shoshana. III. Title.

HV43.G593   2009
361.3'2—dc22   2009001577

Columbia University Press books are printed on permanent and durable acid-free paper.
This book is printed on paper with recycled content.
Printed in the United States of America

c 10 9 8 7 6 5 4 3 2 1
p 10 9 8 7 6 5 4 3 2 1

References to Internet Web sites (URLs) were accurate at the time of writing. Neither the author
nor Columbia University Press is responsible for URLs that may have expired or changed since
the manuscript was prepared.

2/9/10

CONTENTS

Acknowledgments   vii

Introduction   xi

1. The Relational Core of Social Work Practice   1
2. Theoretical and Clinical Contributions: Phase 1   18
3. Theoretical and Clinical Contributions: Phase 2   37
4. Developmental Concepts   54
5. Assessment in Relational Treatment   79
6. Components of Relational Treatment   106
7. Transference and Countertransference: Disruptions
   and Enactments   131
8. Multicultural Issues   148
9. Relational Principles in Brief Treatment   164
10. Couple, Family, and Group Treatment   180
11. The Teaching and Learning Process: In the Classroom
    and Supervision   193

Epilogue   205
References   209
Index   227

ACKNOWLEDGMENTS

Our interest in writing a book about the contributions of relational theories to clinical social work practice grew out of our experiences as clinicians, teachers, and supervisors. We wanted to synthesize the concepts we have found useful in recent years and to show their application to clinical practice with a range of individuals and problems. We appreciate the many clients, students, and supervisees who have shared their struggles with us and from whom we have learned a great deal in the process of our work together.

Another major impetus to our taking on this challenging project was our leadership (Eda G. Goldstein as cochair with Dr. David Phillips) and participation (Dennis Miehls and Shoshana Ringel as members) in the National Study Group of the American Association for Psychoanalysis in Clinical Social Work (AAPCSW, formerly the National Committee on Psychoanalysis in Clinical Social Work) from 2005 to 2008. The professional colleagues who made up the Study Group joined our commitment to providing social work students, classroom instructors, fieldwork supervisors, and other practitioners with a book that encompassed the full range of psychoanalytic relational thinking and its use in today's practice arenas. We thank Marsha Wineburgh, past president of AAPCSW, who supported our efforts, and our colleagues in the Study Group, who encouraged us and contributed their thinking as we developed our ideas.

Writing this book has been a rewarding collaboration. The three authors, who reside in different geographic areas, had not worked together previously. When we began the writing, we did not know how intellectually stimulating and smooth the writing task would be. We believe that the book is much richer than it would have been had each of us written on his or her own. Our collaboration has been enjoyable and lightened the load. Although the three of us had some role in all the chapters, each of us took the major responsibility for certain chapters (Eda G. Goldstein for the introduction and chapters 1, 5, 6, and 7; Dennis Miehls for chapters 2, 9, 10, and 11 and the epilogue; and Shoshana Ringel for chapters 3, 4, and 8, with some assistance from Eda G. Goldstein on chapter 4). Likewise, while all of us contributed case examples in our respective chapters, Dennis Miehls provided numerous case vignettes for chapters 6 and 7.

We thank Lauren Dockett, executive editor of Columbia University Press, for her enthusiasm and valuable assistance in shepherding this volume through all phases of the publication process.

Numerous family members, friends, and colleagues were particularly supportive during the writing. Individually, we are grateful to the following people:

Eda G. Goldstein—I am fortunate to have been associated with New York University's Silver School of Social Work, which has played a vital role in clinical social work education over many years. My colleagues on the social work practice faculty have been an important source of encouragement, and their ongoing dedication to educating students in contemporary psychodynamic theories and practice principles has provided a supportive environment. I am especially thankful for the unwavering support of my partner, Patricia A. Petrocelli, who had to endure my considerable involvement in writing. I am also grateful to the many friends who showed an interest in what I was doing.

Dennis Miehls—I acknowledge my colleagues at Smith College's School for Social Work for continuing to uphold the highest standards in clinical social work education in our master's and doctoral programs. Many colleagues offer support and enthusiasm for my writing projects. I am indebted to the Smith College School for Social Work resident faculty and to a number of adjunct faculty who offer ongoing stimulating dialogues about curriculum content that enrich my thinking. I appreciate the support of Dr. Carolyn Jacobs, dean of Smith College's School for Social Work, who authorized on behalf of the college a sabbatical leave that helped me concentrate on writing. My success in this project and others is largely attributable to my partner, Beth, who is a steady and loving anchor as I complete many professional activities. I also attribute my success to my son James and his partner Alison, who offer support and listen at exactly the right time.

Shoshana Ringel—I would like to acknowledge the University of Maryland School of Social Work for their appreciation of my clinical contributions and for granting me tenure. I also thank Roy for his patience, loyalty, and unconditional support, and my students Rebecca Green, Jessica Myers, John Laur, Miko Masterson, and Jesse Callan for their contribution of valuable clinical material.

INTRODUCTION

This book is about relational theories and their application to clinical social work practice. After tracing the relational thrust of social work practice throughout the profession's history, it will review the writings of major psychoanalytic theorists who have contributed to the relational perspective. Following a description of the key developmental concepts that comprise relational theory today, the book will consider and illustrate the main components of treatment based on relational ideas. It will show their utility in work with a wide range of clients, including those from diverse cultural backgrounds. It also will consider the use of relational theory in short-term treatment and in work with families and groups. It will conclude with a discussion of some of the issues that arise in practicing and learning a relational approach in the classroom and in supervision.

RELATIONAL THEORY DEFINED

In this book we use the term "relational" to encompass numerous distinctive theories that are not well integrated. "Relational psychoanalysts share overlapping but not identical concerns, concepts, approaches, and sensibilities" (Aron and Harris 2005:xiii). Early relational thinking tended to focus on what infants bring to their environmental transactions, on the optimal characteristics of the care-taking environment, and how it nurtures the individual. Later and more contemporary contributions emphasize mutuality and interaction in the relationship between the self and others. Nevertheless, the different frameworks that fall within this rubric have certain commonalities. These frameworks

- recognize that human beings are social animals and emphasize the impact of interpersonal relationships and the social and cultural context on child and adult development
- place importance on creating a human therapeutic environment and tend to view the therapeutic relationship as central to the treatment process, emphasizing the experiential, reparative, and facilitating aspects of the relationship between clinician and client
- underscore the importance of the clinician's empathic attunement to the client's subjective experience and personal narrative. They stress the importance of clinicians putting themselves in the client's shoes and being where the client is, the nature of the collaborative dialogue between client and clinician, and the mutual impact that client and clinician exert on one another during the treatment process
- tend to focus on the here-and-now and how the past becomes alive in the present
- give a prominent role to the impact of gender, racial, cultural, and other major types of diversity on human behavior and in the clinical situation and the process by which clinician and client come to understand one another
- recognize the strengths and resilience of people and their push for growth as well as what goes wrong in the course of development
- offer new perspectives on major concepts such as transference, countertransference, and resistance, as well as on the nature of the therapeutic dialogue

The principles that stem from relational theories can be applied to a multitude of problems. These include life crises and transitions, the effects of physical and sexual abuse and other types of trauma, emotional disorders, substance abuse, physical illness, disability, loss of loved ones, violence, parenting and family problems, and work issues. They have implications not only for individual long-term treatment but also for crisis and short-term intervention and work with couples, families, and groups. Because of their incorporation of contemporary views on gender, culture, race, and sexual identity, relational theories are well suited to work with diverse populations.

In this book we have chosen to include the relational theories and research that have been put forth mainly by psychoanalysts and that reflect psychodynamic thinking. Berzoff, Flanagan, and Hertz (1996) point out that the psychoanalytic and psychodynamic terms, although sometimes used interchangeably, are different. We agree with their view that "psychodynamic" refers to a broad range of theory that reflects a way of thinking about the mind, whereas "psychoanalytic" connotes a more specific theoretical perspective that comprises definite criteria (4–5). These authors acknowledge, however, that the distinction is more difficult to make currently, particularly as numerous psychoanalytic theories have been put forth and have moved far beyond classical Freudian theory and ego psychology.

As chapters 2 and 3 discuss in detail, the evolution of relational theories within psychoanalysis took place in two phases. In the first phase, numerous psychoanalysts attempted to offer alternatives to or expanded Freud's drive-conflict model (Greenberg and Mitchell 1983). It included theorists such as John Bowlby (1988), W.R.D. Fairbairn (1952), Sandor Ferenczi (1932, 1933), Harry S. Guntrip (1969), Karen Horney (1945), Edith Jacobson (1964), Melanie Klein (1932), Heinz Kohut (1971, 1977), Jean Baker Miller and her colleagues at the Stone Center for Developmental Services and Studies in Wellesley, Massachusetts (Miller 1977; Jordan 1997; Kaplan and Surrey 1984); Otto Rank (1928, 1945), Renee Spitz (1945), Harry Stack Sullivan (1953, 1954), and Donald W. Winnicott (1965, 1975).

In the second phase of the development of relational thought, a different group of writers who also rejected Freudian theory and ego psychology attempted to correct what they considered to be the fallacy inherent in earlier relational formulations. The theorists that comprise this group of writers included Lewis Aron (1990, 1991, 1996), Peter Fonagy (2001), Irwin Hoffman (1983), Stephen Mitchell (1988, 1993, 2000), Robert Stolorow and his colleagues Bernard Brandchaft and George Atwood (1994), and many others. These authors argued that the earlier relational frameworks suffer from being one-person psychologies (Aron 1990). Instead, they urged the adoption of a two-person psychology that regards all behavior as determined by a relational or intersubjective field in which self and others are connected and exert a mutual impact on one another. In their view, such a two-person psychology attempts to overcome the separation between a person and others and between past and present. A cornerstone of a two-person psychology is the idea that people cannot be understood in isolation from the interpersonal, social, and cultural context in which they are embedded in the present, although past experience is active in contributing to current behavior. This belief also is important in understanding what occurs in treatment as clinician and client come together and form a relational matrix that shapes the therapeutic process.

Two additional features of the second phase in relational thinking are the incorporation of attachment and other infant research (Ainsworth 1973, 1982; Beebe and Lachmann 1988a, 1988b; Bowlby 1969, 1973; Stern 1985, 1989) and postmodern constructivist ideas about feminism, gender, culture, and race (Benjamin 1988, 1990; Dimen 1991; Dimen and Goldner 2002; Harris 1991; Suchet 2004).

THE RELATIONAL CORE OF SOCIAL WORK PRACTICE

Relational thinking is not new to social work. Chapter 1 shows how social work practice has been relational at its core over the years, even in the period prior to the profession's inception. In addition to being influenced by relational thinking, social workers anticipated many of the theoretical and clinical emphases of recent years, although they are rarely, if ever, given credit for their views by other mental health disciplines (Sheppard 2001). In commenting on this irony, Horowitz wrote, "Like Moliere's Bourgeois Gentlemen who didn't realize that he'd been speaking prose for more than forty years without knowing it, perhaps social workers should consider that we've been relational, postmodern, and cutting-edge for eighty years without knowing it" (1998:378).

SIGNIFICANCE FOR CLINICAL SOCIAL WORK

Perhaps an important reason for the increasing popularity of relational thinking among social work clinicians is that it is in keeping with core social work values and provides a theoretical rationale for many of the tried and true principles that have been characteristic of clinical social work practice over time. Relational theories are holistic frameworks that are consistent with the humanistic stance and values of the social work profession. They value the inherent worth of the human being, the uniqueness of the individual, beginning where the client is, the centrality of the client-worker relationship in the helping process, and the importance of genuineness and mutuality

(Chenot 1998). They embody a person-environmental focus of the social work profession and fit well with the existing body of clinical social work theory and practice. Although the application of relational theories to clinical social work involves advocacy of some practices that are familiar to social workers, such theories provide a rationale for these practices, give them new significance, put them in a different perspective, and extend them in important ways (Ornstein and Ganzer 1997).

IMPETUS FOR THE BOOK

There are several reasons for our choosing to write about the contributions of relational theories to clinical social work. Despite the growing interest in relational thought and the many books on this subject, there are few social work texts that integrate relational theories and show their treatment implications for clinical social work practice. Those volumes that do contain relational content tend to be written by psychoanalysts who come from the fields of psychiatry or psychology, are aimed at those who practice psychoanalytic psychotherapy, and usually address a particular relational theory rather than present an integrative perspective. More significantly, they do not contain case examples with social work populations or reflect the broad range of social work practice. Nor do they consider the empirical evidence for relational ideas and interventions. Yet the majority of social work students want to do clinical work, and both students and practitioners are eager to learn about relational theories and their treatment implications, as is evidenced by the popularity of courses that do offer this content both inside and outside schools of social work.

A second impetus for writing this book stems from our long-standing interest in demonstrating the applicability of the major concepts and treatment principles of contemporary psychoanalytic and psychodynamic theories to clinical social work practice and from our experiences in using relational thinking in our work with clients and students. Employing these frameworks has expanded our ability to understand and relate to a wide range of clients and has produced fundamental changes in the ways in which we listen, what we observe, where we focus, and how we use ourselves in the treatment process. We cannot imagine working without drawing on these perspectives and believe that a knowledge of these frameworks and will help other social work practitioners.

Finally, we are concerned and troubled about the trends that exist in our current academic and practice environments. In contrast to earlier times, currently there is little, if any, curriculum space allocated to the teaching of contemporary psychodynamic theories and their application, and there are a diminishing number of full time faculty who have expertise in this knowledge base. Consequently, students graduate without acquiring even basic understanding of this body of thought. Upon graduation, many social workers take courses in psychodynamically oriented training institutes, but they are taught by members of other disciplines who generally are not conversant or identified with the nature of social work practice and with the types of clients that social workers generally see in agency practice. Many social work graduates begin to feel alienated from and lose their identification with the social work profession. In the practice arena, the health and mental health care systems, constrained by managed care, put less value on relationship-based therapeutic approaches and tend to emphasize cognitive/behavioral approaches. This climate has created a sense of urgency about articulating the contributions of dynamic thinking for future generations of social work clinicians.

Although there is an important place in the clinical social worker's armamentarium for cognitive/behavioral techniques and other evidence-based practice interventions, we believe it is crucial for clinical social workers to operate with a more dynamic understanding of relational principles. Those engaged in clinical or direct practice must be able to make sophisticated assessments, exercise professional judgment, select appropriate interventions, and employ a high level of skill. We want them to be able to assess clients' person-in-situation totality and to plan and implement interventions according to clients' unique needs, problems, life circumstances, and backgrounds in ways that do justice to the complexity of their lives.

PLAN FOR THE BOOK

This book is intended primarily as a guide for clinical social work trainees, practitioners, supervisors, and instructors, and secondarily for individuals from other fields who are interested in learning about relational theories and their use in clinical practice. All of the authors currently are social work faculty, widely published, engaged in clinical practice, and members of the Association for the Advancement of Psychoanalysis in Clinical Social Work. We have provided numerous case examples that illustrate major concepts and treatment process. The clinical material is based on our practice, teaching, and supervision. To protect confidentiality and to present relevant material, the case examples have been disguised and edited and sometimes reflect composite cases.

The plan of the book is as follows:

Chapter 1 discusses the close connection and fit between relational thinking and clinical social work practice. It shows how diverse social work practice models have included many relational principles and techniques throughout the profession's evolution. It also considers issues related to the use of relational approaches in today's world.

Chapter 2 describes the evolution of relational thought in its first phase. It discusses British and American object relations theories, the work of Sullivan and other social psychologists, Ferenczi's contributions, self-psychology, and self-in-relations theory (the Stone Center).

Chapter 3 describes the continuing evolution of relational thought during its second phase. It considers Mitchell's relational theory, intersubjectivity, and empirical findings on the therapeutic relationship.

Chapter 4 describes the major developmental concepts of relational theories and relevant research findings, including those from neuroscience. It considers concepts related to the relational matrix, which is composed of the self, others, and the interactions between them. It discusses the impact of infant studies and Lichtenberg's developmental theory. It also discusses the impact of trauma and other common developmental derailments, gender development, and the influence of society and culture.

Chapter 5 describes how relational thinking shapes the assessment process. It begins by discussing the sources of the data that clinicians utilize, particularly the clinician–client interaction. Then it considers and illustrates crucial aspects of clients' current and past life during the assessment process.

Chapter 6 describes and illustrates major components of the therapeutic process, including the importance of collaboration, the establishment of a therapeutic holding environment, empathic attunement, genuineness and spontaneity, self-disclosure, the mutual impact of client and clinician, bridging subjectivities, therapeutic responsiveness, the encouragement of new types of relational experiences, and the uses of interpretation. It also discusses issues that arise with respect to therapeutic boundaries.

Chapter 7 describes and illustrates the significance of transference and countertransference in the therapeutic relationship. It focuses especially on impasses and enactments that occur during treatment and how these can be managed.

Chapter 8 considers and illustrates the use of relational principles and techniques in work with clients from diverse and multicultural backgrounds.

Major foci will be on how the clinician must understand the client's subjective experience, the impact of the clinician's cultural countertransference that may interfere with this process, and the mutual impact of the client-clinician cultural subjectivities upon one another.

Chapter 9 shows the application of relational thinking to short-term treatment with individuals.

Chapter 10 considers and illustrates some contributions of relational thinking to work with couples, families, and groups.

Chapter 11 discusses some of the issues that arise in learning and teaching relational principles and techniques. It considers such issues as the challenges involved in learning new theoretical and practice paradigms, using a different stance in the therapeutic setting, and participating in and creating a less hierarchical and more mutual interchange in the classroom and supervision.

The epilogue summarizes key issues of the text and discusses the synthesis of relational theory with other contemporary theories, such as neurobiology and trauma theories.

Social work is a profession that values service to others. From our profession's inception, it has been those engaged in direct or clinical practice who have always put themselves on the front lines in working with clients who face a multitude of person-environmental problems, including the effects of poverty, discrimination, and oppression. It is those engaged in direct practice who have always valued the uniqueness of the individual and recognized the reparative and healing power of human relationships. It is those engaged in direct practice who have allowed themselves to get close to and try to ease human pain and suffering, and who have dedicated their working lives to helping others find ways of getting their needs met, overcoming obstacles to their functioning, and increasing their pleasure in living. And it is those in direct practice who know that relationships are core to the helping process, and that short-term, oversimplified, sometimes mechanistic techniques and our fragmented and limited array of empirically based practice interventions usually are not sufficient to help the troubled clients of today. We hope that this book will provide social work clinicians with knowledge that will enable them to be more effective in their work with a broad range of clients.

ADVANCED CLINICAL SOCIAL WORK PRACTICE

1. THE RELATIONAL CORE OF SOCIAL WORK PRACTICE

Social work practice has reflected relational thinking throughout the profession's history and, despite variations in emphasis, has been organized around two main principles. First, social work practice has been grounded on the belief that human behavior develops and can only be understood in the context of interpersonal relationships and social and cultural conditions. Thus, a key feature of social work assessment is its person-in-situation perspective. Second, almost all social work practice models, with the exception of the cognitive-behavioral approach, place importance on the client–worker relationship in the therapeutic process (Turner 1996).

As the social work professional evolved, the originators of different practice models drew on their experience and wisdom and on emerging psychodynamic and social science theory in shaping their approaches. Social work authors incorporated many concepts from the burgeoning body of relational thought into their writings. Today, relational theories provide clinical social workers with a theoretical rationale for many familiar practices but also enrich clinical social work practice with a broad range of clients, including those from diverse cultural backgrounds and those who have been the victims of oppression.

This chapter describes how major social work practice models have reflected relational thinking during the profession's history. This review is selective and does not include family, group, and crisis and other short-term approaches, which later chapters discuss. The chapter also comments on some current issues and controversies surrounding the use of relational approaches in social work practice.

THE EARLY PROFESSIONAL RELATIONSHIP

The friendly visitors and settlement workers of the late nineteenth century before social work became a profession recognized the impact of interpersonal relationships and social conditions on behavior. In the preprofessional period, usually affluent women volunteered to help economically impoverished individuals and families, many of whom had recently immigrated to the United States. During this period, there was little theory on which to draw in order to understand human behavior or to guide the helping process. In reflecting on this period, Gordon Hamilton (1958:13) wrote, "The truth was simply that the causes of behavior were little understood. The culture imposed its morals and values on social work, as well as on all of the humanistic professions." The early social work pioneers drew on their practice experience and wisdom and emerging theoretical frameworks in psychology and sociology to shape the emerging practice methodology (Goldstein 1995:30–31).

Mary Richmond (1917, 1922), who is credited with transforming charity work into a more scientific and professional activity (Germain 1970), focused on helping individuals but showed an understanding of the social determinants of behavior. "At any given time a man's mental make-up is the sum of his natural endowment and his social experiences and contacts up to that time" (Richmond 1922:131). She appreciated the impact of the clients' cultural background on their view of the world and their expectations and behavior in treatment. Likewise, other prominent social workers such as Ida Cannon, Jane Addams, and Bertha Reynolds drew attention to the negative impact of socioeconomic and political conditions on mental and physical diseases, family life, and daily life (Sheppard 2001).

As charity became more scientific and the social work profession emerged, Richmond recognized the significance of the client-worker relationship and viewed it as a lynchpin of the helping process. "The idea that the relationship of worker and client is important in helping people to help themselves—'not alms but a friend'—is one of the oldest in casework" (Hamilton 1940:28). Richmond made repeated references to the teaching functions of the relationship, which she thought should embody such qualities as simple friendliness, tact, goodwill, deep respect, a loving attitude, and mutuality. Unfortunately, during the period in which Richmond wrote, it was not unusual for volunteers to display patronizing, moralistic, and puritanical attitudes and religious values in their work (Horowitz 1998; Sheppard 2001). Moreover, in adopting a medical model in her view of poverty or pauperism as a disease, Richmond likened the friendly visitor to a social physician or general practitioner of charity who is called upon to heal complex conditions (Germain 1970:13). Her emphasis on the development of a method of systematic fact-gathering (study) that would lead to a diagnosis of the problem and a treatment plan took precedence over a focus on relational processes in treatment. Her study-diagnosis-treatment framework became a core feature of the diagnostic model or school of social work, which was developed further by faculty members of the New York (later Columbia University) and Smith Schools of Social Work.

THE NEUTRAL/ANONYMOUS AND TRANSFERENCE RELATIONSHIP

Beginning in the 1920s, classical Freudian psychoanalytic theory and treatment had a dramatic and long-lasting impact on social work practice. Most writers have not considered Freud's views to be relational because he viewed the role of the drives and past early childhood conflict as central and minimized the interpersonal and social determinants of behavior. Likewise, he emphasized the irrational or transference rather than real aspects of the therapeutic relationship. He assumed that the psychoanalyst, like a scientist in a laboratory, could study the client objectively without having an impact on the client. He likened analysts' insight-oriented techniques to surgeons' scalpels and viewed these tools rather than the therapeutic relationship as crucial to successful treatment.

Psychoanalytic treatment aimed at making unconscious conflicts conscious, modifying pathological defenses and character traits, and analyzing clients' irrational attitudes. Analysts were advised against being real and instead were instructed to be neutral in their comments, to refrain from gratifying or supporting the client, and to remain anonymous in order to maximize the irrational or transference aspects of the client-worker relationship. They were taught to minimize, analyze, or eliminate their own feelings and attitudes toward clients or countertransference because these were thought to be potential obstructions to the work caused by analysts' own unresolved problems. They were advised not to divulge personal information that would contaminate their clients' transference or undermine their authority with the client. Freud wrote that "the physician should be impenetrable to the client, and, like a mirror, reflect nothing but what is shown to him" (1912:18). It is somewhat ironic to note that clients, by virtue of coming for help, were supposed to reveal their most personal secrets.

Many social workers became intrigued by Freudian psychoanalytic theory and its focus on the unconscious, and it became the major theoretical underpinning to social work practice for several decades. It appeared to offer an explanation for why many clients had difficulty making meaningful changes in their lives and for their refusal of help altogether. It also offered a new method for helping clients to overcome their problems (Hollis 1963).

The application of Freudian theory treatment principles focused on the inner person rather than the individual in relation to others and to the environment, emphasized the client's psychopathology, and stressed the impact of past rather than current experiences. Moreover, it failed to recognize the importance of the therapeutic power of the client-worker relationship in engaging the client, instilling hope, helping clients feel less alone, providing fuel for the change process, and creating reparative experiences.

The attempt to carry psychoanalytic principles and techniques into social work practice led to what some have described as excesses and wrong turns in the profession (Meyer 1970). Social work practice became "so preoccupied with the inner life as almost to lose touch with outer reality and the social factors with which social workers were most familiar" (Hamilton 1958:23). One critic wrote, "This emphasis on the past and on the efficacy of probing the unconscious mind . . . casts both therapist (social worker) and patient (client) into particular roles. The client is assumed to be psychologically ill, in need of treatment in preparation for which he will be diagnosed and tentatively categorized, and of which he will be the passive recipient. The immediate presenting problem is regarded as merely a symptom of a deeper, all-pervading psychological condition, the proper domain of the caseworker-therapist, who assesses and treats over an indefinite stretch of time, assuming sole responsibility for the goal and direction of treatment . . . but always as a neutral, basically uninvolved figure" (Yelaja 1986:48).

EXERCISING CHOICE AND GROWING THROUGH RELATIONSHIP

Although Freudian theory was a dominant force in shaping social work practice in the 1920s and 1930s, some prominent social workers embraced other theoretical frameworks that had different implications for social work practice generally and for the client-worker relationship specifically. For example, Jessie Taft (1933) and Virginia Robinson (1930), both faculty members of the Pennsylvania School of Social Work, reacted negatively to and actively opposed the diagnostic model and its reliance on Freud's views of personality development and his treatment principles and techniques (Dunlap 1996; Yelaja 1986). The growing revolution against traditional science's static and deterministic view of the physical world and its linear view of causation also influenced them. Moreover, they were students of the philosophy and teaching of Herbert Mead and John Dewey.

Taft and Richmond put forth a new social work practice model, the functional approach, drawing heavily on the writings and teachings of Otto Rank (1924, 1928, 1936, 1941), an early follower of Freud who broke away from him and developed his own theory. Rank served on the faculty of the Pennsylvania School of Social Work and was a strong influence in the social work community there, although he did not personally contribute to the development of the functional model. In Rank's view, "The Ego needs the Thou in order to become the Self" (1941:290). He viewed the birth trauma as the prototype for all later separation experiences and the separation process as instrumental in normal growth and in treatment. He saw "each therapeutic hour as a microcosm of life, a time with its own beginning and end . . . and emphasized the present, rather than the past or future. He encouraged patients to 'experience' rather than to analyze the thoughts, feelings, and behaviors arising from the therapeutic process. . . . Rank is perhaps most famous for setting time limits" (Dunlap 1996:322).

In generating their new practice model, Taft and Robinson incorporated Rank's positive view of the growth process, emphasis on will, self-determination, and relationships, and focus on the use of time as a motivating force in treatment. In contrasting it to the diagnostic approach, Yelaja wrote, "The view of the individual as the hapless product of interacting external and internal forces had given way to a positive, hopeful view: people fashioning their own fate, capable of creatively using inner and outer experiences to shape their own lives. A psychology of illness was rejected and in its place a psychology of positive human potential and capacity for change gave impulse and direction to a new method in social work. Turning its back decisively on the diagnostic preoccupation with the past, functionalism placed new and creative emphasis on the present experience and its power to release growth potential" (1986:51).

The functional school rejected the diagnostic school's emphasis on extensive fact-gathering and diagnosis as a separate phase in the treatment process. Instead they saw it as woven throughout treatment with the client's active participation. More important, the functionalists believed that it was through a relationship process that clients could exercise choice and grow despite past negative growth experiences. "The casework relationship, premised on an implicit trust in the growth potential, provides a unique opportunity for the release of that potential. It provides this opportunity through consistent attitude of respect for and faith in the worth and strength of clients and a consequent creation of an atmosphere in which clients can feel safe and free to be truly themselves" (56).

In contrast to the Freudian-dominated diagnostic model, the functional approach regarded clients' resistance as inevitable and necessary for growth and change. "Resistance, an unavoidable phenomenon in the beginning casework relationship, is not only a natural and essential attempt on the part of the individual to maintain his personality, but is a sign of the strength of the will indispensable to new growth" (57).

It is important to note that the characteristic of the functional model that gave it its name had nothing to do with Rankian theory. Concerned about what they felt was the diagnostic model's focus on the inner person and seeming divorce from reality and the social environment during the period of the Great Depression, when so many individuals and families were suffering economically and social workers were overwhelmed by clients' requests for help, Taft and Robinson viewed the social agency as the link between the therapeutic relationship and growth process and the services that clients sought from social agencies. In this way, the social agency became the bridge between the individual and the interests of society. The functional model was based on the view that the structure and function of the agency defined the focus, direction, content, and duration of service. "Through the therapeutic relationship, the client and the clinician work together to discover what can be done with the help that is offered" (Dunlap 1996:319). The worker represents what the agency can offer, and the client is free to accept or reject the agency's service as a result of the relationship process.

The emergence of the functional model led to heated debate and a deep schism between the diagnostic and functional social workers that pervaded the field for some time. In addition to the controversy over the two models' key features and underlying theories, each approach had its own excesses to which followers of the alternative model could point. Some criticized the diagnostic model for its reliance on a medical and disease model in viewing human behavior, categorization of behavior, pessimism about human nature, robbing individuals of responsibility for moving their lives forward, creating undue dependency, removing itself from the reality of people's lives, and never-ending process of exploration. Alternatively, the functional model was attacked for overstressing client self-determination, individual responsibility, and agency function to the point of depriving individuals of needed services, for engaging in a relationship process as an end itself, and for utilizing withholding and punishing techniques in order to provoke what was thought to be a necessary will struggle in the treatment (Goldstein 1995:33).

THE SUPPORTIVE AND CORRECTIVE POTENTIAL OF THE CLIENT–WORKER RELATIONSHIP

At the end of the 1930s and throughout the post–World War II period, ego psychology gained recognition in the United States and had an important impact on social work practice. Although it had its roots in Freudian theory, ego psychology was more positive and humanistic in its view of human life and potential, growth oriented, and concerned with the impact of the social environment. Numerous social workers drew on ego psychology to correct for some of the excesses of the earlier era.

Gordon Hamilton, a prominent contributor to the diagnostic school, was a major force in transforming social work practice. Writing of the climate at this time, she wrote, "When ego psychology began to permeate psychoanalytic theory caseworkers would no doubt have grasped its importance even if they had not been harrowed in a literal sense by reality stresses of the depression years. The experience of this period helped them to rediscover those inner resources of character to which casework itself had always been attuned. It is part of man's heritage that under the greatest pressure he seems to attain his greatest stature. Perhaps the renewed emphasis on ego strength was a desperate last stand in a world what was crumbling to pieces; perhaps it was part of the vision of man's strength and sturdiness under adversity" (1958:22).

Although Hamilton's writings date back to the 1920s, *Theory and Practice of Social Casework*, a major text that put forth the principles of the evolving diagnostic approach, appeared in 1940. Influenced by the Gestalt emphasis in psychology, Hamilton drew attention to the interaction of phenomena as part of a larger whole or field, to a consideration of multiple causality in human events, and to an emphasis on growth, development, and change. She began to use the term "psychosocial" to describe the model although the term was initiated much earlier. She stressed the person-in-situation configuration. Hamilton taught that, in addition to understanding the client's feelings, the worker must engage him or her as an active participant in change (Germain 1970:19).

Among the most significant changes in the casework process to which applications of ego psychology contributed were those that involved the client–worker relationship. "Ego psychological concepts recognized the reality of the client–worker relationship in contrast to an exclusive focus on its transference or distorted aspects . . . they underscored the importance of engaging the client in a helping relationship in which he or she could exercise innate ego capacities and take more responsibility for directing his or her own treatment and life" (Goldstein 1995:36). Hamilton viewed "a special kind of love," called "acceptance," as a central dynamic in the helping process and "a part of any real healing." She wrote that the relationship "consists of warmth, concern, therapeutic understanding, and an interest in helping the person to get well," that is, to regain control of his or her own life and conduct. Although the worker was to show a "disciplined concern," not "indulgence for oneself," Hamilton recognized that there may be some degree of reciprocity since the worker "may benefit indirectly or incidentally" from the relationship (McCormick 1962:21). She also appreciated the fact that the worker's own personality and values had an impact on clients. Thus, she advised practitioners to cultivate their self-knowledge and to overcome their prejudices. "In any of the professions aiming to help people knowledge of the self is essential for the conscious use of relationship. If one is to use the self, then one must be aware of how the self operates. Not only should the caseworker know something of his motivation for choosing this profession, but he must also surmount another hurdle by recognizing his own subjectivity, prejudices and biases" (1940:41).

The focus on ego strength led to a greater focus on the role of the casework relationship in providing ego support to clients, and the concept of ego-oriented intervention became an important feature of casework practice. In contrast to earlier views that stressed the importance of worker neutrality and objectivity, there was greater emphasis on the worker's ability to show empathy for clients, to engage in controlled involvement, and to convey genuineness. Sometimes fueled by the client's perception of the worker as a benign parental figure (positive transference), the worker provided support by fostering the client's phase-appropriate needs, ego functions, and adaptation. Sometimes the worker functioned as a role model or teacher. Other diagnostic social workers, such as Lucille Austin (1948), Louise Bandler (1963), Grete Bibring (1950), Eleanor Cockerill and colleagues (1953), Annette Garrett (1958), Florence Hollis (1949), Isabel Stamm (1959), and Charlotte Towle (1948), contributed to the refinement of the diagnostic or psychosocial model during the 1940s and 1950s.

Some of these social workers also drew on the work of two revisionist psychoanalysts, Franz Alexander and Thomas M. French (1946, 1963), to expand the use of the casework relationship to include the provision of emotionally corrective experiences, that is, experiences in which the worker functioned in a more benign fashion than did the client's original parents. For example, Austin (1948) wrote of the importance of the worker's attempts at fostering experiences in the client's life situation or in treatment that promoted growth and completion of the maturation process.

PROMOTING ENGAGEMENT AND PROBLEM SOLVING

Helen Harris Perlman's problem-solving model of social work practice (1957) reflected a somewhat different view of the client–worker relationship. She drew on the work of those ego psychologists who emphasized the concepts of ego mastery and growth motivation, and she incorporated some aspects of John Dewey's and Jean Piaget's ideas into her approach. Influenced also by her mentor and friend, Charlotte Towle (1936, 1940), who wrote extensively about the characteristics of the helping relationship, Perlman attempted to correct for what she felt were some of the dysfunctional practices associated with both the diagnostic (psychosocial) and the functional models. Observing the extensive emphasis on history taking and diagnosis, long waiting lists, high dropout rates, the large numbers of "hard-to-reach and "multiproblem" families, and the unfocused and never-ending relationship process as an end in itself, Perlman emphasized the here-and-now impact of the client–worker relationship and the worker's authenticity. She acknowledged the power of the therapeutic relationship in instilling hope and motivating and engaging the client to work on the problems that the client deemed to be important. She placed considerable emphasis on helping so-called resistant or nonvoluntary clients to become positively involved in treatment, and in providing the context in which clients could exercise their own problem-solving capacities with the help of the worker (Perlman 1957, 1979; Turner and Jaco 1996:503–522).

RECOGNIZING THE CONTRIBUTIONS OF CLIENT
AND WORKER TO THE TREATMENT PROCESS

Writing around the same time as Perlman, Florence Hollis was a major figure who systematized and extended the psychosocial model. By the time her major text, *Casework: A Psychosocial Therapy*, appeared in 1964, the diagnostic or psychosocial model had changed significantly. Hollis's thinking evolved over the years, as seen in later editions of the book (Hollis 1972; Hollis and Woods 1981; Woods and Hollis 1990), the most recent of which was published after her death in 1987.

While maintaining emphases on diagnosis and person-in-situation, Hollis recognized the importance of clients' perception of their own needs and difficulties in contributing to assessment. She also acknowledged that workers' attitudes, values, personality characteristics, and background influence their assessment of the client. She made explicit the components of the relationship between the client and the worker. She advised workers to show human concern for clients but to discipline their use of the relationship in keeping with their assessment of the client's needs and intervention goals. She thought that workers should convey certain key attitudes and values, including acceptance of the client's worth, a nonjudgmental attitude toward the client, appreciation of the client's individuality or uniqueness, respect for the client's right to self-determination, and adherence to confidentiality. Hollis wrote that workers must recognize the factors that are influencing the client's participation in the helping relationship during the engagement process. These involve the client's motivation and expectations; previous experiences in getting help; values, gender, religion, sexual orientation, class, ethnicity, and race; ego functioning; current life situation; and the characteristics of the service delivery setting itself. Hollis cautioned that workers, while sometimes functioning as a role model or attempting to provide corrective experiences, must guard against imposing their own values on the client, using the client to meet their needs, or encouraging too much dependence on the worker. When ending the relationship because the work is complete or prematurely disrupted for any reason, workers must consider the meaning the relationship has to the client and help the client deal with the feelings involved.

EMPOWERMENT THROUGH RELATIONSHIP

In the 1960s, the social work profession became more concerned with macrosystems intervention rather than direct practice, and research on the effects of the psychosocial model was discouraging. The civil rights, feminist, and later the gay and lesbian liberation movements contributed to criticisms of the psychosocial model of practice, which was labeled as too intrapsychic and psychotherapeutic. Some accused followers of the psychosocial approach of "blaming the victim" rather than the effects of oppression, poverty, and trauma, and of "pathologizing" the behavior of women, gays and lesbians, and other culturally diverse persons rather than respecting their unique characteristics and strengths.

At this time, new perspectives on women's development and the unique experiences, characteristics, strengths, and coping strategies of African Americans, Latinos, Asians, and other oppressed groups were put forth. An explosion of knowledge contributed to the emergence of practice models that were designed to address the special needs of these populations, particularly their need for empowerment.

All empowerment approaches see clients' personal problems as often reflecting external social, political, and economic realities rather than internal difficulties and emphasize improving coping and adaptation and client strengths. They attempt to improve clients' self-esteem, positive identity, and sense of personal power and control over their lives (Lee 1996). They also urge collaboration in the client–worker relationship in order to help the clients exercise their own strengths and capacities. They advise workers to appreciate the effect of clients' unique life experiences and to recognize how discrimination, oppression, the trauma of multiple losses, and the stresses of acculturation have affected identity formation. They advise workers to recognize and bridge any differences between client and worker stemming from their backgrounds. The treatment relationship provides a space in which there can be validation of aspects of identity that have not been or are not being affirmed by the family and the culture. It is essential for the practitioners to search out and validate the positive aspects of a client's cultural identity. A sense of powerlessness is pervasive among clients who belong to diverse and oppressed populations. Consequently, treatment aims at helping clients to increase their sense of personal control over their lives and to believe that they can have an impact on others and their communities.

MUTUALITY AND AUTHENTICITY IN RELATIONSHIPS

Unhappy with the polarization between macro- and microsystems practice, some social workers attempted to put forth a distinctive and unifying conception of social work practice. The most significant of these approaches, the life model, was developed by Germain (1979) and later Germain and Gitterman (1980, 1996), who also attempted to correct for what they perceived as the psychosocial model's continuing reliance on psychodynamic theory and psychotherapy and lip-service attention to a person-situation perspective. Germain used an ecological metaphor that emphasized the role of social work practice in improving adaptation and the goodness of fit between people and environments. The life model emphasizes a strengths rather than pathology orientation and focuses on helping clients with problems in living rather than their disorders or illness. It asks what is going on rather than investigating the why behind clients' difficulties, and it is more transactional and environmentally oriented than therapeutically oriented in its choice of interventions, including a role for organizational and social change.

Relatedness is a core concept in the life model. "Human relatedness is a biological and social imperative for the human being over the life span. Without relationships, the human infant cannot survive, and without relatedness to others, the human being cannot learn to be human" (Germain and Gitterman 1986:621). In addition to its role in development, relatedness is at the heart of the intervention process. "In life-modeled practice, the professional relationship is conceived of as a humanistic partnership, with power differences between the partners reduced to the greatest degree possible. Thus, the relationship between client and worker shifts from subordinate recipient and superior expert to a relationship characterized by mutuality and reciprocity" (Germain and Gitterman 1996:95). Client involvement in assessment and the sharing of the definition of problems and selection of goals are fundamental to this process.

Anticipatory empathy is an important feature of the practitioner's work with the client. Drawing on the writing of Lide (1966), Germain and Gitterman (1996:63) describe the four steps in anticipatory empathy as: "(1) identification, through which the social worker experiences what the client is thinking and feeling; (2) incorporation, through which the worker feels the experiences as if they were personal; (3) reverberation, through which the worker tries to call up personal life experiences that may facilitate understanding those of the client, and (4) detachment, through which the worker engages in logical, objective analysis." Thus, the worker communicates attitudes of caring and attempts to be emotionally "with" the person (66). This is particularly important in work with clients who come from culturally diverse or oppressed backgrounds or who are different form the worker in other important ways.

The life model incorporates some aspects of empowerment approaches. It recommends the creation of the experience of mutuality rather than unquestioned authority in the worker–client relationship and advises workers to be flexible and authentic in order to empower clients. Germain and Gitterman point out that a worker's favorite theories and assumptions may interfere with the process of individualization, and that a too rigid adherence to standard practices may lead to mechanistic responses and detachment (284).

Another important characteristic of the client–worker relationship is the practitioner's participation with clients as they share their life stories or personal narratives. "The stories that we tell to ourselves and others are . . . our human way of finding meaning and continuity in life events . . . with the empathic, active listening of the social worker, a life story gains increased intelligibility, consistency, and continuity. The teller of the story reinterprets and reconstructs a narrative which ultimately will contain new conceptions of oneself and of relationships with others" (42). Thus, making sense of one's own life story is necessary for one's identity.

Despite its popularity in many social work circles, the life model framework failed to unite the practice community. It lacked appeal to many practitioners who felt that it minimizes in-depth understanding of the personality dimension of human problems, gives short shrift to more severe psychopathology, and does not equip workers with certain types of necessary intervention skills (Goldstein 1996).

DEVELOPING NEW OBJECTS, PROMOTING ATTACHMENT, STRENGTHENING THE SELF, AND THE ROLE OF INTERSUBJECTIVITY

By the time a renaissance of interest in direct or clinical practice occurred in the 1970s and 1980s, more knowledge had accumulated about the needs and problems faced by individuals who were exposed to early experiences of deprivation, indifference, neglect, abuse, trauma, and other types of problematic parenting. Likewise, interest had mounted in how to create an optimal therapeutic environment and process that promoted growth and new personality structures in clients who showed developmental arrests. Many of these individuals showed problems of basic trust and attachment, separation-individuation, a poor self-concept and faulty self-esteem regulation, and serious and repetitive disturbances in the ways in which they related to others and viewed the world. Additionally there were newer perspectives on women and gender, the adult life cycle, the impact of childhood trauma, sexual orientation, cultural, ethnic and racial diversity, and the effects of oppression. Many clinicians who had been trained in the psychosocial approach expanded their knowledge base and experimented with different approaches in their practice, centering, in particular, on the nature and role of the therapeutic relationship. This led to more sensitive and empowering interventions with these populations (Chin et al. 1993; Glassgold and Iasenza 1995; Gonsiorek 1982; Isay 1989; Jackson and Greene 2000; Jordan et al. 1991; Miller 1973).

At this time, there was greater recognition of the importance of the therapist as a real person or as a corrective figure who provided new object experiences that strengthened the personality. For example, more recent developments within psychoanalytic ego psychology, reflected in the work of Gertrude and Rubin Blanck (1974, 1979), recognized the potential of the therapeutic relationship for selectively replicating positive aspects of the parent–child relationship, thus providing clients with opportunities for participation in new, more positive interactions in treatment. In their writings about the treatment of borderline disorders, authors such as James Masterson (1976) wrote about the importance of helping borderline individuals to acquire new object experiences through their participation in treatment. Likewise, British object relations theorists, such as Winnicott (1965) and Guntrip (1975), stressed the need to provide a therapeutic holding environment that resembled the positive aspects of early parenting and the potentially therapeutic effect of new types of relationship experiences. They emphasized the clinician's containment functions and the reparative aspects of the therapeutic relationship. Attachment theorists such as Bowlby (1988) contributed an important dimension to understanding how clients exhibit early patterns of relating in the treatment situation that had major implications for how practitioners respond (Brandell and Ringel 2007).

Many social work practitioners embraced Heinz Kohut's self-psychology (1971, 1977, 1984), which viewed the therapeutic relationship as enabling clients to reexperience their frustrated archaic selfobject needs for idealization, mirroring, and twinship in a more empathically attuned environment. Through the clinician's empathic understanding and responsiveness, clients could have a second chance to develop a strong and cohesive self. Empathy also became an important tool in bridging difference between worker and client, an extremely important idea in work with clients from culturally diverse backgrounds.

The emphasis on the worker's genuineness also led to positive view of clinician self-disclosure. Its selective use began to be regarded as helpful, if not necessary, in enabling clients to engage in treatment, to feel that their needs are understood, to risk relating, to develop a meaningful bond, to remember and explore traumatic or disavowed experiences, or to feel validated in their very existence.

Self-disclosure also took on great significance as intersubjectivity in the client–worker relationship came into focus to a greater degree than previously. Clinicians began to assimilate the view that both worker and client exert a mutual impact on one another (Stolorow and Atwood 1992). Thus, the clinician is never merely an objective observer of the client but is both an observer and a participant who shapes the process. One implication of this model is that a dialogue should occur between worker and client about the ongoing impact of the personalities of each participant on the treatment process. It is important for the worker to bridge the two subjectivities of worker and client. This idea is very similar to the time-valued principle of being where the client is. In order not to be tantalizing, clinicians should disclose at times in order to refute or confirm the client's views and perceptions.

ISSUES AND CONTROVERSIES

This chapter's review of the relational component of selected major social work practice models has shown that they recognized that human beings are social animals and emphasized the impact of interpersonal relationships and the social and cultural context on child and adult development. Moreover, over the years, they moved away from the traditional model of a hierarchical relationship and instead placed importance on genuineness, openness, mutuality, and collaboration. Increasingly, they saw the therapeutic relationship as central to the treatment process, emphasizing the experiential, reparative, facilitating, and empowering aspects of the relationship between clinician and client. Although the models have different emphases, we believe that the relational theories described in chapter 2 provide a powerful rationale that permits many of these diverse views about the nature and uses of the client–worker relationship to be brought together.

In "Social Work Education and Clinical Learning" (Simpson, Williams, and Segall 2007), the authors underscore the importance of two unifying principles that have been present throughout social work's history and that give clinical social work coherence: the person-situation perspective and the concept of relationship. Despite their articulation of these two unifying principles, the nature of social work practice today has become more diffuse and specialized. A popular social work text (Turner 1996) cites twenty-seven different frameworks for practice and does not include additional approaches, such as eye movement desensitization and reprocessing, biofeedback, and spiritually based models, that are being used currently. Although some of these frameworks are relational in their perspective and processes, others tend to be more narrowly focused and emphasize techniques. For example, as a result of a combination of philosophical, political, and economic factors, certain segments of the social work profession and the vast network of social agency and health care settings are urging the adoption of cognitive-behavioral and other evidence-based approaches in social work practice. This view is being promulgated by major segments within the profession and by the demands of managed care. This emphasis tends to negate the importance of relationship-based practice and favors the use of cognitive-behavioral and other more readily measurable and researchable techniques. Thus, an important issue is how to maintain the core principles that have defined social work practice amid this abundance of diverse, sometimes highly specialized, and even at times mechanistic approaches, and in a service delivery atmosphere that places little value on relationships.

Although there is an important place in the clinical social worker's armamentarium for cognitive/behavioral techniques and other evidence-based practice interventions, in our view it is crucial for clinical social workers to operate with the concepts of person-situation and relationship as major organizing principles of their practice. This means that the practitioner may draw on diverse technologies in the intervention process but must integrate these into an overall approach that has the client's relational world and the worker–client relationship at its core. Obviously, social workers who are engaged in direct practice must fit what they do to the requirements of the agencies in which they are employed. This does not necessitate abandoning one's core values but instead demands that practitioners find ways of integrating relational thinking into their work, whatever the setting and client population.

A related issue is whether to use and teach only those approaches or interventions that have been verified empirically or to be guilty of unethical practice (Gambrill 2003; Thyer 1994, 2001). In today's world, the demand for accountability requires that clinical social workers become knowledgeable about and competent in utilizing evidence-based interventions, evaluating outcomes, and contributing to research. There are enormous gaps, however, in the research base of practice. Likewise, there are shortcomings in the use of intervention manuals that do not reflect the realities of practice. Moreover, some of the evidence that underpins relational theories and practices has been minimized or ignored. Finally, there has been a noncritical elevation of the quantitative research paradigm as the gold standard for practice research (Goldstein 2007).

Social work is a humanistic profession that necessitates the education of current and future generations of clinical social workers to make professional judgments and to engage in a professional practice rather than to be trained as technicians. Practitioners must be able to assess clients' total person-in-situation and to plan and implement interventions according to clients' unique needs, problems, life circumstances, and background in ways that do justice to the complexity of their lives. They need to be able to offer clients the opportunity for experiencing a human relationship that can instill hope, decrease loneliness and isolation, help them exercise their strengths, promote development and growth, and empower their sense of themselves. We agree with Reamer, who cautions that "empiricism can be taken too far. . . . While [it] can certainly inform and guide intervention, we must be sure that it does not strip intervention of its essential ingredients—a keen sense of humanity, compassion, and justice and the ability to engage and work with people. . . . Truly enlightened practice integrates the systematic method of empiricism with the valuable knowledge that social workers have once regarded as . . . practice wisdom and professional intuition" (1992:258).

2. THEORETICAL AND CLINICAL CONTRIBUTIONS: PHASE 1

As described previously, there is a rich historical tradition and compatibility of relational thinking with social work values and practice that has spanned many decades. Relational ideas themselves have expanded and changed over time and have gone through different phases. Although early relational theorists moved away from the "drive-structural model" of classical Freudian theory (Greenberg and Mitchell 1983), their formulations initially still adhered to what has been termed a "one-person" psychology that views development as an "individual" activity that is aided by the presence of a caregiving other. A second group of more contemporary theorists have put forth concepts that are broadly referred to as "two-person" psychologies that emphasize mutuality and interaction. This chapter discusses the theoretical contributions in phase 1, whereas chapter 3 elucidates the contributions in phase 2.

LOCATING THE SHIFT TO RELATIONAL THOUGHT

With the publication of their classic text, *Object Relations in Psychoanalytic Theory* (1983), Greenberg and Mitchell synthesized concepts of a number of psychoanalytic writers who proposed relational ideas that departed significantly from the traditional Freudian drive-structural model. These authors did not actually define themselves as relational theorists. It was Greenberg and Mitchell, "as historians and scholars of the development of psycho-analytic theory, who categorized them retrospectively as belonging to the relational turn in psychoanalysis" (Aron and Harris 2005:xv). Their seminal text highlighted some of the deep conceptual rifts that were occurring in the American analytic community in the early 1940s. In contrast to Freud's drive-structural model, the relational model, initiated by Fairbairn and Sullivan, among others, suggests that one's individual relations with other people contribute to the structure of one's mind, and that generally one's relationships with other people shape personality. What follows is a discussion of the contributions of a range of writers that began the shift in the United States to relational thinking in clinical practice. Since "relational psychoanalysis is a complex phenomenon constantly on the move," DeYoung (2003:26) uses the metaphor of streams and tributaries to "try and capture the motion and fluidity of its development." This chapter shows how numerous schools of thought shifted thinking to a relational model. These are ordered to reflect the historical timeline of the contributions:

- British object relations theorists (Klein, Fairbairn, Bowlby, Ainsworth, Winnicott)
- The Interpersonal School (Harry Stack Sullivan)
- American object relations (Jacobson, Mahler, Kernberg)
- Self-psychology (Kohut)
- Self-in-relation theory (Jordan, Miller, Stiver)

THE BRITISH OBJECT RELATIONS SCHOOL

Somewhat before Sullivan theorized his main tenets of interpersonal theory, the psychoanalytic community in the British Isles was shifting the conceptualization of human development and clinical work. Although the interpersonal theorists certainly challenged the modernist views of psychoanalysis and therapy and the American object relations school began to underscore the importance of object relations in human development, it was the ever-expanding influence of the British object relations theorists that consolidated a shift toward relational thinking in the United States. Many authors contributed to the shifting views. Although they often wrote in isolation from each other, they arrived at similar conclusions. Generally speaking, these theorists built relational ideas into psychoanalytic thinking by suggesting the following.

- Infants crave relatedness with others.
- Attachment to others is crucial for species survival.
- One's libidinal energy is object seeking, not pleasure seeking.
- Humans are primarily relational by intent.
- Caregivers shape children's sense of self and others by providing a holding environment.
- Individuals develop internal object relations worlds that fundamentally shape the nature of one's interpersonal relationships.
- Faulty object relations worlds lead to unsatisfying and troubled interpersonal relationships

What follows is a discussion of the ideas of the main contributors of the British Object Relations School.

MELANIE KLEIN   Although Klein is considered to be part of the British School of Object Relations and was the first person to build a relational component into psychoanalytic theory, her writings were controversial. She kept allegiance to some of Freud's principles but departed from him in significant ways. Trained as a child psychoanalyst, Klein developed her concepts about children as a result of close observation of her young clients' worlds. She became immensely interested in the "contributions of the early mother-infant relationship to their pathology" (Goldstein 2001:30). Her early writings suggested that infants and small children had the capacity for elaborate mental capacity, including development of fantasy and projection of fantasy. Like Freud, she articulated the importance of instincts, but she shifted fundamentally from Freud when she "argued that the goal of life was relationships with others (objects) rather than instinctual gratification" (Goldstein 2001:31). One major difference between Klein and Freud was in their understanding of the psyche-mind. Freud thought that the psyche was "shaped through the oedipal conflict into stable and coherent structures, with hidden recesses and illicit designs" (Mitchell and Black 1995:87). Klein, on the other hand, thought of the psyche as being unstable, fluid, and continuously fending off psychotic anxieties (ibid). These anxieties are fundamentally linked to fantasies about the child's caretaker/parents and take the form of annihilation (paranoid schizoid) or abandonment (depressive) anxieties.

Klein became a controversial figure in the British analytic society when she was invited by Ernest Jones to move there to work with his children (and those of other analysts). While in London, her writings became more widely known, and this notoriety led to an intense rivalry between Klein and Anna Freud and their respective followers. Essentially, the theoretical differences between Klein and Anna Freud were organized around the structure of the mind and its stability, coherence, or lack thereof (in Klein's views). Ego psychologists tended to view the adult mind as highly stable and structured, with highly developed defense mechanisms that contribute to adaptation when an individual experiences anxiety. Kleinians, however, viewed the child (and adult) mind as "beset with deep, psychotic-like terrors, as unstable, dynamic, and fluid, and as always responsive to 'deep' analytic interpretations" (Mitchell and Black 1995:88). Citing Greenson (1974), Mitchell and Black go on to say: "The Kleinians tend to view ego psychology as concerned with shallow dimensions of emotional life. The ego psychologists tend to view the Kleinians as widely interpretive, overwhelming patients with concepts they cannot possibly understand or use." It is interesting to note that Klein published articles explicating the notion of projective identification, which became a major concept in relational theory.

Though spawned in England, this political acrimony migrated to the American psychoanalytic community where Klein's ideas and "writings were considered to be heretical among American psychoanalysts until recently" (Goldstein 2001:31). Nonetheless ideas of object relations began to make their way into American thinking, as typified by the work of Edith Jacobson, Margaret Mahler, and Otto Kernberg, who will be discussed later in the chapter.

W.R.D. FAIRBAIRN   W.R.D. Fairbairn was a Scottish analyst who maintained close connections with the British psychoanalytic community. His geographic isolation from the others, however, afforded him the opportunity to conceptualize theory that was independent of the thinking of his contemporaries. Fairbairn elaborated a model of object relations theory that clearly emphasizes that individuals are driven to be connected to others (Basham and Miehls 2004; Goldstein 2001; Greenberg and Mitchell 1983; Mitchell and Black 1995; St. Clair 1996). Challenging Freudian concepts, Fairbairn envisioned "a unitary, integral ego with its own libidinal energy, seeking relations with real and external objects" (Greenberg and Mitchell 1983:183). He proposed that one's ego stays intact as long as one's relationships with significant caretakers are healthy.

Making observations while doing clinical work with abused children, Fairbairn noted that children maintained an alliance with their parents, in spite of being physically abused. In fact, the abused children whom he studied often characterized their parents as being good. Fairbairn came to conceptualize this as the child's ego adaptation to the abuse. He thought that if the individual is frustrated, abused, or disappointed by significant caretakers, the ego splits, and this splitting is seen as the ego's adaptation to the pathological real relationship with the caretaker. Basham and Miehls (2004:105) note, "Fairbairn's 'endopsychic structure,' as it is called, is determined by the individual's need to find homeostatic responses to frustrating objects." In the endopsychic structure, the ego is split into a number of parts or characteristics that seem to be at odds with each other. In other words, the ego is the site of internal conflict, and Greenberg and Mitchell (1983:106) note that these parts are characterized as "the ideal object (the gratifying aspects of the mother); the exciting object (the promising and enticing aspects of the mother); and the rejecting object (the depriving, withholding aspects of the abuser)." Basham and Miehls (2004:106) elaborate, "The part of the ego that continues to hope for positive contact and relatedness to the exciting object is termed the 'libidinal object.' The part that stays connected to the rejecting object is termed the 'anti-libidinal object,' or 'internal saboteur.'" Finally, the central ego, whose function it is to adapt to the external world, forms interpersonal relationships with real people and relates to the frustrating parent as an idealized figure (Goldstein 2001; Greenberg and Mitchell 1983).

Fairbairn's views of the internal conflicts of the ego shaped his understanding of the analytic treatment situation. He suggested that the prototypes of human connection established historically are preserved in internal object relations. These object relations shape the interaction with the therapist, and Fairbairn suggests that clients eventually experience the clinician as the old, bad object (Mitchell and Black 1995:122). Fairbairn also suggested that no one can give up their ties to their bad objects unless there is some promise of new objects. In other words, "For the analysand to renounce the old, transferential forms of connection to the analyst, she must begin to believe in new, less constrained patterns of relatedness" (Mitchell and Black 1995:122). To change, not only insight but a new relationship are necessary. This concept became a cornerstone of contemporary relational thinking. Alexander and French (1946) were among the first theorists to suggest that analysis works as a result of the interpretations of the analyst in conjunction with the analysand's experience of having some primary interpersonal needs met in the treatment relationship. Alexander argued that the analyst should deliberately try to create a relationship that would be specifically healing for each client, and this then would necessitate a move away from analytic neutrality or abstinence. Horowitz (1998:371), a social work writer, echoes this sentiment when she says: "the treatment relationship is primary, real, and potentially healing in itself, although not the whole of what is required to help." In summary, then, Fairbairn (1952) clearly theorized the importance of object relations in one's development. St. Clair (1996:55) suggests this his version of objects relations is the most pure—"that is, free of a biological emphasis and purely psychological—a model that is very different from Freud's model of motivation and personality."

JOHN BOWLBY   John Bowlby and his followers furthered the move toward relational theory with the explication of attachment theory through its developmental research and its eventual application to child and adult development. Bowlby also explicitly turned his back on classical drive theory when he suggested that infants seek attachment relationships with caregivers as a matter of survival of the species. He wrote very powerfully about the need for attachment, and his writings demonstrate his allegiance to behavioral observation. While Bowlby was not a pure "behaviorist" at the time, his writing does emphasize the impact of real interactions on infants, children, and adults. Classical psychoanalytic theorists demeaned his work, but he did attract the attention of researchers who began to test out his theory systematically in research studies examining child/caregiver interactions.

Bowlby and his colleagues chronicled the tragic impact of separation experiences of infants from their parents. Witnessing the psychological and physical deterioration of institutionalized children, Bowlby (1958, 1960, 1973, 1980) and Spitz (1945, 1959) strongly suggested that attachment of infant to caretaker was crucial for healthy child development. Bowlby noted that children develop internal working models of self and other (this is his language for internal object relations), and that one's attachment schema becomes activated when one is threatened or separated from caregivers.

In keeping with Bowlby's work, Mary Ainsworth and her colleagues systematically researched child responses to separation experiences and formulated a research protocol that is known as the "Strange Situation Experiments." In a laboratory setting, Ainsworth recorded the reunion experiences of children and parents, and she developed a typology of attachment styles including secure, ambivalent, and avoidant attachment. In later studies, a fourth category of disorganized/disoriented attachment was also observed in children when their parents had unresolved trauma histories and/or an unresolved grief experience. Mary Main further strengthened the ideas of Bowlby when she developed a research tool called the Adult Attachment

Interview. Main and her colleagues developed a semistructured interview that yields classification of adults—these parallel the child classifications that Ainsworth described in her work. Attachment theory continues to be very influential in contemporary investigations, elucidating the importance of relationships contributing to healthy or maladaptive mental health. (See chapter 4 for an elaboration of attachment theory constructs.)

DONALD D. WINNICOTT   Donald W. Winnicott was initially trained as a pediatrician, and one witnesses this influence in his theorizing about human development. Having observed many mother–child interactions, "he developed strikingly innovative and enormously provocative ideas about both the sort of mothering that facilitates healthy development and the sort that leads development astray" (Mitchell and Black 1995:124). Winnicott's writings are highly relevant for contemporary psychotherapy practice today (Applegate and Bonovitz 1995; Goldstein 2001; Greenberg and Mitchell 1983). Basham and Miehls (2004:109) note that "His emphasis on early development and the importance of environmental influences [is] compatible with development across diverse cultural groups."

Winnicott (1965:52–54) postulated that pregnant mothers develop a primary maternal preoccupation with their baby, and that increasingly in the last trimester of pregnancy the mother becomes very focused on the developing child within her. This preoccupation continues after the birth of the child, and Winnicott says that "there is no such thing as an infant; there is only an infant and its mother" (39). This of course implies that a caretaker is exquisitely attuned to the needs of the infant. One can clearly see that Winnicott considered the mother–infant bond to have ultimate primacy and importance for child development. He noted that parents need to provide a good enough environment so that children can blossom psychologically, and that from these beginning interactions the child develops a core sense of himself or herself in the world. His theory describes how many aspects of a child's internal structure, such as the capacity to be alone, come about as a result of positive relational experiences with the mother. In this respect, Winnicott differed from Fairbairn, who was concerned about how frustrating relational interactions resulted in the development of the intrapsychic structures.

One of Winnicott's important contributions is his discussion of the results of parental impingement. Winnicott suggested that the infant may develop a false self-adaptation to the caretaker if the latter is not attuned to the infant's needs and imposes his or her own on the child. In this instance, the child suppresses her own needs and tries to anticipate the needs of the caretaker. This sort of interaction leaves the child's sense of self to be vulnerable; the false self-adaptation gives the illusion that the child is emotionally in tune with the caretaker, but this is at the expense of the child's development of his or her authentic or true self. Winnicott's developmental model does not imply that the caretaker has to be perfectly attuned to the child's needs in order for the child to develop a positive sense of self. On the contrary, he believed that it is the caregiver's gradual failures of attunement with the child that facilitate a more complex and mature understanding of relationships within the child.

Winnicott clearly saw the therapeutic process as an opportunity for the client to reintegrate split-off experiences of the child into a more complex sense of self. With the provision of the holding environment, the therapist offers the opportunity for the client to gradually reveal his or her emotional needs so as to give up his or her false self-adaptation. In Winnicott's therapy, clients need to reexperience a relationship that is restorative and specifically healing of earlier impingements. His therapy strategy relies less on interpretation of unconscious material and is best understood as offering a corrective emotional experience to the client (Mitchell and Black 1995:134).

TREATMENT PROCESSES OF BRITISH OBJECT RELATIONS THEORISTS

The thesis that one's early relationships fundamentally shape our intrapsychic world leads to the following conceptualizations about treatment.

- Clinicians offer a holding environment that permits a reshaping of early object relations impairments.
- Aggression is viewed as a response to ruptures in early caregiver relationships (it is not an innate drive).
- Conflict is viewed as arising from faulty relationships (it is not an internal conflict between parts of the mind).
- Clients develop transference reactions to their clinicians, attempting to re-create patterns of their primary caregiver relationships.
- Goals of treatment are to improve the client's capacity for and satisfaction in relationships.
- Clients change by updating their internal object relations world as a consequence of a corrective experience with the clinician.
- Clinicians use their countertransference responses as a means to understanding the clients' internal world.

- Clinicians maintain a sense of neutrality with the client and rarely use self-disclosure as a therapeutic tool.

HARRY STACK SULLIVAN AND THE INTERPERSONAL SCHOOL

In the United States, authors from the interpersonal school of psychiatry (Sullivan, Fromm Reichman, Thompson) contributed to a paradigmatic shift in psychoanalysis In fact, De Young (2003:29) notes, "Interpersonalist theory taught 'relational psychoanalysis' that pathology is located in faulty patterns of making meaning out of interpersonal interactions, and that these patterns are best addressed directly and in the present, so that the patient can come to understand what's going on and take responsibility to deconstruct the old meanings and construct new ones." Even though members of the interpersonal school wrote extensively, their ideas were somewhat dismissed by those supporting traditional forms of psychoanalytic thought as the interpersonal school tended to "de-emphasize the internal world and internal psychic structures" (Mitchell and Aron 1999:x). The Interpersonal School advanced relational thinking by suggesting the following.

- One's personality/character is shaped in interaction with family members or other environments.
- The individual psyche is always part of a social matrix.
- Personality is made manifest only by interpersonal relationships.
- Anxiety is purely relational in nature.

To put the above main points in context, it is important to understand that Sullivan's earliest work focused on the experience of individuals with schizophrenia. In the 1920s the psychiatric community conceptualized schizophrenia as a biologically based disorder that worsened over time to the point of the individual being nonfunctional. Sullivan, however, disagreed with this purist biological explanation of schizophrenia and noted that "these concepts were strikingly inapplicable to his own experience with schizophrenic patients, whom he found to be extremely sensitive and responsive to their interpersonal environment" (Mitchell and Black 1995:61). Arising from this basic stance, Sullivan (1953) suggested that the study of an individual, as a separate entity, does not capture the complexity of lived experience. Rather, he postulated that an individual's personality is not something that "resides" within an individual but rather is shaped in continual interaction with others in one's family or other environments.

Elucidating the notion that each individual has a complex identity, Sullivan suggested that "a personality is not something one has, but something one does" (Mitchell 1988:25). This suggests that humans interact differently depending on the situation, the audience, and other people; in other words, the individual is fully understood only in the context of interpersonal relationships. This notion is similar to the postmodern view that individuals have complex identities and that identity is fluid and dynamic, dependent on the social context that frames interactions. It is interesting to note that once again, views of schizophrenia as a biologically based disorder dominate the mental health field; while there is certainly some validity to this understanding of etiology, we once again witness a diminution of the importance of interpersonal relationships in many aspects of managed-care mental health services. Rather, a model that advocates for insurance companies mandates pharmacological and short-term treatments.

Sullivan attracted some core followers, including Frieda Fromm-Reichman (1950), who discussed the benefits of psychotherapy for seriously mentally ill patients. Likewise, Harold Searles (1979, 1986) developed a series of publications in which he talked about the powerful interplay of transference and countertransference feelings that become enacted in psychotherapy. Clara Thompson, another interpersonal thinker was initially trained at the New York Psychoanalytic Institute. Later, she also came under the influence of Sandor Ferenczi, a Hungarian analyst. Thompson adopted an allegiance with Ferenczi's understanding that children experienced real trauma as a result of sexual abuse (challenging Freud's fantasy theory of childhood sexuality), and she then placed a great deal of emphasis on real relationships in the development of personality style. Mitchell and Black (1995:78) comment that Thompson also synthesized some concepts of Erich Fromm's humanistic psychoanalysis into her theory, writing that societies are comprised of different types of people who are "forced" to perform certain functions to maintain a social structure. She thought that individuals fear isolation and thus do not express an authentic experience of oneself—rather, there is a collusion with what the broader structure expects of the individual. In summary, in spite of their later marginalization, the Interpersonal School became institutionalized by the development of the William Alanson White Institute (for psychoanalysis) and the Washington School of Psychiatry. These programs offered training structures that fostered the continuing ideas and influence of interpersonal thinkers on traditional psychoanalytic theorists.

INTERPERSONAL THEORY AND THE TREATMENT PROCESS

One can summarize the contributions of interpersonal theory to shaping the treatment process as follows.

- There is more focus on the "here-and-now," with the understanding that relationships shape the present.
- There is an emphasis on the interaction of transference/countertransference feelings, manifested by a shared unconscious world.
- There is an emphasis on interpretations about the nature of one's relationship patterns.
- The personal relationship between the client and the clinician is the most important aspect of the therapy change process.
- Individuals need to reorganize their personality configurations in order to make changes.
- Therapists' use of self is crucial in terms of understanding client dynamics.
- Countertransference feelings are welcome and used as an aide in understanding the client (see chapter 7).

THE INFLUENCE OF AMERICAN OBJECT RELATIONS THEORISTS

The American School of Object Relations grew out of the theoretical formulations of ego psychology. Ego psychologists had begun to deviate somewhat from drive theory principles, by attempting "to correct for Freud's instinctual emphasis, minimization of the strength of the ego, focus on the unconscious, and inattention to the impact of reality" (Goldstein 2001:18). In addition to paying more attention to the individual's innate capacities, ego psychologists focused more attention on the impact of interpersonal relationships, the environment, and culture in the development of individual strength and/or pathology. Edith Jacobson and Margaret Mahler were major American object relations theorists, and Otto Kernberg synthesized concepts of both the American and British object relations theorists. Some general considerations of these theorists moving us toward relational thinking are as follows.

- Mother/infant dyads are unique in each constellation.
- The infant's experience of pleasure/unpleasure is fundamentally linked to the mother/infant relationship.

- Developing children have a dual wish of yearning for autonomy while wishing for connection with the caregiver.
- Achievement of certain developmental milestones facilitates the development of healthy adult relationships.
- Interpersonal exchanges are affected by four components—the real self, the ideal self, the real object, and the ideal object.

When Jacobson published her groundbreaking book *The Self and Object World* (1964), Goldstein (2001:27) notes that she "showed how infants acquire self- and object-images or representations based on their relationships with others and how these affective experiences are linked to and consolidate libidinal and aggressive drives." Rather than suggesting that there is an objective phenomenon of "good" mothering, for example, Jacobson suggested that mothering might feel good to a particular baby depending on his or her temperamental predisposition, the fit between mother and infant, the affective matching of the dyad, and the mother's capacity to respond differentially to the baby's changing developmental needs (Mitchell and Black 1995:50). She suggested that these factors, among others, would shape an overall affective response within the infant, and that the child's basic drive constitution would be predicated on the cumulative impact of many experiences. Mitchell and Black explain that "she argued that the balance in the subjectively registered feeling tone of earliest experience not only contributes to the consolidation of libido and aggression as drives, but also lays the groundwork for ongoing tendencies in the ways we feel about ourselves and others"—hence her focus on the self and object world. Jacobson's work foreshadowed the contemporary idea that the "fit" between client and clinician is a crucial factor in overall treatment success.

Initially Margaret Mahler (1968) studied emotionally disturbed children, which led to her formulations of childhood autism and symbiosis. In New York, she and her colleagues established a center that functioned as a research laboratory. Basham and Miehls (2004:94) note that they invited young mothers and their children to attend their center. In this setting, the mothers benefited from socialization and support with other new mothers while the research team made observations of mother–child interaction that shaped the foundation theory of the separation-individuation process. Their findings were published in 1975 in the book *The Psychological Birth of the Infant: Symbiosis and Individuation*. In this work, "the term *separation* refers to the infant's gradual disengagement from a fused state with the primary love object, and the term *individuation* signifies the development of the child's unique characteristics" (Goldstein 2001:28, italics in original). The theory describes a series of psychological phases of development, with the young toddler eventually attaining a sense of object constancy—implying that the child can understand complex images of his or her caretakers (as neither all good or all bad), even when his or her needs are being frustrated. Though she believed that drives were part of the infant's psychological world, Mahler also viewed the child's relationship with the primary caretaker (mother) to be fundamental in shaping human development. Ego psychologists and classic psychoanalytic practitioners embraced her writings because she kept some allegiance to certain concepts of Freudian drive theory. Nevertheless, Mahler's theory fundamentally shifted the emphasis of human development to the relationship between child and parent.

Although born in Vienna, Otto Kernberg was educated in Chile. After moving to the United States, he received further psychiatric training at the Menninger Clinic in Topeka, Kansas, and then moved to New York, where he spent a considerable amount of his professional life. His work focused on theory development regarding the diagnosis and treatment of borderline and narcissistic personalities. His contributions played a major role in the development of object relations theory in the United States. St. Clair (1996:131) notes that Kernberg had two fundamental goals in his theory development: "(1) to integrate object relations theory with psychoanalytic instinct theory, and (2) to understand the borderline conditions (and a subgroup of the borderline condition, the narcissistic personality) by using a conceptual model that integrates object relations and instinct theory." Kernberg is often described as a synthesizer of theory (St. Clair 1996) as he drew from concepts of Freud, Jacobson/Mahler, and Klein. He saw himself as keeping an allegiance with the drive structural model of Freudian theory, and he does describe how internal object relations structures (of self and other) are built up with the influence of aggressive and libidinal drives of drive derivatives (St. Clair 1996:133). Nevertheless, his writings show the profound influence of Melanie Klein's ideas.

Kernberg wrote extensively (1975, 1976, 1980) and was a widely sought-after speaker. His influence on psychoanalytic thinking was far reaching in North America and beyond. He outlined a developmental theory that describes "a series of sequential stages that trace the infant's acquisition of internal self- and object-representations and affect dispositions under the influence of libidinal and aggressive drives" (Goldstein 2001:29). Essentially he suggested that "good affective experiences accumulate and are the basis for libidinal drives, and bad affective experiences serve as the basis for aggressive drives" (St. Clair 1996:134). Though this notion of building up drives is significantly different from Freud's initial ideas about drive, Kernberg's use of *drive* language and seeming adherence to Freud's structural model afforded him some recognition in traditional psychoanalytic circles.

Kernberg is perhaps best known for his rich description of borderline personality disorders. He articulated the developmental pathway of borderline individuals and also wrote extensively about treatment principles of working with this group of clients. He clearly delineated the pathological object relations of borderline individuals, but here, too, he framed his discussion in drive language. St. Clair (1996:144) points out that Kernberg's "borderline personalities fail to integrate loving and hateful images of self and objects because of the presence of this *intense early aggression*" (emphasis added). In other words, Kernberg suggested that individuals are not able to integrate aspects of good and bad feelings about objects when they experience too much aggression or frustration. Kernberg also expanded Klein's ideas about projective identification, and he described that this process is really a powerful negative transference that the client develops in the treatment relationship. The client projects unconscious aggressive impulses onto the therapist and then behaves as if the therapist is indeed a powerful, sadistic person whom the client must try to control. We mention this concept as the reader can see the parallel of Kernberg's projective identification with relational theory's focus on understanding and working through treatment impasses, especially of negative transference/countertransference phenomena. So, although Kernberg did not directly discuss the role of the therapist in the development of the client's projective identification, he did certainly understand the power of the unconscious worlds of each participant in the development of the therapeutic relationship.

TREATMENT PROCESSES OF AMERICAN OBJECT RELATIONS THEORIES

While there is some similarity in treatment processes of the British and American schools of Object Relations, the following are specific to the American school.

- There is a recognition of how the "fit" between client and clinician influences the development of the treatment alliance.
- There is an expectation that clients will recreate the phases of separation-individuation theory in the clinical relationship.
- A fundamental goal of treatment is for the client to attain a sense of object constancy, that is, the ability to hold complex images of

others (including the clinician) even when their needs are being frustrated.

- Clients will also develop a mastery of ambitendency in the clinical process, that is, the ability to form close relationships with others without the fear of engulfment by them.
- Clients will resist the change process by holding onto and utilizing lower-level defenses.
- Clients will use the defense of projective identification in their unconscious effort to have the clinician enact their object relations world.
- The clinician will use countertransference responses to the diagnostic profile of the client.

SELF-PSYCHOLOGY

Heinz Kohut was the founder of self-psychology, a distinctive perspective that has attracted many followers and strong adherents to its tenets. Although generally considered to be a one-person psychology because of its emphasis on the self as the organizing principle of human behavior and its recognition of the importance of an innate self-structure, self-psychology views the caretaking environment as essential to self-development, bringing it closer to a two-person relational theory. Moreover, many contemporary intersubjective theorists initially were trained in self-psychology and contributed to its development.

Before developing his theory of the self, Kohut was closely identified with classical psychoanalytic training and theory throughout most of his career. In fact, he was president of the American Psychoanalytic Association at one point. In a series of publications (1971, 1977, 1984), Kohut began to systematically challenge traditional drive theory and explicated a theory of self-development. As he developed his theory over time, he increasingly departed from classical drive theory. The following aspects of self-psychology furthered relational thinking.

- While the individual is born with an innate sense of self, the child needs a responsive and empathic environment (caregivers) to achieve a coherent sense of self.
- Individuals need close relationships to perform certain empathic responses in order for the child to develop optimally.

- Individuals will have opportunities for growth across the life cycle.
- This theory holds relevance and applicability for a range of individuals, including oppressed populations.
- Individuals are encouraged to be fully expressive of individuality and creativity, regardless of societal sanctions or value judgments.

There are certainly similarities between Kohut's views and those of the British Object Relations School, but some differences are also present. In common with object relations theorists, however, he articulated a developmental theory of normative narcissism, and his theory explicates a departure from Freud's concept of narcissism. Kohut's developmental model is predicated on the idea that "the individual is born with an innate sense of self, which is the central organizing and motivating force in the personality but also requires an empathic and responsive selfobject environment in order to unfold optimally" (Goldstein 2001:42). Kohut mapped out a developmental schema in which children have three main types of relationship (selfobject) needs met. First, children need to have a sense of mirroring that facilitates a reinforcement of their innate grandiosity; second, children develop an idealized image of their caregivers—this idealization allows the child to bask in the strengths of the parent and to borrow from them, a sound sense of self; third, children also develop a more complex sense of self by developing a twinship with others who are similar to them. In essence, the child has innate potentials that are actualized as a result of an empathic relationship with caregivers.

Kohut's theory differs from the American Object Relations School in that he emphasized "self deficits instead of internalized pathological object relations structures and his view of aggression and narcissistic rage as reactive to frustration and misattunement rather than being innate" (Goldstein 2001:43). In other words, he viewed an individual's aggression as secondary to empathic failures on the part of the caregiver and did not see it as an innate drive.

Kohut suggested that individuals in analysis will develop transference relationships with the analyst that indicate the site of narcissistic vulnerability. Based upon the three development needs of mirroring, idealization, or twinship, the client will develop the transference relationship with the analyst, consistent with the unconscious attempt to have the analyst emphatically respond to this need. Through the process of transmuting internalization, Kohut suggested that the therapy process will be reparative when the client can utilize the therapist as a corrective selfobject.

TREATMENT PROCESS IN SELF-PSYCHOLOGY

The following offers a summary of the treatment process framed in self-psychology theory.

- Individuals will develop revised self structures with successful treatment, including shifts in self-esteem and self-concept.
- Individuals will lessen somatic symptoms as healthier self structures are built.
- Individuals will become more creative and experience an increased capacity for pleasure.
- It is understood that individuals will develop a series of three transference responses to the clinician in order to have self needs met in the treatment relationship.
- Change processes occur when the clinician disappoints the client and the client is able to gradually build up a sense of self that is narcissistically able to manage such disappointments.
- Clinicians tend to avoid direct confrontation of the client.
- Clinicians need to monitor their unempathic responses to clients, recognizing that these lead to potential transference ruptures in the relationship.
- Clinicians may experience some countertransference feelings of boredom or frustration when working with narcissistically oriented clients.

STONE CENTER SELF-IN-RELATION THEORY

The last group of writers to be considered in this chapter is a group of feminist scholars who primarily collaborated and wrote out of the Stone Center in Wellesley, Massachusetts. Their "self-in-relation" theories have been expanded since the early 1990s, and the group has published three books over the last fifteen years (*Women's Growth in Connection*, 1991; *Women's Growth in Diversity*, 1997; *How Connections Heal*, 2004). There are a number of other publications by these authors, many published as "works-in-progress." This implies the fluid construction of theory and an effort to move away from essentialist, modernist theorizing and thinking.

Integrating some concepts from Gilligan (1982) and Chodorow (1978), key Stone Center authors are Jean Baker Miller, Janet Surrey, Judith Jordan, Irene Stiver, Alexandra Kaplan, Maureen Walker, and Wendy Rosen,

among others. Their writings suggest that development (especially female development) proceeds through relationship elaboration rather than
through separation or disengagement (Jordan et al. 1991:87). As such, their
views contradict some tenets of Mahler's separation-individuation theory.
They do not see mental health as the achievement of autonomy and separation but rather regard it as being defined by the ability to deepen connection
and relationships throughout the life span. Some ideas from this school of
thought that further relational thinking are listed below.

- Women experience positive self-esteem or self-regard when they
  are in connected relationships with others.
- Individuals feel understood when they are seen or recognized by
  others.
- Men often feel threatened by their own needs for connection and perhaps project their negative judgment of "dependence" onto women.
- There is an opportunity for deepening connections, across the life
  span.
- Individuals develop a sense of agency and/or power out of close
  relationships

These points have been expanded over the last number of years. The initial writings of the Stone Center were critiqued somewhat when others commented that this group of scholars was writing about the experience of white,
middle-class women. However, the study groups and scholars have taken up
this critique and have expanded their theorizing to include development of
lesbian women, oppressed women, and disabled women. As examples, chapters on fusion in lesbian relationships (Mencher 1997), clinical application
of Stone Center theory to minority women (Turner 1997), and racial identity
development and relational theory (Tatum 1997) all demonstrate the application of the above theoretical concepts to diverse populations.

The most recent publication, edited by Maureen Walker and Wendy Rosen,
expands the Stone Center theory even further by integrating models of intervention related to community and culture (*How Connections Heal: Stories from
Relational-Cultural Therapy*, 2004). They note that "culture has everything to
do with psychological growth and development" and "a culture that does not
provide a growth-fostering impetus for everyone sets in motion forces that can
end in psychological problems—and the therapeutic relationship, itself, reflects
the surrounding culture in both obvious and subtle ways" (ix). Later in this
book, we devote a chapter to the interface of culture and relational theory.

TREATMENT PROCESSES AND SELF-IN-RELATION THEORY

Treatment based on self-in-relation theory reflects the following components.

- A treatment relationship that is characterized by deepening connection and mutual empathy is the cornerstone of the change process.
- Psychological growth is seen as a function of action in the relationship.
- The goals and focus of the treatment is to enhance connection in a myriad of relationships.
- Treatment does not privilege the notion of independence as a hallmark of maturity.
- Transference relationships are discouraged, and psychological growth is enhanced by the sense of equal agency and power between the client and clinician.
- Clinicians are very attuned to their own countertransference responses so as to not contribute to relationship ruptures.
- The clinician does use self-disclosure, at certain times, in the treatment process, particularly self-disclosure of affect or personal experience if it furthers the client's progress toward a deepening relationship.

CONCLUSION

This chapter has described the early phase of relational thinking that is characterized by a one-person psychology. Although the schools of British Object Relations, Interpersonal Psychiatry, American Object Relations, Self-Psychology, and Self-in-Relation Theory all contributed to the paradigmatic shift to relational thinking in psychoanalysis and psychodynamic theories, it is only through the explication of the intersubjective or "two-person" psychologies that one fully grasps the main tenets of contemporary relational theory in clinical social work. The treatment emphasis was similar. Drawing on theories of intersubjectivity, social constructivism, contemporary feminist theory, attachment theory, and neurobiological theory, contemporary relational theory emphasizes mutuality in the developmental and treatment process. The next chapter describes these later theoretical developments.

3. THEORETICAL AND CLINICAL CONTRIBUTIONS: PHASE 2

In contrast to the "one-person" relational theories that were discussed in chapter 2, the more contemporary "two-person" intersubjective theories that characterize phase 2 of relational thinking place central importance on the mutual and interactional process that occurs between infants and caretakers during development. These theories have contributed significantly to new understanding and innovative approaches to the therapeutic process. Chapter 4 will describe the most important of the developmental concepts that comprise this phase in relational thinking, whereas this chapter discusses their treatment implications. Contemporary relational treatment puts a great deal of emphasis on the clinician's subjective feelings, thoughts, and reactions, and on the mutual interaction between client and clinician as two open and authentic human beings.

The numerous theories that constitute current relational-intersubjective thinking emanated from three different streams of thought. A group of clinicians in the New York University postdoctoral program in psychoanalysis, who were greatly influenced by interpersonal theory, intersubjectivity, and social constructionist and feminist theories, comprise one stream of relational thinking. This stream includes the relational theorists Stephen Mitchell and Lewis Aron. A second stream flowed from the work of the intersubjective theorists, Robert Stolorow, George Atwood, Bernard Brandchaft, James Fosshage, and others, who originally embraced self-psychology. Yet a third stream of relational thinking stemmed from a number of self-psychologists and developmental researchers who were influenced by infant studies and attachment research. These theorists included Daniel Stern, Joseph Lichtenberg, Frank Lachmann, and Beatrice Beebe.

This chapter draws on these relational and intersubjective concepts as they shed light on the therapeutic relationship. It discusses the clinician's participation; the nature of resistance; the importance of the clinician's subjectivity and authenticity; mutuality and asymmetry; the therapist's use of self-disclosure; the mutual regulation between therapist and client; the role of enactment; and the concept of the third space between client and therapist. It will conclude with a discussion of the research literature on the working alliance between client and clinician, suggesting that the therapeutic relationship is an important factor in treatment outcomes.

THE CLINICIAN'S PARTICIPATION

A significant difference between traditional psychodynamic theories and relational theory is the emphasis that the latter places on clinicians' participation in the therapeutic interaction. Treatment based on traditional theory sees the therapist as an observer who remains outside of the therapeutic encounter. From this vantage point, the therapist's main functions are to serve as a transference object, provide interpretations, and serve as a container for the patient's affects. This point of view assumes that the therapist is able to maintain a neutral, objective, and anonymous presence, "uncontaminated" by the therapeutic interaction. The therapist's own feelings, reactions, and thoughts are excluded from the therapeutic situation.

In contrast, from a relational viewpoint, the therapist's neutrality and anonymity are seen as unrealistic, and impossible to uphold. Renik (1993) refers to the therapist's "irreducible subjectivity," meaning that therapists' affects and attitudes are inevitably an integral aspect of the treatment, even if these remain nonverbal. According to the relational view, clinicians possess their own personal history, inner conflicts, and opinions and bring these to their clinical practice. It regards every therapist–client interaction as unique, influenced by both participants' contributions and coconstructed from moment to moment (Hoffman 2006). Rather than standing outside the interactions and maintaining their personal anonymity and neutrality within their ivory tower (Mitchell 1997), the therapist is seen as an active participant through nonverbal signals, words, and actions. The therapeutic interaction rests on the coming together of the subjectivities of both client and clinician and their mutual influence (Hoffman 1996). Clinicians play an active role in the therapeutic interaction by contributing their subjectivity, or their unique personal attitudes, feelings, and thoughts.

THE NATURE OF RESISTANCE

The notion of resistance, an important concept in classical theory, illustrates one important shift resulting from relational thinking. In earlier psychodynamic formulations, especially drive theory and ego psychology, the term "resistance" implied that clients developed a variety of unconscious defense mechanisms to avoid facing their intrapsychic conflicts. From this perspective, one of the therapist's functions was to interpret the client's resistance and to bring it to the client's conscious awareness. One of the drawbacks of this approach is that almost everything clients say or do can be seen as resistance to the treatment, thereby pathologizing the client and setting up the therapist as the expert who is the ultimate authority on truth and meaning (Hoffman 1996).

The relational point of view sees resistance in a more complex manner that brings into consideration the clinician's role in regard to the client's response. Resistance may mean that the client does not feel safe with the therapist, not only because of who the client is, but also because of the therapist's behavior and personal style (Aron 1996). Resistance also may have positive and protective attributes, as some clients may need time to learn to trust their therapists before they open up, or they may feel too fragile to face painful experiences at a particular time. Thus, their so-called resistance may indicate a healthy sense of self-protection. From the relational view, it is important to investigate the therapist's own contribution to a specific interaction and its meaning from the client's perspective, rather than imposing the clinician's point of view or theoretical paradigms on the therapeutic process. In McLaughlin's words (1996:217), his client's hesitation and difficulty in expressing himself "struck me far less as resistance and more as the inherent tensions inevitable to intense collaborative effort."

THE THERAPIST'S SUBJECTIVITY AND AUTHENTICITY

The concept of therapist authenticity and subjectivity is linked to greater therapist participation. Relational theory emphasizes clinicians' authenticity, that is, their ability to be honest and relatively open regarding their subjective reactions to the therapeutic process. Relational therapists are encouraged to be more transparent with their responses and opinions, with the focus remaining, of course, on clients' issues. As stated previously, traditional treatment discouraged clinicians' display of their subjectivity or countertransference (Freud 1912). As Renik (1995:507) states, "neutrality on an analyst's part does not facilitate dialectical learning process. It is an analyst's capacity to apprehend the essence of a patient's struggles and to engage with the patient about them that contributes to successful clinical investigation."

Countertransference became more central to the treatment with Melanie Klein (1952) as a result of her conceptualization of projective identification, which her followers later elaborated on. Although Klein believed that projective identification stemmed from the client's fantasy, her followers included the therapist in the concept. Thus, they viewed projective identification as affect states that the clients projected onto the therapist, and therefore as a kind of unconscious communication from client to therapist inducing the therapist to feel and act in certain ways. Through focusing on what was being projected, therapists could thereby gain a better understanding of the client's dissociated feelings and experiences. Although Kleinian theory is still considered a one-person approach in the sense that the exclusive focus is on the client, its emphasis on the role of countertransference contributed to a greater appreciation of the therapist's internal feeling states and the value of using them to understand the internal world of clients.

Many relational clinicians added an important dimension to this idea. They suggested the importance of not only focusing on the therapist's countertransference in order to better understand their clients (Jacobs 2007), or to mirror the client and reflect what the client brings to treatment as in self-psychology, but also advocated the use of countertransference self-disclosure. As Hoffman (1996:110) states, "there is no way to reduce one's involvement to being merely that of a facilitator of self awareness . . . there is no objective interpretation and there is no affective attunement that is merely responsive to and reflective of what the patient brings to the situation. There is always something personal and theoretical that is coming from the therapist." Relational practice emphasizes therapists' greater transparency with their affect states, thinking process, and reactions, for example, their honesty and authenticity with their clients. Therapists are more likely to admit their mistakes, thereby validating their clients' perceptions of them, and showing their clients that they are also flawed human beings capable of making errors. The following example illustrates some of these ideas.

A young male social worker was assigned as a case manager to a twenty-three-year-old client who was diagnosed with severe spinal muscular atrophy. The case manager's job was to make regular home visits to the client to provide him with companionship and support and address any concrete or other needs as they might arise. The client was bed-bound, and his only contact with the outside world was through online communication. The social worker, on the other hand, was a tall, robust, and athletic young man in excellent health, which the client idealized and looked up to. One day the case manager did not feel well and called to cancel his appointment with the client, who sounded angry and disappointed. As they resumed their visits, the client became very critical and mocking, utilizing any opportunity to put down the case manager and belittle his abilities.

The clinician felt hurt and angry. He deeply empathized with his client's disability. He also admired his intelligence and talents and treated him with respect. He believed that they had developed a mutual relationship based on trust and friendship. He nevertheless thought that the client had been selfish and inconsiderate, unconcerned about the case manager's well-being, and instead punished him for the missed visit. As the clinician reflected more deeply, he began to understand that he represented all that the client wished he could be—strong, athletic, independent, and popular, having a girlfriend and a successful career. He represented an ideal that the client wanted to emulate. The social worker's illness, however, was a profound disappointment. It reminded the client of his own vulnerability, which he hated and felt others did not accept, and projected his self-hatred onto the case manager, who found himself in a dilemma. Should he keep these reflections to himself, or share them with the client? His countertransference response helped him gain a deeper understanding of the client, but he also felt that the client might benefit from a mutual discussion of this process. During their next meeting, after the client had again criticized him, the case manager suggested that his client must have been very disappointed when he became sick, as he recognized that his social worker was imperfect and vulnerable to physical frailties, just like him, and that must have been difficult for him to accept. The client admitted that he was indeed disappointed; he conveyed that he was also concerned that the case manager would stop coming and abandon him, just like the previous one had done, and would forget about him as the case manager continued with his own normal life. This discussion was a breakthrough in their relationship. The client stopped idealizing the case manager and accepted that he was fallible and made mistakes. He also became more open in sharing his fears and concerns, rather than putting on a bravado appearance. The case manager became more at ease admitting his mistakes and revealing his thoughts and responses to the client, even when these were not what the client wanted to hear. Both started to use humor and play in their interactions with each other.

MUTUALITY AND ASYMMETRY

The therapist's participation, subjectivity, and authenticity contribute to a more egalitarian relationship between therapists and clients. Meaning and truth are not seen as emerging from the therapist's expertise and knowledge, but rather are coconstructed between client and clinician based on mutual interactions and are contingent upon each therapeutic dyad's unique relationship.

Ferenczi's contributions greatly influenced the concept of mutuality (Aron and Harris 1993). He developed what he called "mutual analysis" with his patients. He believed that it was important for both client and clinician to be completely open and honest with each other, and to express their inner thoughts and feelings to each other, taking turns as clients and clinicians. Many of Ferenczi's patients were sexual abuse victims, and he believed that the only way he could gain their trust was by being completely honest and open with them, and by validating their experiences. Although Ferenczi went too far in his approach of mutual analysis and was ostracized at the time by Freud and his followers, his idea of greater mutuality between clients and therapist has gained increasing attention, and its use has contributed to reducing the power differential and hierarchical structure between client and therapist upon which earlier psychoanalytic models were built.

Another aspect of mutuality is the concept of mutual recognition (Benjamin 1995). According to Benjamin, the child does not reach maturity until he or she is able to recognize the parent as a separate other, with his or her own needs, affects, and limitations, separate from themselves. The caregiver is no longer perceived as only the provider of emotional and material provisions, but as a separate being. Benjamin elaborated on Winnicott's concept of the mother who is able to survive the infant's rage and destructiveness, thereby showing the infant that she is not part of him or her, and is able to survive the infant's aggression and maintain her separate integrity (Winnicott 1965). With regard to adult treatment, this means that clients have reached a developmental stage whereby they can view the therapist as a unique individual, rather than as a part of them or as an object onto which they project their thoughts and feelings. In the therapeutic interactions, both client and clinician are interconnected yet autonomous, and the client is capable of appreciating and accepting the therapist's difference and humanity.

Relational clinicians try to convey more transparency in their thinking and responses. They may share their own affective reactions to the client's material, may let clients know the impact they have had on them (Ehrenberg 1992), and may articulate dilemmas with regard to therapeutic interactions (Aron 1996). According to Aron, relational practice is based not only on words, that is, the client's free association and the therapist's interpretation, but also on nonverbal and at times unconscious communication and interactions between client and therapist. This will be covered in more detail later in the chapter.

According to Aron and Harris (1993), Ferenczi understood the value of mutuality, but his mistake was that he did not grasp the importance of asymmetry in terms of maintaining appropriate boundaries with his clients. His formulation of the therapeutic relationship was that therapist and client played equal roles in the therapeutic process. Although relational practice advocates greater interaction and mutual investigations between therapist and client (for example, the client is encouraged to wonder about the therapist's reactions, or to ask questions about the therapist's thinking and responses), the relationship is not symmetrical. Relational theory proposes that client and therapist roles are always different and asymmetrical, with the focus of investigation on the client, rather than the therapist. There are set rules that govern the therapeutic interactions and ensure that professional boundaries are kept. These include ethical guidelines, meetings at a regular time and place, the therapist's compensation for his or her service, and the therapist's assumed knowledge and expertise. These rules protect the integrity of the relationship and show that it is not really possible for symmetry to exist.

Modell (1991) discussed the paradoxical nature of the therapeutic relationship that is both real and unreal. It is a relationship between two people who engage with each other, and in many ways may care for one another; however, it exists in a rarified and special time and space and does not take place in the real world. This dialectic allows for the therapeutic relationship to be a safe space where boundaries and trust are not violated. These ethical considerations cannot exist if the notion of asymmetry is denied, as when the professional relationship is mistaken for a real relationship and boundary violations occur. Although relational theorists tried to create a less hierarchical therapeutic relationship, they understood that it was important to emphasize therapists' responsibility to practice based on their professional code of ethics, and to protect the client and the sanctity of the therapeutic endeavor. Some of these concepts are illustrated in the following case.

An African American social work intern worked in a hospice for terminally ill clients. One of her favorite clients was a fifty-five-year-old African American woman diagnosed with terminal cancer. This client was fiercely independent and found it difficult to rely on others now that she had become increasingly incapacitated. This was apparent in her relationship with the social worker, who was considerably younger that she was. She treated the clinician as if she were her daughter, and despite the fact that she shared with her much about her life and history, she insisted on trying to reciprocate by asking about her health and well-being, about her family, and complimenting her on her appearance and abilities. The social worker felt increasingly uncomfortable, not sure how to maintain boundaries in this delicate relationship which was not quite psychotherapy in the traditional sense, as she met the client by her bedside, at times with her family and friends present, in a more or less casual manner.

One day, toward the end of the social worker's internship, the client told her that she wanted to give her a goodbye gift. The social worker explained that in accordance with agency policy, she was not allowed to receive gifts from clients, although she appreciated the intention and was quite grateful. The client became very upset and told the social worker tearfully that giving the gift would mean a lot to her, that she wanted the social worker to remember her even after they parted ways. The social worker was in a quandary. She shared her dilemma with the client, saying that she appreciated her gift and obviously felt that it was important for the client that she accepted it, but she added that she was bound by the agency's policy and had to refuse the gift. As the client continued to press the gift upon her, she finally accepted it but also felt some anger and resentment (which she did not share with the client) that the client had forced her to act against the agency's policy.

When the social worker opened the gift, she found a letter of gratitude and a photograph of the client as a beautiful young woman, very different from the way she looked now. She wondered why the client gave her this old photo, and as she reflected on what happened she understood that the client wanted to be remembered as an attractive, healthy, and independent young woman, her inner self that she had such a hard time letting go of. The client entrusted this younger self to the social worker, whom she trusted to hold that precious part of herself that she was now losing, but hoped that the social worker would remember through their long talks with each other. The social worker shared some of these insights with the client, who was deeply touched and reiterated how much their relationship and the memories she had shared with the social worker meant to her.

THERAPIST SELF-DISCLOSURE

Self-disclosure is an aspect of mutuality, subjectivity, and therapist participation. In more traditional psychodynamic models, self-disclosure was rigorously avoided because of the belief that it violated the notion of therapist's neutrality and objectivity, and because therapist self-disclosure risked shifting the focus from the client to the therapist. Burke and Tansey (1992:361) suggest that from a drive theory perspective, "since counter-transference disclosure is antithetical to the drive-conflict theory of therapeutic action, revelation of the thoughts and feelings experienced by the therapist would only serve to gratify the patient's pathological wish rather than analyze the wish to know, with all its attendant anxieties fears, pleasure, and so on. Disclosure in this light amounts to a foreclosure of the opportunity to analyze the transference neurosis."

In relational practice, however, therapist self-disclosure is an important aspect of therapeutic action and, if skillfully done, an expression of the therapist's subjectivity (Aron 1996). Relational theory maintains that because the therapist's subjectivity is inevitable and is impossible to hide or ignore, it would be dishonest to pretend that therapists do not have subjective responses during the session (Renik 1995), and that it makes no sense for therapists to withhold their inevitable thoughts, feelings, and opinions as if they hold no influence on the client. Even if therapists do not discuss their responses with clients, clients may pick up nonverbal cues that are always available, such as facial expressions, tone of voice, and silence. Therapists may retraumatize their clients by repeating previous experiences of rejection, invalidation, and emotional withdrawal by not responding to their clients' impressions and perceptions of them.

Therapist self disclosure, which will be discussed in more detail in chapters 6 and 7, does not necessarily mean that clinicians discuss their personal life, past experiences, or demographic facts with the client. It can involve clinicians' sharing of their countertransference (Chused 2003), dilemmas they are struggling with in an effort to understand and help the client, or a disclosure of their thinking process in relation to the client. Nevertheless, self-disclosures should always be related to the client's needs. As Ehrenberg suggests, "in those instances where interpretation might be experienced as a form of rape or violation of the patient's inner space, or where silence might be experienced as sadistic, cruel, or abandoning, judicious use of counter-transference disclosure can be much less invasive, threatening or dangerous than either . . . it can also become a valuable tool toward turning a potential impasse into an analytic opportunity" (Ehrenberg 1992:214–215).

Writers such as Aron and Renik discuss at length their struggles with the decision of whether, how, and when to disclose. Self-disclosure inadvertently may also serve to reduce the hierarchical structure of the therapeutic relationship and help clients view their therapist as a regular person like themselves. Goldstein, for example, relates how she disclosed to her client, in answer to her question, that she played the piano but was not very good at it. According to Goldstein, this helped the client relax her perfectionist standards toward herself and become more self-accepting (Goldstein 1994).

Relational therapists may disclose their countertransference reactions to the client in order to help clients recognize their impact on others, and shift from a self-centered stance to awareness of others, and of other experiences and points of view besides their own. The therapists' disclosure of their countertransference response to clients may help clients improve interpersonal relationships with others based on greater accommodation for differences and a more realistic perspective of their impact on others. Ehrenberg (1992:43) gives examples of disclosing her affective responses to her clients. For example, she describes how, with a patient called Edward, she admitted to being "upset with myself for not being more perceptive about the degree of his withholding." Following this disclosure, Edward states that he suddenly saw Ehrenberg as "more 'human' than before and that he now felt 'more equal' than he ever imagined he could feel." Nevertheless, self-disclosure does not always have positive consequences.

In the following vignette, the clinician disclosed aspects of her ethnic identity. An Israeli clinician worked in a college-counseling center. She was assigned a Palestinian student during the intifada in Israel and the Palestinian territories. She did not know if the client knew she was Israeli and was in a quandary whether to disclose her identity to him. The more the client shared his feelings toward his family and his struggles as an immigrant and a Muslim in a mostly secular American society, the more uncomfortable the clinician became about withholding her national identity from him. When the client started to discuss his conflicts with an American girlfriend and with American women in general, whom he felt did not understand him and looked down on him, the clinician thought he might be referring to her.

She decided that it was important to address her identity so as to provide this client with more choice and agency in the treatment.

The clinician asked the client whether he wondered where she was from. He looked up, smiled, but did not say anything. She then continued that she thought it would be important for him to know at this point that she was an Israeli, and that he might have already known that based on her Israeli name and accent. The client smiled and stated that he suspected as much. The therapist asked if he felt comfortable continuing to work with her. The client stated that he had already told her much about himself and felt comfortable and did not want to be referred to someone else. Nevertheless he seemed uncomfortable and soon left, canceling his next appointments and ending treatment.

In this example, the therapist faced an ethical dilemma. If she had withheld her identity, the client may have continued the treatment for a time but may have felt misled and manipulated. By disclosing her identity, the therapist allowed the client to have an active choice and a sense of agency in his treatment. Perhaps she should have disclosed her identity much earlier in the treatment based on the unique circumstance of their ethnic origins? When she did disclose her identity, the client may have experienced a sense of betrayal and anger that he was encouraged to share intimate aspects of his life with a therapist who, under other circumstances, would have been his enemy. It is also possible, however, that the ethnic differences between therapist and client meant more to the therapist than to the client, and that the therapist's self-disclosure suggested to the client that she did not want to work with him and made him feel unwanted. Thus, there are risks to self-disclosure that will be discussed in later chapters.

MUTUAL REGULATION

The concept of affect regulation was developed based on infant studies by Daniel Stern, Beatrice Beebe, and others. Their findings regarding bi-directional interactions between infant and caregiver were then applied to the client–clinician relationship (see chapter 4). Previous theories emphasized the provision of a corrective experience, a holding environment (Winnicott 1965), containment (Bion 1963), or a self object function (Kohut 1971) as the means of regulating the client's affects. As infant researchers started to recognize that infant-caregiver interactions are reciprocal, with infants exercising their own agency, taking their own initiative, and having a considerable influence on interactions with their caregivers, more recent relational theorists viewed therapist and client as providing mutual regulation for each other through their reciprocal interactions (Beebe and Lachmann 2002; Lichtenberg et al. 2002). From the intersubjective perspective, both client and therapist are seen as influencing one another and contributing to the creation of a unique pattern of mutual regulation in the client–therapist dyad. The client's verbal and nonverbal communications affect therapist verbal and nonverbal responses as much as the therapist's communications affect the client. Patterns of mutual regulation that may develop include a certain ritual of greeting, saying good-bye, mutual laughter, and reciprocal gestures and gaze.

Mutual regulation is of particular concern in clinical practice with traumatized clients, whose capacity to self-regulate has been compromised, and the therapeutic situation allows them to recognize maladaptive regulatory behaviors through interactions with the therapist. The therapeutic relationship is also a space where both therapist and client develop and practice new, more adaptive mutual and self-regulatory skills, based on greater trust in self and others, greater tolerance for frustrations, disappointments, and relational conflicts, and greater acceptance of oneself.

Infant researchers, including Meltzoff (1990), Trevarthen (1989), Stern (1985), and Beebe and Lachmann (2002) note that in addition to the pattern of disruption and repair during verbal and nonverbal communication, there is a pattern of correspondence and matching between the infant and caregivers, which starts when infants are as young as a few weeks old. According to these authors, "cross modal correspondence enables either patient or analyst to bring internal process and behavior into correspondence with the internal process and behavior of the partner" (Beebe and Lachmann 2002:7). They write that matching regulates both client's and therapist's inner states and thus contributes to mutual regulation. They note that intersubjectivity is initially preverbal and only later becomes symbolized through verbal communication. Stern et al. (1975) note that changes occur moment by moment, through matching to each other's rhythm and intensity, nonverbally. Beebe and Lachmann add that matching and correspondence between infant and caregiver, client and therapist are incomplete without the concept of "contingency." One's behavior, either client or therapist, is predicated upon previous signals and behavior by the other, and thereby the partners mutually regulate and change each other. The following two vignettes provide examples of correspondence and matching, and of disruption and repair between client and therapist. The following example shows how both client and clinician contribute to mutual regulation, often through nonverbal and even unconscious interactions.

The client was a man who sustained considerable verbal and psychological abuse throughout his life both from his family members and from others. In addition to his diagnosis of depression, the client also suffered from obsessive-compulsive disorder (OCD). Whenever this client became excited, he would start talking very quickly, garbling and swallowing his words, and raising his voice with excitement. In response, the therapist slowed down her own words and spoke more softly. The client then responded by slowing down his speech as well and lowering his voice, and a new rhythm was created between them. His pressured and unregulated speech pattern became more regulated and responsive. During these times the therapist helped regulate the client's excitement and agitation; at other times the client regulated the therapist.

This client was particularly sensitive to any nonverbal signals from the therapist and would pick up immediately when the therapist was distracted, inattentive, or sleepy. In response, the client would proceed to repeat the same sentence again and again, until he was sure that he captured the therapist's attention again and the two returned to their mutually regulating cycle. These interactions occurred without attempts to explain, interpret, or point out the process, and they seemed to be a recurring spontaneous pattern of interaction.

One day, however, the client described how his OCD was exacerbated around people at work who were unable to follow his instructions and were incompetent in their work. The client found himself having to second-guess himself, question his competence, and repeat his instructions in order to make up for the incompetence around him. Both he and his therapist joked that his OCD came in especially handy during those times. The therapist thought that this was a good opportunity to ask the client whether this pattern occurred with her as well—that because of her own seeming incompetence and lack of attention at times, the client found himself having to second-guess what he had said and repeat himself. The client sighed deeply and admitted that the therapist was indeed a handful and at times very taxing for him, and both laughed.

ENACTMENT

As chapter 7 will discuss in more detail, relational theorists place importance on recognizing and addressing enactments in treatment. In enactments client and clinician take on roles that are analogous to the client's early relational patterns, typically with their parents (Sandler 1976). The interaction between client and therapist is experienced not only through verbal communications and interpretation, but through actual behavioral interactions. For example, clients may exert pressure on therapists unconsciously to enact early relational configurations with them, in which the clinician takes on the role of an abusive parent, a victim, or a savior (Black 2003; Davies and Frawley 1994). It also is possible, however, that that the clinician, rather than the client, stimulates the enactment, and thus it is not always easy to know how each member of the therapeutic dyad is contributing to the enactment.

Although it is advisable that clinicians try to prevent enactments from escalating, they are an unavoidable aspect of the therapeutic interaction. They present opportunities for client and therapist to understand and process painful relational dynamics through a mutual experience that goes beyond words. This experience in the context of a safe and trusted relationship with another may help clients gain insight into maladaptive patterns of interactions, as well as practice new relational patterns. By working through enactments, clients may learn how to resolve relational conflicts and miscommunications without ending the relationship, withdrawing, or retaliating (and being retaliated against).

With traumatized clients, enactments take on a poignant role. Davies and Frawley's (1994) book about their work with victims of sexual abuse discuss the range of enactments that can occur. It is only through the therapist's ability to recognize and help process these role enactments that clients can gain insight into habitual patterns of relating and thereby have the choice to react differently to new relational situations, as well as to old ones. They acquire the capacity to move out of binary positions of victim and perpetrator, neglectful parent and neglected child, and gain greater integration and internal coherence of fragmented internal parts and polarized relationships.

In the following example, the client was a forty-year-old single woman, with a history of rejection by her family. She reported that her father had always ignored her, unlike her other sibling to whom he paid careful attention. He was not interested in talking to her and would spend as little times on the phone with her as he could get away with. In addition, he became uncomfortable with any expression of feeling on her side, whether it was anger, sadness, or anxiety. He would discourage her from expressing her feelings and would become immediately uninterested and withdrawn.

During a session, the therapist was expecting an important business call and forgot to warn the client. During an emotional discussion regarding her father's and family's most recent rejection of her, the telephone rang. The therapist asked for the client's permission to respond for a few minutes, and she then returned to the room to continue the session. The client was livid. She was so enraged that she picked up her bag and left, despite the therapist's repeated apologies. She then called the therapist from her car's cell phone to berate her about her lack of professionalism, concern and empathy. The therapist experienced a mixture of intense emotions. She felt guilt, responsibility, a sense of incompetence, and helplessness. On the phone, she encouraged the client to come back so that they could process what had occurred.

The client agreed to return. She seemed very distant and distrustful of the therapist. The therapist acknowledged to the client that she had made a mistake that had disrupted the client's sense of trust. She tried to repair this with the client but also thought it was important to explore the dynamic nature of this interaction between her and the client. She asked the client if what had occurred between them made her feel as she did with her father—that she was not worthy of the therapist's time and attention. The client admitted that that is exactly how she felt. She started to cry and stated that she had started to trust the therapist, who, like everyone else in her life, became an insensitive, rejecting presence that she could no longer count on.

This interactions had a particular resonance to this client, who brought with her a history of dismissal and rejection by her significant others. The therapist's mistake placed her in the role that mirrored the client's past relationship with her father. The therapist became the rejecting, neglecting parent, with the client experiencing herself as the rejected, abandoned child. The client also became the rejecting, dismissive other, making the therapist feel like the rejected, criticized child. Their ability to process what had occurred and move on to reconnect in a new way would ultimately determine the outcome of this treatment.

THE THIRD SPACE

The notion of the third is related to Winnicott's concept of the transitional space. Winnicott described the transitional space as a symbolic space in the therapeutic sphere that serves as a link between the inner fantasy life of the client, and the objective external reality they have to learn to adjust to. The transitional space between therapist and client is a safe space that allows the client to develop their sense of creativity and play, at times through reciprocal play between client and therapist. The transitional space allows the client to practice new ways of interacting with another and thereby adapt to the external social and cultural reality.

The concept of the third from a relational, two-person perspective has evolved considerably. Writers such as Ogden and Benjamin each understood the meaning of the third in somewhat different ways. For Ogden (1997), the third is the therapeutic space between client and therapist. For Benjamin (2002), the third is inspired by Sandler's work with infants and their mothers, in which he discovered that a unique rhythm develops between mother and infant as they adjust to each other and create a pattern of interaction unique to them. Benjamin describes the third as a pattern of sounds, gestures, or other nonverbal signals that develops between therapist and client, the creation of their unique mutual interaction. For example, one therapist developed a pattern of singing a song with his client whenever she came in a particular mood. Both of them knew what the song alluded to and would laugh with each other in mutual enjoyment.

Mattei (1999) also elaborated on the third as a social cultural and racial phenomenon. The client's race, ethnicity, or culture and the therapist reactions, preconceived ideas or stereotypes, race, ethnicity, and culture become the third in the treatment room that needs to be talked about (Gentile 2007:576).

In the following example, a student intern found a third space with his client through a shared interest in the Rolling Stones. A male social work clinician worked in an adolescent residential treatment facility. He was assigned a thirteen-year-old adolescent female client. Her mother was a crack addict. When the client was eight months old, she was taken from her mother and sent to live with her maternal grandmother until she was eight years old. Then she returned to her mother, where she witnessed her mother being beaten by her boyfriend and was raped by a boy when she was ten. The client was guarded and uncooperative with the therapist and initially extremely distrustful and resistant to any friendly overtures and attempts to establish a relationship. Because she was impulsive, she frequently got into trouble at the group home and eventually started to seek the therapist's advice about how to avoid getting into trouble. Eventually, the therapist found a way to elicit her cooperation. He would tell her, "Remember what Mick [Jagger] said. 'You can't always get what you want but if you try sometimes you get what you need.'" He would sing this phrase with her to suggest that she had to learn to tolerate not always getting her way, and they would start to sing the song together and laugh. This interaction became a familiar pattern between them, a "third" that they both shared and infused with special meaning that only the two of them understood.

EMPIRICAL BASIS FOR A RELATIONAL APPROACH

There is a large body of research that supports the value of a relational approach to treatment, most of it focused on a variety of measurements of the therapeutic alliance between client and clinician.

Quantitative and qualitative measurements of the therapeutic alliance include the California Psychotherapy Alliance Scale (CALPAS, Gaston 1991), the Helping Alliance Questionnaire (HAQ, Luborsky et al. 1985), and the Working Alliance Inventory (WAI, Horvath and Greenberg 1989). These instruments are highly correlated with one another and show high levels of reliability.

Most studies show that the therapeutic alliance contributes to positive treatment outcomes (Horvath and Symonds 1991; Martin et al. 2000). Some studies showed a significant relationship between a positive alliance in psychodynamic therapy and clients' posttherapy symptoms (Piper et al. 1991). One study, however, did not report a significant relationship between the alliance and treatment outcomes (Windholtz and Silberschatz 1988). A study of a twelve-session dynamic therapy showed that for clients with low motivation, a positive alliance was associated with better outcomes, but for clients with higher motivation, an emphasis on the alliance produced poorer outcomes or showed no correlation with outcome (Piper et al. 1991). Barber et al. (2000) found a direct causal role between the alliance and therapeutic outcomes in a study of supportive expressive psychodynamic psychotherapy. Based on most of these studies, it appears that there is a consistent influence of the alliance on therapeutic outcomes in psychodynamic therapy.

In conclusion, these studies show that the relationship between client and therapist, both from the client and from the therapist's perspective, is a significant factor in the treatment and in treatment outcomes, and that a relational approach may provide more specific dimensions of therapeutic interaction that can be studied and evaluated. For example, Safran et al. (2005) developed a model of Brief Relational Therapy, based on contemporary relational principles, and designed specific interventions designed to address therapeutic alliance ruptures (such as enactments). Predictably, they found that when these ruptures were addressed, therapeutic outcomes improved (less untimely termination, higher patient satisfaction, etc.).

4. DEVELOPMENTAL CONCEPTS

Chapters 2 and 3 show that early relational thinking tended to focus on what the baby brings to the world and on how the caretaking environment nurtures and influences individual development, whereas later contributions emphasized mutuality and interaction in the relationship between the self and others. The ideas put forth by the full range of relational theorists are not fully integrated so that there is not a unitary relational developmental theory. Drawing on both theoretical streams, this chapter describes what we consider to be major developmental relational concepts. It also will draw on recent research findings that provide some empirical support for a relational view of development.

The following discussion classifies the concepts in terms of what Mitchell has called the relational matrix, which refers to the self, others, and the nature of the interactions between self and others (Aron and Harris 2005:xvi). Additionally it will describe common derailments or psychopathological developments that may occur. Finally, it will comment on gender development and the influence of cultural diversity and oppression on the developmental process.

PERSPECTIVES ON THE SELF

Although a hallmark of relational thinking is the interaction between self and others, some writers have focused mainly on what infants bring to these transactions and the processes that affect the growing child's relationships to the environment.

THE TRUE SELF AND THE CORE NUCLEAR SELF   According to Winnicott (1965), the true self represents an individual's core potentialities and develops when there is good-enough mothering. Also emphasizing the self, Kohut (1971) regarded it as the center of initiative of the person that organizes experience and regulates self-esteem. Although Kohut believed that it exists in a rudimentary way from birth, like Winnicott, he recognized that the core nuclear self crystallizes as a result of the caretaking environment's *empathic attunement and responsiveness* to the growing child's innate potentialities and needs. As a result of attuned parenting, the self gradually achieves cohesiveness and stability as an enduring structure. A strong cohesive self gives the person a sense of vigor, inner harmony, and self-esteem.

SELFOBJECT NEEDS   According to Kohut, the self of the infant exhibits needs for others to fulfill vital functions from birth all through life. Kohut identified three main types of selfobject needs: the need for *mirroring* that confirms the child's sense of vigor, greatness, and perfection; the need for an *idealization of others* whose strength and calmness soothe the child; and the need for a *twin or alter-ego* who provides the child with a sense of humanness, likeness to, and partnership with others. Other selfobject needs that have been suggested are the need for *merger experiences* with someone who is totally subject to the child's initiative and who functions as an extension of the self; the need for *an adversary* who provides a supportive but oppositional relationship in the service of autonomy; and the need for *efficacy* in having an impact on others and in being able to evoke desired responses. Although not all types of selfobject needs may be gratified in a particular child's life, rewarding experiences with at least one type of selfobject give the child a chance to develop a cohesive self (Wolf 1988:55).

STAGES OF SELF-DEVELOPMENT   Daniel Stern's infant studies provided empirical support for the view that infants bring with them a basic awareness of self that needs and is shaped by ongoing interactions with the caretaking environment. In contrast to Mahler, Stern found that the formation of an infant's self did not arise as a result of symbiosis and gradual separation from the mother or main caretaker but instead preceded attachment and made possible a "sense of merger like experience" (Brandell and Ringel 2007:70).

Stern described three discrete developmental stages: the emergent self, the core self, and the subjective self. During the stage of the emergent self, infants as young as two months of age made direct eye contact, began to smile responsively, and chuckled at their mother. Almost from birth, infants began to turn their head, look around, and display an emergent sense of agency and autonomy. Stern theorized that at the age of two to three months, infants become more social and able to focus more fully on interactions. They appear to have a more integrated sense of self even at this early stage in their development.

Stern also formulated four qualities of a core self, which infants could achieve at this stage: self-agency, or the authorship of one's own actions; self-coherence, or a sense of being part of a whole; self-affectivity, or an experience of inner self, feelings, and states of mind; and self-history, or sense of continuity and history. Another important aspect of the core self was the developing ability to be with others, which Stern saw as an important factor in self-integration.

MOTIVATIONAL SYSTEMS As an alternative to viewing the drives as the major motivating forces in human behavior, some relational theorists drew on empirical observations of infants to put forth motivational concepts that emphasize infant–caretaker interaction. For example, Lichtenberg, Lachmann, and Fosshage (2002) proposed the existence of five motivational systems, each having its own developmental line that is codetermined by individual need and environmental responsiveness:

- *The Motivational System Based on the Regulation of Physiological Requirements*, in which the infant is dominated by the need to have his basic bodily needs responded to, regulated, and fulfilled
- *The Attachment-Affiliation Motivational System*, in which the infant and toddler seeks connection, closeness, likeness, and intimacy
- *The Exploratory-Assertive Motivational System*, in which the infant and child forcefully express curiosity in and efforts to have an affect upon and be competent in dealing with the environment
- *The Aversive Motivational System*, in which the infant and toddler react to frustration and fear with attempts to avoid, flee, or oppose painful situations. This system gives rise to defense formation.

- *The Sensual-Sexual Motivational System*, in which the infant and child express their needs for affection and soothing, on the one hand, and sexual excitement and relaxation, on the other

Personality develops in relation to how the growing organism evolves the mechanisms and coping strategies for dealing with each of these motivational systems. Certain forms of psychopathology reflect the dominance of a particular motivational system and problems in getting the need associated with it met.

INTERNALIZATION   Internalization refers to the mechanism by which infants and young children take in the outer environment and make it part of their inner structure or experience. Internalization goes beyond imitation of others and involves more than taking on the characteristics of the external environment. Children actually make what is external to them a vital part of what is internal. Children internalize what they experience around them — parental and societal attitudes toward the self, parental characteristics and styles of relating, and interactional patterns between themselves and others and between others.

A distinctive variation of the term "internalization" is reflected in the self-psychological concept of *transmuting internalization*. This refers to a child's gradual taking over the selfobject functions that others have provided and building up his or her ability to self-regulate. It occurs as a result of inevitable nontraumatic empathic failure on the part of the caretaking environment in the context of its general attuned responsiveness to the child's needs. Transmuting internalization renders the actual presence of the selfobject less vital or even unnecessary. Thus, what is outside becomes internal and alters the original or archaic structures that exist. An example of transmuting internalization via optimal frustration can be seen at times when a mother who sings to her child at bedtime withdraws prior to the child's falling asleep. If this change is timed correctly and thus is not too traumatic, the child may soothe himself or herself through singing, playing, or talking, thereby identifying with and taking over the mother's function (Goldstein 2001:83).

SELF- AND OBJECT REPRESENTATIONS   Infants begin to form images of themselves (self-representations) and others (object representations) by taking in experiences with those close to them. Once formed, self- and object representations are fundamental internal structures that affect the ways in which individuals view themselves and others. Theorists differ with respect to whether they believe that these self- and object representations are based on the internalization of objective reality exclusively or are influenced by children's' fantasies. For example, the presence of frustrating interactions with the mother may make her appear more "monstrous" than she is in reality. Likewise, children may imagine that their "badness" is causing their caretakers to neglect or abuse them.

There are different phases of the internalization process. In *introjection*, which arises earlier than identification, fantasies or images of real frustrations and dangers in relationships with others are taken in under the impact of highly charged primitive impulses and affects. These images often are experienced as consuming and frightening. For example, the infant may take in an ominous and powerful image of the mother's angry face that is associated with the infant's intense hunger. This part-object image may terrify the infant. Likewise, the infant may introject of the mother's smiling face that is associated with soothing and warmth and that exerts a comforting influence. Introjects begin to cluster into "good me" and bad me" depending on whether the infant is experiencing pleasurable or frustrating interactions with the environment.

Identification, the second and later mechanism that affects the internalization process, rests on the child's ability to recognize his or her separateness from the mother and to take on or model the different functions that the caretaking object plays in important interactions. For example, a little girl whose mother sings to her in a loving and soothing way when she is going to sleep takes in a positive image of the mother in relation to the child's fatigue and bedtime routines. Later she may take on the mother's role by singing to her doll when she imagines the doll is tired. Her imitation of the mother's interaction with her may eventually become a more stable part of her internal organization and repertoire of behavior. The child acquires many diverse introjects and identifications based on his or her interactions with others.

Because early self- and object representations are based on part-object experiences, they do not result in a coherent conception of the self and others until later in the developmental process. An important milestone is the child's ability to integrate his or her part-object experiences. The completion of the internalization process involves a consolidation of self- and object images into a stable and coherent whole.

MULTIPLE SELVES In contrast to the view describe above that sees the developmental process as leading to a cohesive, unitary sense of self, some relational theorists (Bromberg 1998; Mitchell 2003) view the self as reflecting discontinuous states that reflect different aspects of personal history and relational experience. Thus, the self may be composed of various selves that manifest themselves at different times as the individual interacts with others.

PROJECTION Just as infants take in external experiences through introjection, they also project certain internal states onto others. When good or pleasurable feelings are projected, infants experience the object of their projections positively. Alternatively, when infants expel bad, unpleasurable, or frightening feelings and impulses, they experience the object of their projections as threatening and persecutory. Repetitive cycles of introjection and projection result in the building up of internalized object relations.

An important early defense mechanism is *projective identification*, which is more extreme than projection. In projective identification, not only is an aspect of the person put onto an external object, but also the object begins to feel or behave in ways that are keeping with what has been projected. For example, a woman who experiences her rage as intolerable may not express it directly but may act in ways that induce her husband to behave in a very angry manner. She then feels justified in responding to him with retaliatory anger.

AFFECTS Although she was more wedded to traditional psychoanalytic theory than others, Edith Jacobson (1964) introduced the idea that infants experience certain feeling states (affects) that are linked to their interaction with others. When their external relationships are internalized, the resultant self- and object representations and the relationships between them contain affective colorations. For example, the infant may internalize an object representation of a loving mother in relation to a positive self-representation of the infant's own loving and dependent feelings. The infant also takes in a self-representation that is positive with respect to loving and dependent feelings. Alternatively, an infant might internalize an object representation of an angry mother in relation to a negatively tinged self-representation involving the infant's neediness, which becomes equated with "badness."

INTERNAL WORKING MODELS Based on his observations of young children, Bowlby used this concept to refer to the patterns of attachment between the child and the caregiver that become internalized and that determine later relationships (Brandell and Ringel 2007). For example, children who grow up in secure environments internalize secure relationships with their parents. They are later able to maintain a balance between closeness and intimacy, and autonomy and independence. Parents who are insecure transmit a pattern of anxious attachment to their children, who then have difficulty forming healthy attachment relationships with others. The different attachment patterns will be discussed in more detail below.

ORGANIZING PRINCIPLES   Writing about an idea that is similar to Bowlby's view of internal working models, Stolorow thought that the internalization of infant–caregiver patterns of interaction result in certain fixed principles that organize the child's subjective experience and influence later interactions with others (Stolorow and Atwood 1992). He argued that these structures are the essential building blocks of personality development, but that they also are affected by current and ongoing transactions with the environment.

PERSPECTIVES ON OTHERS

Early relational theorists also tended to focus on how the caretaking environment nurtures and influences development and on delineating the optimal features of caretakers and significant others.

THE GOOD-ENOUGH MOTHER   According to Winnicott (1965, 1975), the infant's mother is the first representative of the facilitating environment that he believed is essential to human growth. In his view, the "good-enough" mother is one who adapts to and responds to her child's changing individualized needs and provides for the child sufficiently to help the child to grow. There is not one type of optimal mother because children exhibit a variety of needs at different times and require individualized handling or responsiveness.

Winnicott thought that pregnant mothers are biologically prepared for parenting, displaying what he called *primary maternal preoccupation* with their infant's particular needs. He placed considerable importance on the concept of *ego-relatedness* between the mother and infant, which sets the stage for the child's ability to develop a strong sense of self. Ego-relatedness is a type of emotional bond between two individuals who both exist as separate people but who are intimately connected. This connection begins when the good-enough mother and child interact. The mother's provision of good-enough care results in the child developing a sense of continuity, history, and uniqueness or *going on being*. The growing child's *capacity to be alone* also can be attributed to ego-relatedness or, in other terms, to the child's experiences in being alone in the presence of an attuned other. Likewise, Winnicott drew attention to the child's *capacity for concern*, an outgrowth of the infant's basic sense of ego-relatedness with the mother and the infant's realization that the mother who may at times be frustrating is the same mother who is sustaining and holding.

THE MATERNAL HOLDING ENVIRONMENT Infants are completely dependent on the mother, who supplies the baby with all its physiological and emotional needs. Winnicott's good-enough mother provides a holding environment that makes the child feel safe and secure and does not intrude or impinge on the infant. The baby gradually moves from complete dependence and immersion in the mother into a *transitional space* between the mother and the outside environment. The child can practice and play with another, typically the mother, until the child is prepared to move into the objective external world (Goldstein 2001; Mitchell and Black 1995; Winnicott 1965).

THE SELFOBJECT ENVIRONMENT Like Winnicott, Kohut (1971) recognized that the child brings certain potentialities to life but needs relationships with others, or what he termed selfobjects, to help the child achieve his or her potential and develop cognitive and emotional structures. Selfobjects are empathic or attuned caretakers and significant others who perform vital functions for the infant that it cannot carry out itself, for example, soothing. Thus, the mother may not be the only important selfobject in the child's life, and moreover, selfobjects are necessary throughout life. They can include mentors, friends, and others in the person's life.

MATERNAL SUBJECTIVITY More recent relational theorists have pointed out what they consider to be limitations of Winnicott's emphasis on the maternal holding environment and on Kohut's stress on the caretaker's selfobject functions. "The holding metaphor ignores, even implicitly *deletes*, the reality of the mother's subjectivity. . . . There is little room in this model for those aspects of a mother's experience that are not congruent with the needs of her baby" (Slochower 2005:31–32). Benjamin (1988, 1990) argues for a more complex view of mothering in which there is an important role for the mother's subjectivity in the child's development. She argues that it offers the mother more emotional breathing room and helps the child to recognize the needs of another person and to acquire the capacity for empathy. Aron (1991) takes this idea further and draws on the developmental view that children observe and study the parental personalities, need to make contact with the parents' inner world, and must come to recognize the parent as a separate other.

INTERACTION BETWEEN SELF AND OTHERS

Rather than focus on the characteristics of the self, on the one hand, or on the impact of the caretaking environment, on the other, there are numerous concepts that emphasize interactional processes.

INTERSUBJECTIVE FIELD   In drawing attention to what he called the myth of the isolated mind, Stolorow wrote that all human behavior is codetermined by two interacting and mutually influencing worlds of experience, the intersubjective field (Stolorow and Atwood 1992; Stolorow, Brandchaft, and Atwood 1994).

MUTUAL EMPATHY   Optimal development requires not only the mother's or caretaker's empathic attunement to the child's needs but also the cultivation of the child's empathy for the caretaker. This flows out of a reciprocal interchange between caretaker and growing infant. Incorporating the idea that there is a role for the mother's or caretaker's subjectivity, the emphasis on the development of mutual empathy requires that the caretaker be not only a need-gratifier but also someone who has to be considered in his or her own right (Freedberg 2007:254).

PATTERNS OF ATTACHMENT   In her studies of children and their mothers in a range of situations around separation and reunion in what she called the "Strange Situation," Ainsworth identified three distinct attachment styles in children (Brandell and Ringel 2007). The first is called a *secure attachment*.

Children who were characterized as having a secure attachment cried when their mother left the room but seemed happy to see her when she returned and adjusted relatively quickly, resuming their play and exploration in the laboratory room. The second attachment style was called *insecure-ambivalent or resistant attachment*. These children cried when their mother left but were difficult to sooth when she returned. They demonstrated an ambivalent behavior, alternately seeking to be close to and held by their mother, and pushing her away. The third group was called *insecure-avoidant*. These children engaged in playing and in an exploratory behavior when mother was in the room with them, when she left, and when she returned, showing little interest in her presence (Ainsworth and Bell 1970; Ainsworth et al. 1978).

These observations of mother–child dyads also led Ainsworth to conclude that the mother's behavior was closely related to the child's attachment style. For example, mothers who were secure themselves, accurately attuned to their child's needs, and at ease both with the child's attachment-seeking strategies and exploratory behavior, had secure children. Alternatively, mothers who were insecure and behaved unpredictably, sometimes attentive to their child and sometimes ignoring the child, had ambivalent children who devised a range of strategies to gain their mother's attention. These children had a highly activated attachment system but were less interested in exploring and investigating their environment. Finally, mothers who were either rejecting of their children's attempts to seek their attention or overly controlling had children with an avoidant style. Seeming to realize that their needs will remain unmet, they learned to pretend that they were independent and autonomous. Sometimes they developed a defensive strategy to ward off their mother's controlling and intrusive behavior.

These observations suggested that children's behavior was directly related to their interactions with their parents. It appeared that both the children and the parents developed a relational pattern contingent on dyadic, reciprocal interactions with one another. Later infant studies confirmed and elaborated on this mutuality and role responsiveness between children and their caregivers. Another researcher, Mary Main, and her colleagues developed the Adult Attachment Interview and showed that the parents' attachment style is closely linked to their children's attachment style. The autonomous-style parents had secure children, the preoccupied parents had ambivalent-resistant children, and the dismissive parents had avoidant children, with an average overall high correlation of approximately 84 percent (Main and Hesse 1990; Main, Goldwyn, and Hesse 2002).

AFFECT REGULATION   Affect regulation has an important role in child–caregiver interactions. It is an important part of self-regulation, which includes the capacity to manage emotional arousal through self-soothing behaviors, regulate emotional arousal, respond appropriately to emotional stimuli, and regulate aggressive and sexual impulses (Applegate and Shapiro 2005; Beebe and Lachmann 2002). Initially, developmental psychologists viewed affect regulation as unidirectional, a function transmitted from the parent to the child. Later researchers found that affect regulation was bidirectional and intersubjective (Tronick et al. 1998). Recent research findings suggest that infants already have a primitive self-regulatory mechanism in utero (Beebe and Lachmann 2002), but infant–parent interactions provide the necessary modeling and systems to help the child self-regulate at a more mature developmental stage.

Moment-by-moment observation of mother–infant interactions, both verbally and nonverbally, showed that the infant is an active agent in initiating, responding to, and regulating mutual interactions (Beebe and Lachmann 2002). These interactions include both self-monitoring of each partner in the interaction and mutual monitoring of one another. A number of researchers (Sander 1977, Tronick et al. 1998) investigated this bidirectional internal system. It requires constant adjustment and readjustment between infant and caregiver in terms of vocalization, eye contact, touch, facial expressions, and other nonverbal signals. Both partners shape and are shaped by the interaction concurrently.

Parents initially help children regulate their affect through accurate attunement to their child's verbal and nonverbal cues. Affect regulation also is promoted through the provision of a secure base and a safe haven that provides the child with support and nurturing at times of threat, and the space to play, explore, and engage at other times. These interactional patterns provide the child with positive internal self-representations that the child can access during times of difficulty and stress in later childhood and adolescence. Internal representations include both the child's self-image as valued, loved, and worthwhile, and the representation of others as supportive, encouraging, and available. The ability to regulate affect is therefore learned from the caregiver, is internalized, and then becomes the basis for mutual regulation with peers, friends, and romantic partners. Children whose caregivers are not available, or are abusive and rejecting, internalize negative representations. Those people who tend to have an anxious attachment style need constant reassurance from others, and those with avoidant style learn to become self-sufficient and are fearful of depending on others.

Clients with disorganized attachment styles may engage in self-destructive behaviors such as cutting, substance abuse, sexual addiction, and eating disorders as self-regulating techniques, and need to learn to self-regulate through self-soothing, accessing internal positive representations, and developing supportive relationships.

Affect regulation is closely linked with attachment, as the quality of attachment bonds is related to the parent's capacity to help regulate the child's affects through attuned responses. As Mikulincer and Shaver (2004:168) suggest, "interactions with security enhancing attachment figures contribute to the formation of self representations that include or evoke the positive and soothing consequence of actual interactions with these figures. In contrast, interactions with unresponsive and rejecting figures contribute to the formation of insecurity based self representations that include or evoke the frustrating and painful consequences of actual interactions with these figures." Despite early negative attachment experiences, the accumulation of later positive experiences with mentors, friends, and romantic partners can become a reservoir of positive memories that one can choose to access that can override earlier negative experiences. Main refers to this development as "earned security." It refers to people who are able to overcome difficult and depriving childhood based on later positive experiences, including therapy (Main, Goldwyn, and Hesse 2002).

Neurobiological research provides another validation for affect regulation as an important developmental concept. Memory research suggests that there are two types of memory, both engaged in self- and mutual regulation. The declarative memory informs verbal and cognitive interactions between infant and caregivers, for example, when the mother comments on the child's behavioral responses, such as "so you are smiling now," or "you want to play," and articulates states of mind, expressions, and behaviors. The second type of memory, the procedural memory, informs nonverbal and unconscious interactions such as mutual gazing, vocalizations, and other facial expressions. Mothers' abilities to be attuned to, respond to, articulate, and mirror their children's mental states and behaviors without impinging, controlling, or imposing their own states of mind are crucial to development. They allow children to internalize an accurate picture of their own inner worlds, undistorted by parental affects such as anger and fear.

Brain imaging studies (EEG) showed that the infant's brain responds to the caregiver's facial expressions, such as smiling (Meltzoff 1990). More recently, mirror neurons in the frontal cortex have been associated with the mirroring process between infant and caregiver initially suggested by

Winnicott (1971), and later integrated in self-psychology (Kohut 1971). The development of the child's mirror neurons through mirroring interactions with the caregiver contributes to the development of the capacity for empathy toward others and the ability to identify others' mental states (Applegate and Shapiro 2005).

Schore (2003) and others (Dawson et al. 1992) did extensive research to show that maternal response is an important factor in the infant's developing brain. For example, infants with depressed mothers showed brain organizations that were different from those of other infants. Moreover, early trauma can alter the development of right brain, which is "responsible for unconscious processing of information, the regulation of bodily state, the capacity to cope with emotional stress, and the corporeal and emotional self" (Schore 2003:113).

METACOGNITION AND MENTALIZATION   Metacognition refers to the ability to observe and reflect on one's own thinking process, notice changes in one's perceptions over time, and observe differences between self and others, typically parents (Main, Goldwyn, and Hesse 2002). It is one of the hallmarks of an autonomous attachment style and demonstrates a capacity for insight, reflection, and empathy.

More recently, Peter Fonagy (Fonagy et al. 2002) broadened the term to include developmental factors, calling this broader function the capacity for mentalization. According to his research, mentalization is not an innate capacity but rather develops based on the interactions between children and caregivers. Through these interactions, parents model for their young children how to identify and articulate their feeling states, so that they can communicate them to others. They also learn to read others' feelings and states of mind and respond to them empathically.

Fonagy conceptualized a process of mentalization that develops from the initial stage, which he calls "psychic equivalence," where children mistake their internal states of mind and beliefs for objective reality. For example, fear of the monster may translate to a belief that the monster is lurking under the bed. The second stage is called "pretend play," when children exclude external reality and their play, both solitary and collaborative, becomes their reality. This developmental stage is important in developing social skills, creativity, and fantasy life, but it may also result in dissociating and ignoring reality.

Parents can help children move from pretend play to mentalization by participating, and mirroring their play and fantasy, but also providing a separate other rooted in reality, and thereby helping their children to differentiate, but also link pretend activities with external reality (Wallin 2007). Fonagy and his associates (2002) also found that children with secure attachment show good mentalization capacities. He notes that "pretending requires a mental stance involving the symbolic transformation of reality in the presence of, and with a view to, transformation of reality in the presence of, and with a view to, the mind of the other" (48). This requires that the adult or parent be able to both represent the reality as well as mirror the child's internal mind state.

Similarly to affect regulation, mentalization is an important learned skill that is transmitted from parent to child through empathic and attuned interactions. The development of mentalization is contingent on the parent's ability to mentalize and reflect on his or her own thought and feelings processes, and to be sensitive to the child's mental states. The parent's verbal and nonverbal response to the child, and the ability to articulate the child's internal feeling states, help the child to develop his or her own mentalization abilities with himself or herself and with others. Along with being able to be attuned to their own states of mind, these children develop empathy and understanding for others and become skillful at social interactions that determine the quality of their later social relationships. Verbal communication from parents to children and the parents' ability to discuss their mental states and verbalize the child's mental states also are linked to reflective functioning in the child (Fonagy et al. 2002). Secure mother–child dyads were found to be more verbally communicative, able to engage in interactive play and mutual comforting. Peer group interactions have also been shown to enhance mentalization capacities. There is research to suggest that peer competence is associated with children's secure attachment history (Elicker, Englund and Sroufe 1992). Peer interactions help children learn to read others' states of mind, develop empathic capacities, and learn from peers about the functions of the mind. "Through participation in activities of their culture they come to share their culture's way of regarding others' and their own actions" (Fonagy et al. 2002:51).

Neuroscience findings suggest that brain functions also develop as a result of these interactions. Of special interest are the recently identified mirror neurons, named so because they develop as a result of mirroring interactions between parents and children. These neurons deepen the capacity for empathy and emotional attunement with others' states of mind (Applegate and Shapiro 2005). Neglected children were found to have difficulty recognizing emotions in faces, and physically abused children were found to display heightened response to angry facial expressions and therefore have difficulty recognizing, interpreting, and accurately responding to others' social and emotional cues (Pollack et al. 2000).

DEVELOPMENTAL DERAILMENTS OR PATHOLOGICAL DEVELOPMENTS

There are many ways on which the development process becomes compromised resulting in serious derailments that affect later functioning.

VULNERABILITY IN THE SELF According to Winnicott (1965), maternal failure, particularly in the form of impingements on the child as might be reflected in overly strict expectations, results in the child developing a "false self" as a defense for the vulnerable and unsupported "true self." The false self adapts to the mother and the surrounding environment at the expense of the true self. As the false self, which is a facade aimed at pleasing others, becomes more rigid, it becomes split off and the person becomes alienated from his or her true self, which remains hidden. Thus, the false self is a defensive organization that both hides and protects the true self at the expense of its full expression. It can be more or less severe depending on the nature of early mother–child interactions, in some instances leading to psychosis.

Kohut also believed that disabling self-disorders occur when the child's protracted exposure to a lack of parental empathy in at least two areas of selfobject need leaves the child unable to develop the compensatory structures essential to a cohesive sense of self (Elson 1986:50). When there is selfobject failure of this intensity, transmuting internalizations do not occur and the self remains enfeebled. Those who remain fixated at the level of the grandiose self may develop inordinate needs for affirmation and attention, withdraw entirely from interpersonal relationship and appear cold, haughty, and self-sufficient, or dwell on unrealistic fantasies of stardom, wealth, or power, sometimes in the absence of any efforts to function in the world or any real accomplishments. Difficulties in transforming the archaic parental imago may lead to later tendencies to idealize others at the expense of one's own self-regard, extreme dependence on others for the regulation of self-esteem, or an inability to depend on others due to fears of disillusionment or loss. Problems in fulfilling twinship selfobject needs may result in longings to be in close proximity to another person with whom one shares everything, difficulties tolerating separateness or difference from another person, and wishes to have one's thoughts and feelings known without having to communicate. In those who show narcissistic vulnerability, depression, shame, humiliation, rage, and even fragmentation and suicide result from even minor criticisms, lack of appreciation, disapproval, rejection, or failure to live up to one's own or others' expectations. Secondary disturbances of the self, which include temporary reactions of a structurally undamaged self to the vicissitudes of life, may result.

Among the self-states that Kohut and Wolf (1978) described are the *understimulated self*, in which the person is driven to engage in exciting, distracting, and sometimes compulsive and dangerous activity in order to ward off inner deadness, the *fragmented self*, in which the person experiences chronic or recurrent loss of cohesiveness even in the face of minor rebuffs or blows to self-esteem, the *overstimulated self*, in which the person becomes easily flooded by unrealistic grandiose fantasies or anxiety when encountering even small successes or attention, and the *overburdened self*, in which the person lacks self-soothing capacity and experiences the world as unduly frightening, anxiety-producing, and dangerous.

In addition to the self-states that may occur in response to the deprivations or excesses of the caretaking environment, there are some character types that develop in order to deal with circumscribed selfobject failures and resultant weakness in the self. Certain individuals become

- *mirror-hungry*, in which they continually search for applause and affirmation to overcome an inner sense of worthlessness and lack of self-esteem but can never be satisfied
- *ideal-hungry*, in which they always seek out those they can admire for certain qualities, such as beauty, power, and intelligence, in order to feel worthwhile themselves but always wind up deidealizing others and renewing their search
- *alter-ego hungry*, in which they try to find others who are just like them in certain ways in order to affirm their fragile sense of self but cannot sustain the twinship for long and look elsewhere
- *merger-hungry*, in which they need to lose themselves in others who are always available and who have difficulty tolerating even the slightest frustration or separation
- *contact-shunning*, in which they avoid others out of fear that they will be swallowed up and destroyed because of their intense needs for merger.

PARANOID/SCHIZOID AND DEPRESSIVE POSITIONS Maintaining a much greater emphasis on the importance of aggression than is characteristic of later relational theorists, Klein (1948, 1957) described the paranoid/schizoid and depressive positions. The paranoid/schizoid position occurs in the first six months of life when infants' rage, envy, and greed are heightened by experiences of frustration and they vent their impulses on the object or part object that frustrates them. Because the ego is immature and easily threatened, infants become terrified of their own primitive and overwhelming destructive impulses toward the objects or part objects upon whom they are dependent. They are capable of using defenses to protect themselves and project their anxiety-provoking angry impulses onto the mother. This results in their developing persecutory fears of the environment. Once their impulses are projected, infants experience the outer world as being as threatening as were their original impulses, but they now can control their external enemies. Although Klein considered the paranoid/schizoid position a normal rather than pathological development, she thought that early experiences could intensify the child's aggression, persecutory fears, and primitive defenses to such a degree that they drastically distort an individual's relationships to others.

Beginning at approximately six months of age, the infant becomes more able to perceive the mother as a whole person (object) that is separate from and outside of the infant and enters the depressive position. Loving feelings toward the mother temper the uncomfortable and threatening aggression and hatred that the infant experiences toward her. Instead of fearing retaliation, children feel guilt and anxiety about the damage they have done or can do in fantasy. In order to preserve the mother as a good object, the infant makes reparation for aggressive fantasies and impulses and experiences gratitude and guilt. The infant then introjects the more caring and guilt-ridden relationship with the mother. The depressive position strengthens the infant's ego and ability to relate to reality, but it never fully replaces the paranoid/schizoid position, with which individuals continue to struggle all through life.

Klein believed that infants experience the continuing conflict between their rageful impulses toward and persecutory fears of the mother associated with the paranoid/schizoid position and their need to love and protect her, which is related to the depressive position. Consequently, they fear that they will not be able to succeed in keeping the mother safe and that she will be destroyed.

INTERNALIZATION OF BAD OR PERSECUTORY OBJECTS Fairbairn (1952) believed that environmental failure and abuse resulted in the internalization of bad objects that persecuted the individual. He viewed the child as coping with environmental failure by splitting its experiences with real bad objects into different internal parts, the totality of which is referred to as the endopsychic structure:

- An *idealized object*, which reflects some elements of good object experiences and is satisfying and which represses the frustrating object
- A *rejecting object*, which represents the mother's denial of the infant's needy self
- An *exciting object*, which stimulates but frustrates the infant
- A *central ego*, which adapts to the external world and relates to the parent as an idealized object
- An *antilibidinal ego*, which directs aggression toward the ego and relates to the parent as a rejecting object
- A *libidinal ego*, which seeks out the exciting object and represses feelings of need and longing

Children pay a price for the split that occurs and is repressed. Their endopsychic structure becomes a closed system that exerts a powerful force on relationships with others in the real world. It operates to tempt a person into relationships that are destined to repeat the frustration of earlier connections. The child and later the adult cannot relinquish or escape from the control of internal bad objects that sabotage the ability to get one's needs met. The individual maintains a repressed tie to these bad objects, which substitutes for the connection to the originally frustrating external object, who often continues to be idealized. Giving up this tie would leave the person profoundly alone. The endopsychic structure impedes further personality development and prevents the individual from progressing from infantile dependence to mature dependence, and from establishing loving and satisfying bonds with others. For example, a man may be attracted to a woman whom he idealizes and finds exciting but elusive and unavailable, and with whom he cannot experience a mutually loving relationship, while he rejects another woman who is attentive and responsive to his emotional needs. In this example, the man is pulled by his idealized and exciting objects but winds up being frustrated while his antilibidinal ego acts to spurn the woman who meets the needs of his libidinal ego. The creation of these splits in the endopsychic structure allows abused children, believing that they themselves were bad, unlovable, and responsible for the abuse, to continue to love their parents.

THE SCHIZOID STATE OR PROBLEM Fairbairn (1940) wrote extensively about those who exhibited a schizoid state, in which they displayed attitudes of omnipotence, isolation, and detachment and were preoccupied with fantasy and inner reality. Standing apart from others, they never become truly involved, although they may learn to play a social role appropriately. Fairbairn thought that at a deep level, schizoid persons fear that their love will destroy others and also hold the belief that they can control their inner bad objects (Seinfeld 1996:67).

Guntrip (1969, 1975) held a somewhat different view of the schizoid state or problem, which he saw as reflecting a final split in the ego (or self) in which children and later adults withdrew from objects altogether. He called this split the *regressed ego*, which exhibits attitudes of omnipotence, isolation, detachment, and hopelessness. The regressed ego is split off from the person's need for others, which still exists deep within the person. The schizoid individual may have conscious or unconscious longings to relate to others but is so fearful of the hurtful and frustrating experiences inherent in relationships that the person cannot overcome his or her isolation and feelings of emptiness.

LOSS, DISORGANIZED ATTACHMENT, AND TRAUMA In his studies of orphaned and hospitalized children, Bowlby (1969, 1973) discerned the impact of separation and loss on young children. He was influenced by Spitz (1945), who observed that orphaned and institutionalized young children seemed apathetic, depressed, and unable to thrive both physically and psychologically. Bowlby observed that children who were separated from their parents were deeply affected, and that their grief and mourning process could last for a long time (Brandell and Ringel 2007).

Based on their studies, Main and Solomon (1990) identified a fourth attachment style, disorganized attachment. They observed that children who came from neglectful or abusive homes, or had mothers who suffered from mental disorders such as depression and schizophrenia, behaved in bizarre ways at certain times. They engaged in ritualistic and repetitive movements, appeared dazed and frozen, or alternated between avoidant and ambivalent responses. Main and others thought that fear played a significant role in these children's behavior. They either were afraid of their caregivers or believed that their caregivers were afraid of them. These children had no apparent strategy to solicit a loving response or to protect themselves against intrusion (Liotti 1995; Main and Hesse 1990). This disorganized attachment style is closely associated with early attachment trauma and may result in a dissociative disorder later on.

It also was shown that other types of attachment trauma exerted a long-term impact on children's lives. For example, longitudinal studies by Allan Sroufe and his colleagues in Minnesota found that children's attachment styles predicted their success in school, the quality of their peer relationships, romantic relationships, and feelings of self-esteem and self-worth (Sroufe, Egeland, and Kreutzer 1990). Children with disorganized attachment styles were found to have difficulties in relating to others and achieving academically.

There are three distinct types of developmental attachment trauma: trauma due to fear for the survival of the self; trauma because of fear of abandonment or loss of the caregiver; and trauma due to abuse (Kobak, Cassidy, and Ziv 2002). Even a brief separation may have a serious impact on a young child, who is not yet able to hold a mental representation of the absent parent, or to understand why the parent is away or for how long (Bowlby 1973). The fear of loss of a parent can be just as devastating as the fear for the safety of the self because of the complete dependence of young children on their parents for physical and emotional survival. Abuse perpetrated by a parent also presents a complex dilemma for the abused child: the source of love, nurturing, and protection is also the source of fear and threat, as described by Fairbairn and discussed earlier.

Studies in neuroscience suggest that severe attachment trauma, such as neglect or abuse, may "override any genetic, constitutional, social, or psychological resilience factors" (Schore 2003:124). Schore notes that unregulated stress in infants and toddlers resulting in disorganized, disoriented attachment patterns predicts long-term dysregulation of affect, stress management, and aggressive behavior. Gross impingements or disruptions due to the parent's own dysregulated affects, for example, their inability to contain anger and depression and the parent's early experiences of abuse and neglect, may cause the child to internalize distorted internal representations of their affect states. They also may compromise the development of neuronal growth (Fonagy et. al. 2002; Applegate and Shapiro 2002). Infants learn to adapt the caregiver's responses and affect states and to perceive them as their own. This explains such phenomena as identification with the aggressor and abused children's sense of badness and desire to remain with their abusive parents.

It is noteworthy that attachment trauma and Post-Traumatic Stress Disorder share several characteristics. In both, there is a failure to integrate the memory of a traumatic experience into a coherent narrative, an avoidance of the painful emotion associated with traumatic memories, and a hyperarousal and increased reactivity to stress (Kobak, Cassidy, and Ziv 2004:398). Children who grow up with abuse or neglect, absent caregivers, or caregivers whose own affects are dysregulated may not be able to learn affect regulation from interactive experiences. This difficulty may later be expressed in inability to manage anger, aggressive behavior toward self or others, and self-destructive behaviors such as self-harm, eating disorders, substance abuse, and sexual addiction that play the role of self-regulatory mechanism during times of anxiety, anger, or grief.

The abusive/neglectful caregiver induces extreme levels of arousal in the child, rather than modulating the child's affects. Because the caregiver does not provide "interactive repair," the child's traumatic affective states endure and become toxic and "continue to escalate in intensity, frequency and duration" (Schore 2003:124). One of the possible long-term effects of the parent's lack of provision of affect regulation is dissociation, through which the child learns to "disengage from stimuli in the external world and attend to an internal world" (125). Schore suggests that paternal neglect and an insecure attachment with the father would be especially damaging to the boy and inhibit the boy's access to the unique impact of paternal regulation with affects such as anger and aggression.

Children who experience abuse or neglect may develop internal representations of being bad, incompetent, unworthy, or a belief in a threatening world and dangerous others. These children may then develop a "psychic equivalent" of a frightening, unsafe world in which they are constantly threatened. Children who are at the "pretend" stage may likewise develop a world of fantasy and play and ignore others, or external reality to build their own safe space. Research with disorganized attachment shows that fear plays an important part in children's development of this particular style. Children's perception of their caregiver as frightening, or as frightened of them, contributes to an inability to develop an integrated, organized pattern of behavior and cognition based on distorted representations that they internalize from their environments (Liotti 1995). Fonagy (Fonagy et al. 2002) suggests that while disorganized children may have mentalizing abilities, they are too focused on their caregivers' states of mind to attend to their inner states, their caregiver does not provide them with mirroring and attuned responses but evokes intense anxiety in these children. Therefore, while they develop highly vigilant perceptions of others' states and behaviors, they are poorly attuned to their own.

If children grow up with neglecting, abusive, or otherwise compromised environments due to the parent's mental illness, substance abuse, or other factors, their capacity to mentalize does not develop. They show limited ability to identify their feeling states and to verbalize them, or to accurately interpret social and emotional cues in their social environment, which leads to poor capacity for interpersonal relationships.

GENDER DEVELOPMENT

Some feminist psychoanalytic writers, especially Chodorow (1978), are considered essentialist theorists because they focus on the unique characteristics of women, including their relational skills, capacity for caregiving, and the unique bond between mothers and daughters, fathers and sons (Zerbe-Enns 2004). In contrast, others, including Benjamin (2002), Dimen (2002),Goldner (2002), and Harris (2002), are among those who argue that the essentialists' views are limiting because they emphasize women's gender difference, rather than critiquing the way culture and society shape women's behavior and expression. They perceive gender to be a social construction, apart from any innate or biological characteristics of males and females. For example, certain characteristics such as relationality, nurturing, passivity, caretaking, and emotional expression, which are associated with women, and qualities such as aggression, domination, and competitiveness, which are associated with men, may be the results of upbringing and sociocultural attitudes and norms. Dimen, for example, sees gender as a "social institution" (Dimen 2002:43), assigning women the passive role and males the active role. Goldner (2002:64) suggests that the difference between gender and sex is that "gender emphasizes the particular and the symbolic over the generic givens of biology," and that gender is unstable and ambiguous rather than binary. Harris argues for a multiplicity in theory of gender, where multiple expressions would be considered and acknowledged as valid (Harris 2002). Finally, Benjamin (2002) argues for a new theory of identification. Rather than subscribing to the traditional oedipal model developed by Freud, where the male and female child identify with the same-sex parent, she offers a model of identification with difference. In this view, the girl may identify with the "masculine" characteristics of her father, and the boy with his mother, thereby creating a greater range of gender-based expression and behavior.

Recent developments in neuroscience show that male and female brains are different from birth and may account for some gender differences between the sexes. For example, Ackerman (2004) notes that women's brains tend to have more neuronal connections between the right and left hemispheres, suggesting that they are better at multitasking. In contrast to men, women's right hemisphere is more developed, and therefore they are better at interpersonal communication and emotional expression. In addition, hormonal differences between men and women under stress were found. While men respond with fight-or-flight response and typically secret adrenaline, women respond to threat with "tend-and-befriend" response, seeking closer proximity to each other and to their children, a more adaptive response from an evolutionary point of view. These studies contribute to a greater complexity in the determination of how biology and culture contribute to the development of gender, and whether each factor can even be teased apart.

CULTURAL DIVERSITY AND OPPRESSION

Finally, it is important to note the important role that cultural diversity and oppression play in the developmental process. Through their social and cultural environment, children internalize a sense of who they are, and culturally accepted patterns of interactions with their caregivers. For example, while Western society promotes autonomy and independence, Japanese, Chinese, and other non-Western cultures promote a sense of self that is contingent on a larger family and community structure. All too often, the distinctive needs, strengths, cultural patterns, and life course issues of people of color and of multicultural and other diverse groups have been ignored. These groups have been viewed in the light of the dominant culture's norms or cultural stereotypes that have prevailed.

Moreover, people of color, many of whom are recent immigrants, women, gays and lesbians, the elderly, the mentally and physically challenged are examples of groups who have been the subject of marginalization, discrimination, and oppression. Many members of these groups are vulnerable to identity diffusion resulting from cultural conflict, feelings of dissonance or difference with respect to others, and the taking in of unfavorable societal attitudes. Some may have been victims of hate crimes, genocidal acts, and discriminatory policies. They may have sustained losses of significant others. Family members may have been killed during internal disputes and wars, been brutally murdered or imprisoned, or died of starvation. They may have endured other traumatic events and experiences, such as natural or manmade disasters, homelessness, inhumane physical conditions, and sometimes torture. Many women may have been raped or subjected to childhood sexual abuse and past or ongoing domestic violence. For all these reasons, they grow up with reality-based distrust, lack of positive expectations, anger, apathy, alienation, and fear of intrusion. They may be prone to low self-esteem, depression, anxiety, substance abuse, and other maladaptive behaviors.

IMPLICATIONS FOR TREATMENT

The concepts described in this chapter not only are important for understanding the relational developmental process but also have had a significant impact on the clinical situation, as will be discussed and illustrated in the following chapters.

A major paradigmatic shift in treatment has occurred. Treatment that incorporates relational thinking draws on the optimal aspects of the developmental process to shape what transpires between clinician and client. Clinician and client are now seen as mutually interacting systems, both coconstructing relational patterns and behavioral interactions, and mutually regulating one another. Collaboration takes precedence over the clinician's adoption of the role of authority and expert. Empathic attunement and attention to the client's subjectivity and own "truth" guide the clinician's interventions. The clinician prizes genuineness and transparency. Dialogue plays a greater role than interpretation. The clinician moves beyond being an observer and becomes a more active figure, bringing his or her own history, personality, and opinions to the therapeutic situation and acknowledging possible mistakes and shortcomings. Holding, nurturing growth, and supporting strengths through the clinician's use of self play as important a role as interpreting and modifying deeply embedded personality characteristics and ways of relating to others. Developing new objects by means of the therapeutic relationship occupies a major place alongside helping clients to lessen the effects of old objects that cause them to enter into and repeat destructive interactions with others.

The client's history is an important factor in this mutually regulating and coconstructing dyadic interactions in that the client's early attachment history and neurobiological development shape their perceptions, expectations, and patterns of relating in treatment. These characteristics, combined with the clinician's own background, values, expectations, and relational history, contribute to the unique quality of each client–therapist dyad.

In the clinical situation, it is crucial that the clinician be aware of and understand the development of the client's self-structure, motivation, and self-regulation; the characteristics of the caretaking environment; the client's attachment patterns and trauma history; and the nature of the derailments that have occurred. All of these influence not only the client's current difficulties but how the client relates to the clinician. It also becomes crucial for clinicians to understand the nature of their own personalities and behavior on clients and to create opportunities for discussion of the mutual impact of clinician and client on one another.

Gender and culturally based assumptions and behaviors can be a fertile source of investigation in the treatment. In what ways are therapist and client constricted by their differences and sameness? Can these beliefs and behaviors be treated as fluid, dynamic constructs subject to change, rather than rigid categories within which client and therapist are trapped? Seeing life through the eyes of our clients who come from diverse backgrounds and engaging in a dialogue with them about areas of difference and sameness require that we transcend our own cultural and professional training. This is hard to do because there is a tendency to take for granted what is deeply embedded in us and to experience our own view of the world as right and our ways of doing things as proper. We also do not know what we do not know.

5. ASSESSMENT IN RELATIONAL TREATMENT

The relational theories and developmental concepts discussed in chapter 4 have significant implications for assessment and intervention in clinical social work. Assessment goes beyond understanding the nature of a client's presenting problem or clinical diagnosis. In social work practice, assessment is biopsychosocial in nature and more holistic. It includes both current interpersonal and environmental and past developmental and cultural factors that have bearing on a client's problems, personality, motivation, and strengths. Although it is important for clinicians to develop an initial, tentative understanding of clients and the likely causes of their difficulties right from the beginning of treatment, assessment is a continuous and changing process as clinician and client work together and coconstruct clients' life stories. This chapter will describe and illustrate the foci of a relational assessment, which constitutes a part, but not the whole, of a broader and more inclusive biopsychosocial assessment. A relational focus in assessment is relevant whether clinicians are working under the pressure of managed care to establish appropriate goals and a method of intervention or instead are practicing in a more relaxed atmosphere that can allow the client's story to unfold over a longer period of time.

SOURCES OF DATA

Although information about the client that comes from others, such as referral sources, other professionals, or family members, may be instructive, it should not constitute the final word. Such information needs to be clarified with the help and participation of the client. For the purposes of assessment, a relational perspective utilizes what clients share about their lives, reformulations of the client's story as both client and clinician work together, what transpires between client and clinician during the treatment process, and how clinicians use their own feelings to understand clients.

UNDERSTANDING AND COCONSTRUCTING THE CLIENT'S STORY

As the clinician invites clients to share what concerns them and their stories or personal narratives, the clinician engages in empathic listening and sensitive exploration and efforts at clarification. The clinician tries to understand the subjective experience of his or her clients and to balance the act of seeking crucial information with the need to be attuned to the client's pace and style of relating. It is usual for the clinician to question clients about areas that they do not mention spontaneously or to explore, reframe, and sometimes offer new ideas about what clients say. In so doing, clinicians may help clients to deepen, expand, and sometimes reshape how they understand their life stories. The following two case examples illustrate this collaborative process.

AN ANXIOUS MAN WITH A TRAUMATIC PAST   Mark, a thirty-three-year-old editor in a small publishing firm, entered treatment at the urging of his girlfriend, Lisa, who asked her therapist, Dr. A, for a referral for Mark. When Dr. A called a colleague to ascertain her availability, she said that Lisa felt concerned about Mark's tension, anxiety, trouble sleeping, and difficulty enjoying himself and also felt that he was overinvolved with his parents. She said that the couple wanted to marry, but Lisa worried about what it would be like to be with Mark if he did not "chill out."

In his first session with a Dr. G, a woman clinician in her late fifties, she asked Mark what had prompted him to call the therapist. Mark replied that although his life was going well, he was a "worrier' and found it hard to relax. He actually looked tense and stiff as he spoke. Mark described his relationship with Lisa as fine, his new job as promising, and his interactions with his divorced parents and sister as good. He explained that he had always been "a tense sort of guy," but he attributed this to "just being who I am. I want to do well and make something of myself, not necessarily make a lot of money but do work that I can be proud of. But I have been realizing that not everyone worries or works as hard as I do. Lisa has made a lot of progress in therapy and thinks that I could benefit. I decided to give it a try." In response to Dr. G's question about whether anything had been causing him to worry more lately, Mark thought a moment and said that the only thing new in his life was his job. He had received a promotion recently. "It's more responsibility, but I know I can handle it. It's what I was doing before really, but I'm always concerned about what others think and not making any mistakes. Sometimes I really get bad and I can't sleep or wake up at the slightest noise. I get up in the middle of the night to check on things I have to do for work. I know it's stupid but that's how I am." The therapist asked if Mark had any physical symptoms. "As a matter of fact, I do." Pointing to his neck, Marks explained that his neck was often painful. Dr. G. commented that what Mark was saying wasn't stupid, and that he seemed to be experiencing a lot of discomfort. She wondered if Mark expected something bad to happen. Mark looked a little surprised and replied, "That's a good way to describe how I feel most of the time. I guess I'm always waiting for the worst. I don't know why."

Dr. G explained to Mark that it would be helpful for their work together if he could talk about the important people in his life and what his background and upbringing was like so that she could understand him better. Mark described his relationship with his Lisa and his family members as close and supportive. Despite their divorce when Mark was nineteen, his parents kept in contact with one another. He described their having grown apart after coming to the United States from Europe. In seeing the quizzical look on the therapist's face, Mark, who had no trace of a foreign accent, explained that he was born in the Ukraine in the former Soviet Republic and immigrated to the United States with his family when he was nine years old. In response to Dr. G's questions about what it was like for him to be uprooted as a child and to have to adjust to a new culture, Mark responded that he never missed the Ukraine. He described being happy when he came to America and that he looked forward to his life being better. He threw himself into his schoolwork, learned English quickly, and felt accepted by his peers. "Even so, I used to worry a lot even then." In replying to the therapist's question about what his life was like in the Ukraine, Mark acknowledged that it was very hard for everyone under the Communist regime. "I was just a kid so I didn't really know everything that was going on. I think my parents tried to protect me and I had school and my friends . . . my parents worked very hard and we did not have very much." Dr. G asked if Mark ever felt that he and his family were in danger. He sighed and responded, "Of course. Everyone was afraid. You couldn't trust your neighbors or friends because people were encouraged to spy on one another. You never knew who was at the door. . . . Sometimes people were arrested for no reason."

When Dr. G commented that Mark had had to endure and learn to cope with a very frightening existence that he had to push away, Mark readily agreed but said that he had tried to put it behind him. Dr. G said that he had gone through some pretty harrowing experiences and wondered if Mark thought that the fear he had earlier in his life was still affecting him despite his new surroundings and good life. Startled, Mark said, "I never really thought of it that way."

In the next session, Mark and Dr. G spoke about other aspects of Mark's background that shed light on his coping and resulted in his thinking about his "worrying" somewhat differently. Mark spoke about his sense of responsibility for his younger sister when they were children. He recalled that his parents put him in charge of making sure she was safe. He also talked about his trying to be "a good son" who did not do anything to burden his parents, whose life "was hard enough." In response to the therapist's comment that Mark must have felt a lot of pressure, he shrugged and said, "That was just how it was... . Lisa tells me that sometimes I seem much older and more serious than other guys my age. She likes my sensitivity but wishes I would lighten up... . Maybe my past does have something to do with how I'm feeling."

AN UNFULFILLED, ASHAMED WOMAN HOPING FOR A SECOND CHANCE Upon her primary care doctor's urging, Angela, an unmarried, sixty-year-old, Italian American office manager, sought help as a result of what she called "a crisis" in her personal life that was causing her considerable distress. "I'm an emotional wreck and I need to get myself together in six weeks. I'm ashamed to even tell you about it but I know I have to." Angela launched into an account of the past month. She described having met Anthony, an interesting and exciting man who was close in age to her. He came to her office to meet with her employer. Previously, Angela had telephone contact with Anthony, and when they met for the first time, Anthony was very warm and chatty and told Angela that she should call him if she ever came to the West Coast where he lived. He said he would show her around. Angela was immediately attracted to Anthony and found herself thinking about him. Several days after their chance encounter, Angela found a reason to e-mail him, and they began exchanging friendly e-mails. Coincidentally, Angela's employer decided to send her to California for a meeting, and Angela and Anthony had a plan to meet for lunch in six weeks when she arrived in Los Angeles. After arranging this date, Angela had become so agitated that she could hardly concentrate, sleep for more than several hours a night, or eat without getting sick to her stomach. She thought about Anthony all the time, had uncontrollable crying jags, and isolated herself from friends for fear that they would laugh at her. She sent frequent e-mails to Anthony and was afraid this was turning him off. Her doctor had prescribed something to help her calm down and sleep, but she didn't like the way it made her feel. "I'm so ashamed. I am a sixty-year-old woman who is acting like a teenager or worse. I don't even know if Anthony is interested in me that way. I may be reading too much into a friendly meeting and invitation, and what man would be interested in me anyway? I thought of canceling my trip but I can't really do that, and I want to meet Anthony for lunch. I have to grow up in the next six weeks so that I can meet him and not act like a total idiot. You must think I am totally pathetic for thinking this man might be interested in me in the first place and then for losing it like this in the second place. I know I am over the top."

After listening intently to Angela's account, Dr. K, a sixty-three-year-old woman therapist, replied, "I don't think you are crazy at all for being excited about the possibility of having a relationship of some kind with Anthony. Nor is it hard to believe that a man could be interested in you. Meeting someone unexpectedly can bring about strong emotions, but I do agree that your reaction is overwhelming you. Meeting Anthony seems to have stimulated something in you that is causing you to feel out of control, and we need to try to understand what may be contributing to your feelings. I know very little about you or your past relationships with men."

Several important issues emerged as Angela began to relate her history. First she "confessed" that she had an out-of-wedlock child whom she gave up for adoption when she was in her early twenties, shortly after her father died. She tried to keep the pregnancy from her mother and delivered the baby in another town. She said that her shame about the pregnancy and her feelings of rejection by the infant's father led her to feel wary of men and sexual intimacy. In addition to fearing further disappointments, she was convinced that if she told a man the "truth" about her pregnancy, he would not want to be with her. Alternatively, if she kept her secret, she would feel fraudulent. At times she berated herself for having had sex before marriage and getting herself "in trouble." Although she dated a lot, she did not become seriously involved with another man and often felt like a failure for never marrying.

A second issue for Angela was that she had spent ten years of her adult life taking care of her mother who was seriously ill and who died two years earlier. During this time she continued to work but was isolated from friends and did not date. After her mother's death, Angela began to feel a surge of yearning to be with a man romantically and sexually. "I felt free and alive for the first time in as long as I could remember, but I was almost sixty. What was I to do? I didn't know where to begin." Feeling unattractive and old, Angela underwent some cosmetic surgery, which did make her feel prettier. She wanted to date but thought she was too old. "I felt angry at myself for having let life pass me by."

At one point during Angela's outpouring of her life story, the therapist commented that Angela seemed to have sacrificed and suppressed many of her own needs most of her adult life. Angela replied that she was old when she was young and had been a parent to her mother. At another point, the therapist said that it must have seemed like a second chance when Angela met Anthony—an opportunity to make up for lost time and to get what she had not had in her life. Angela responded, "I do feel that way and I don't want to be alone any more, but I'm also terrified that I'm going to mess it all up or that I am living in a world of fantasy." Dr. K asked, "Is it any wonder you are so stirred up? Perhaps your thinking about Anthony constantly is a way you are dealing with living with the uncertainty of it all? What will happen between the two of you is an unknown. It is not crazy to have hope because he has shown an interest, but it is true that you don't really know how this will all turn out and you need to give your friendship time to develop." Angela replied that she was glad the therapist said what she did. "I have to remember that this is about friendship and that I have to slow down. I can't make up for my whole life on one date."

In the next few sessions, Angela became somewhat calmer and began to share other information that seemed important in understanding her current emotional upheaval. From a young age, she had always parented her mother and felt torn between wanting to be independent and her responsibilities to her mother. In talking about this to the therapist, Angela realized that as much as she had wanted to marry, she didn't really feel that her mother wanted her to leave her. With great embarrassment, Angela also said, "I don't have a clue about how to even make friends with a man, let alone have a romantic relationship. I dated but I never got involved. I don't even know what it means to have a relationship." The therapist commented that it was not hard to understand that meeting Anthony had thrown Angela into a panic and that she might be fearful that Anthony was interested in her because she did not know if she could handle his attention. Angela nodded vehemently and said she couldn't even imagine what she would talk about with Anthony at lunch. "I have nothing to offer." This led to a discussion of Angela's deep-seated feelings of being "different" from other girls, to her envy of women who had achieved more than she had, and to her conviction that a man would not be interested in her. In exploring what Angela might talk about at lunch with Anthony, the therapist commented that Angela seemed to negate any of her interests or accomplishments. Angela replied, "I've always felt that I was not as good as other girls."

CLUES FROM CLINICIAN–CLIENT INTERACTION

The clinician–client interaction is a major source of data about the client in a relational assessment. The therapist is not only an empathic and attuned listener but utilizes the roles and patterns the therapist and the client enact in order to understand clients' past and current relational patterns. It is important to bear in mind, however, that clinicians' personalities, theoretical biases, and interventions influence how they perceive and interpret clients' feelings and behavior and also influence how clients behave in treatment. Thus, therapists must be self-scrutinizing about the impact of their attitudes, belief systems, and actions on the assessment process and cautious in forming conclusions about the client without the client's active involvement. Although chapter 7 will discuss these ideas further, the following two vignettes illustrate how the clients' interactions with their therapists provided clues to their characteristic relational patterns.

A WOMAN WHO CREATED DISTANCE TO PROTECT HERSELF Trisha, a thirty-five-year-old single woman who worked as a loan officer in a bank, sought treatment after Dan, a man whom she was dating, stopped calling her. Although she did not think they were good for each other, Trisha nevertheless continued to think about Dan and to fantasize about their getting back together. She was concerned that she never seemed to find a man who wanted to be with her whom she wanted to be with. She began to think that she was doing something wrong but didn't know what it was. When she confided in a former roommate, who was a former student of the therapist at a local university, the friend urged Trisha to seek treatment. She described the therapist as a smart, tough, dynamic, and successful woman.

In early sessions, Trisha said she wanted to get the therapist's "input." She spoke about her ruminations about Dan, her job situation, which was causing her stress, and her dates with men, most of whom she found "boring." Not used to being self-reflective, she appeared to be disinterested in going beyond a description of current events and seemed out of touch with her feelings. She related to the therapist as a coach whom she looked up to and whom she expected to give her advice about her life. She often seemed uninvolved emotionally in what she was saying but initially attended the sessions regularly and was always on time.

Trisha described a long series of brief relationships that ended either because she did not feel excited about the relationship or because the man whom she liked a lot would suddenly break off with her. In an example of the first type, Trisha dated Timothy, who was an Irish American like her. He proposed marriage, but Trisha feared that she would feel trapped by the kind of life they would lead. She viewed Timothy as lacking in ambition and too passive. He wanted to live in the small town in upstate New York where he was raised. In contrast, Trisha spoke about Keith, whom she really was "crazy" about. "He was like Dan. I just didn't feel he put me first. He wanted me to do what he wanted to do, was very involved with his family, and always wanted to see his friends. I wanted my space too, but he didn't make me feel special despite what he said. He also was very opinionated and didn't respect what I think." In response to the therapist's question about whether she had told Keith how she felt, Trisha replied that she kept her feelings to herself and knew this was a problem. She explained that although she really liked Keith and wanted to be with him, she often acted cool toward him when he got around to calling her, or she told him she had other plans. She said that sometimes he would pout and not call for a while. "I think he just got tired of our relationship." The therapist asked Trisha whether she thought that she had contributed to the demise of the relationship in some way. Trisha replied that she realized that she wasn't being honest with Keith but didn't think he was really interested in her despite what he said.

In the next few sessions the therapist learned more about Trisha's work life, family background, and personality. Ambitious and hard working but self-critical and filled with self-doubt, she had a tendency to leave jobs if she felt she was not getting ahead fast enough. She often felt fraudulent and not as smart as others. In response to the therapist's question about whether she thought there was anything more behind her leaving her jobs, Trisha said that she sometimes felt that she left too soon and that she might have been promoted if she had given her job a greater chance. She couldn't say anything more about this.

Trisha described being close to her mother and siblings and as having had a strained, if not distant, relationship with her father, whose advice and approval she nevertheless sought. A very successful, critical, and opinionated man who strove for perfection, he made her feel stupid and worthless. In response to the therapist's question about whether Trisha had ever felt close to him or thought he had good qualities, she acknowledged that when she was younger, she had admired his strength and wanted to please him. In fact, she continued to ask him for advice until recently when she decided to try to be more independent. Trisha said that her parents divorced when Trisha was a teenager. She felt that her mother was good hearted and nurturing but overprotective and smothering. According to Trisha, after her mother divorced, she became involved with an alcoholic man who was a "nice guy" but whom Trisha viewed as "weak and dependent." When the therapist asked Trisha how she thought her relationships with her parents might be affecting her now, she said she really hadn't thought about it.

In her relationships with the men who seemed to like her a lot, Trisha saw herself as often judgmental and opinionated like her father, whereas she tended to be passive and eager to please with those she found exciting but who treated her badly. She acknowledged never being sure if she ever really loved any of her boyfriends despite feeling "crushed" if a man broke off with her. She described wanting to have her own space when she dated someone. She tended to be compliant initially, however, and then would find herself distancing although she did not know why.

In several sessions, the therapist explored Trisha's relationship with her parents and suggested that there might be a link between Trisha's feelings about being criticized by her father and suffocated by her mother and her relationships with men. Right after these meetings, Trisha canceled because she had to work late. When she returned, she brushed aside any suggestion that there might be another reason for the cancellation. Soon after, Trisha asked to change her appointment time so that she could go swimming after work and again dismissed the idea that there was any connection between her request and her feelings about treatment.

The therapist began to ask herself what pattern was expressing itself in her interactions with Trisha. It seemed possible that Trisha was finding ways to create distance by giving other activities greater priority than her therapy. The therapist wondered if this was coming mainly from Trisha or whether the therapist was triggering some kind of reaction in Trisha that was contributing to her attempts to distance. She thought that Trisha might either be unaware of this or unable to bring it up directly. When the therapist explained her thinking to Trisha and asked her reactions, Trisha seemed surprised but acknowledged that the therapist's description of their interaction did "ring a bell." In response to the therapist's asking if Trisha was aware of feeling upset after any of her sessions, she first said no but then commented that she had been feeling very down on herself recently. The therapist learned that Trisha felt upset with herself for letting her parents influence her. The therapist replied, "Perhaps you felt that I was blaming you when I suggested that your experiences with your parents were affecting your relationships with men? Maybe you began to criticize yourself, and instead of being able to tell me what you were experiencing, you tried to put some space between us?" In response, Trisha said, "I want you to tell me what I am doing wrong. Maybe I did feel criticized. It's confusing. I don't think it's anything that you are doing, but maybe I do see you as knowing more than I do. I looked you up on Google and saw you had written a lot." The therapist commented that Trisha seemed to expect criticism. She then realized she was putting all the responsibility on Trisha and was blaming her in a way. She asked Trisha if she thought the therapist was being judgmental. Trisha commented that she guessed she expects people who are smart and successful to find fault with her. The therapist replied, "If you feel I am judging you, it's understandable that you might want to cancel your sessions." The therapist asked if she was doing anything that made it hard for Trisha to tell her what she was feeling. Trisha responded that she didn't always know what she was feeling. "Creating distance is second nature to me." The therapist asked if it were possible that what had occurred between Trisha and her is similar to what happens with some of her relationships with men. Trisha thought a moment and said, "I do put certain guys on a pedestal and I don't understand what they see in me, especially if they don't give me a lot of attention or say something critical. I don't tell them how I feel. Maybe I do start acting distant. They probably think I'm not really interested in them when the opposite is true. I guess I try to protect myself." The therapist commented that it would be important for her and Trisha to work on helping Trisha to identify her feelings and to share them.

A MAN WHO PERFORMED AS A WAY OF ELICITING A POSITIVE REACTION   Bob, a twenty-five-year-old single veterinarian's assistant, entered treatment following the death of Dan, his male partner of five years, from HIV. Bob attended a bereavement group, but the group leader thought that Bob could benefit from individual counseling. Bob felt that he and Dan had a loving relationship for the most part, except for the stress due to Dan's illness. Since Dan's death, Bob felt lost and was drinking too much in order to ease his emotional pain. His ex-lover, Doug, had been his first long-term gay relationship. Bob and Doug met a year after Bob "came out" to himself as a gay man, and Bob had not had much experience dating. In addition to his feelings of grief, Bob blamed himself for not having been able to keep Dan alive. He also feared being alone and starting over.

Despite his sadness, soon after he began seeing the therapist, a woman in her fifties, Bob showed an interest in the therapist's tastes and interests. He commented on the posters, books, and decorative objects in her office and tried to engage her in conversation about them. He asked her questions about current events and told her humorous stories about the "weird" people he encountered in his work life. If the therapist tried to deflect Bob's questions and discourage efforts at chitchat, he would shift to another tactic to engage her. If she remained silent or focused on exploring Bob's background, he would become more withdrawn and negative until he regrouped and tried to engage her anew. If the therapist responded by answering some of Bob's questions or by enjoying his stories, he seemed pleased and would become more cooperative and involved in exploring his issues. On one occasion early in treatment, when the therapist had a cold, Bob was solicitous and recommended symptom-relieving remedies.

The therapist learned more about Bob's relationship with Dan and his background during this initial phase. With respect to the latter, Bob described how he grew up with an older, apparently alcoholic single mother who left him to his own resources and was not available to care for him or his younger brother either physically or emotionally. Bob remembered spending much of his time alone, or with a baby-sitter who sometimes "forgot" to feed him or even give him water. He expressed anger and resentment toward his mother for her drinking, neglect, self-involvement, and lack of validation of him. He portrayed himself as passive and powerless in his relationship with her. He has always been protective of his brother, with whom he still is in contact, but the brother has had a lot of drug problems and isn't doing too well.

In contrast to Bob's memory of his life with his mother, Bob's initial interactions with the therapist showed him to be active in trying to get her positive attention and in taking care of her. The therapist recognized that the interaction between Bob and her likely had an important meaning. When she felt able to bring up their interaction, the therapist explained to

Bob that often what transpired between a therapist and client was a clue to understanding experiences the client had earlier in his life. She asked if he was aware that he seemed to be very active and persistent in attempting to find out about her and engaging her, and that his reactions to her fluctuated based on her responses. "I wonder what this tells us? It seems different from what you have described about your relationship with your mom, for example. Bob shrugged these comments off initially, but later in the session he spontaneously remembered that his mother loved flowers, and he learned as a child to take care of their garden, thereby gaining his mother's attention and forming a bond with her through their mutual interest. Bob became tearful when he thought about this and said that he wished he had more of those times with her. When the therapist asked if he had other positive memories, Bob laughed and replied that there were times when, as a very young child, he enjoyed throwing his spoon down from his high chair again and again so that his mother could pick it up for him. "It was fun." When Bob grew silent, the therapist asked him what he was thinking. He said, "It's funny. I was missing Dan. He was a florist and was playful. He used to make me laugh. I don't know if I will ever find someone else like him." The therapist commented that perhaps Bob had sought and reached for the better parts of his relationship with his mom when he met Dan, and that was a real strength. "Even though your relationship ended sadly, you can find someone else."

CLINICIANS' USE OF THEIR OWN FEELINGS

Another way that clinicians develop an understanding of clients is by using their own countertransference feelings as an assessment tool. Thus, in addition to the therapists' interactions with clients, their emotional responses can provide clues to clients' feelings, about which they may not be consciously aware, to what they have experienced in past relationships, or to their interaction with others. Clinicians also have an impact on clients or react to clients because of their own attitudes and personal vulnerabilities and blind spots. Consequently, it is difficult to know who is doing what to whom, and clinicians must proceed cautiously in assuming that a client is "inducing" the therapist to feel a certain way. Usually the client–clinician interactions reflect a mutual impact. Even if a client is contributing to what a therapist is feeling toward the client, clinicians bear the responsibility for managing their feelings in therapeutic ways.

In the case of Trisha above, the therapist began to feel dismissed and unimportant when Trisha first canceled her session and then wanted to change her time in order to go swimming after work. At first she thought that Trisha was engaging in a characteristic pattern of creating distance. Then she wondered if she was inadvertently doing something that was triggering Trisha's behavior. It was only when she raised the issue of what was occurring between them that she learned that Trisha felt criticized by the therapist's statement that it was likely that Trisha's relationships with her parents were having a negative impact on her relationships with men. When she had time to reflect on the session, the therapist recognized that her seemingly innocuous and probably accurate comment did reflect some growing impatience she was feeling with Trisha's unquestioning attitude about her relationships. Consequently, the therapist may have prematurely tried to get Trisha to see what she was doing, which, in turn, contributed to Trisha's feeling judged. In response, Trisha engaged in her usual behavior. Instead of recognizing what she was experiencing and speaking up, she created distance. Understanding the mutual impact of therapist and client helped the therapist to more fully comprehend some of Trisha's relationship difficulties. The following example is illustrative of a similar process.

AN ANGRY AND BURDENED MAN WHO DENIED HIS OWN NEEDS   Kurt was a fifty-five-year-old hospital transportation manager when his employee assistance counselor (EAP) referred him for treatment following a poor performance review by Kurt's department head. Although the review complemented Kurt for the efficiency and excellence of his task performance, it noted that several staff had complained about his exacting work standards, harsh criticisms of them if they seemed to not performing up to his expectations, reluctance to approve time off, and punitive scheduling. Kurt received a warning that unless he improved in his people skills, he was in danger of losing his job. He reluctantly sought advice from the EAP and was referred to Dr. K., an older male therapist.

In his first sessions, Kurt expressed resentment that his immediate supervisor did not appreciate his efforts or help him manage difficult employees. He also was angry with many of his staff for not "pulling their weight" and "being lazy." Despite his unhappiness on the job, he did not want to leave. Having been an assistant manager for many years, he had been passed over for promotion several times because of his difficulties getting along with others. Finally, a year earlier, he was given a chance. "This is the farthest

I can go. I have great benefits, and I'm not getting any younger. Besides, what would I do?"

Kurt saw himself as a strong and independent man who had to make his way in life without the help of his parents. He did not like weakness in others. Kurt described feeling more pressured recently as his two children needed financial help from him to pay for college, his household expenses were increasing dramatically, and he was approaching an age that made him think about his future retirement. He had recently been diagnosed with high blood pressure and high cholesterol and was taking medications for both conditions. He felt angry that he did not have more in the way of work success or financial assets in view of his long career, and he thought he would need to continue working for many years. He said that his wife was emotionally supportive but recently had been undergoing treatment for breast cancer, which was taking a lot out of her. She had a good prognosis but was struggling with her diagnosis. Although discussing these things in a matter-of-fact way in response to the therapist's questions, Kurt did acknowledge that he had been feeling burdened recently and that it was possible that his stress was carrying over to his work life.

In sharing his background, Kurt spoke about having grown up in an economically unstable family. He described his parents as depressed, emotionally unavailable, and verbally and physically abusive, and his younger siblings as draining their energy. He never had been able to count on anyone in his family. Kurt left home at an early age and, except for one sister, has not had much contact with his family in his adult life. His father died when Kurt was nineteen, and his mother died a few years ago.

Kurt used his sessions to vent his anger and resentment and seemed to feel accepted and understood by the therapist. After a month of sessions, the therapist had to be away for a week and was unable to give Kurt much notice due to illness in the therapist's family. Upon resuming their work, Kurt became very critical of the therapist, finding fault with and challenging anything he said. He would make comments such as, "You just don't understand." "Why did you say that?" "I don't think you're really listening." "You people don't know what it's like to really have to work hard." When asked to elaborate or explain what he meant, Kurt would ignore the question. When the therapist commented that Kurt had seemed different since the therapist's absence, which must have upset him, Kurt responded, "Don't flatter yourself that you are that important." When the therapist pursued Kurt's likely distress, Kurt said that the only thing that bothered him about the therapist's vacation was that he obviously could afford to take one. The therapist found himself to be increasingly defensive and frustrated when he saw Kurt, who kept coming to his sessions. He did not know how to reach the client. His uncomfortable feelings mounting, the therapist knew he had to address what was occurring between the two of them. The therapist was able to get control of his own feelings enough to comment, "I know you may dismiss what I am going to say but I think it is important for us to understand what is happening between us. What goes on in therapy gives us clues that can help us work on the issues that come up elsewhere in your life." Kurt asked, "What do you think is going on? You're the expert." The therapist responded, "I'm not sure. I know that lately you seem very angry and impatient with me. It makes me feel that I am doing something wrong. I wonder if I have done something to provoke you, but I need you to tell me what it is. I know that it has made you angry when you have felt that people have not been there for you or appreciated your efforts or not worked hard enough. Could something like that be occurring here? I really want to understand." Kurt blurted out, "I just don't know if you realize how bad I have been feeling. I'm used to being able to handle everything. When you were away, I felt overwhelmed and alone and it seemed like you didn't give a damn, just like everyone else. Why should I trust you anyway?" The therapist replied that perhaps he had not handled his going away very well and that he knew it would be difficult for Kurt, but he should have communicated that and even made some kind of arrangement for Kurt and him to have contact. Kurt said, "You must think I'm really needy. I hate that." The therapist responded that Kurt was carrying a lot of responsibility and deserved some help. "Why do you think you became very critical and challenging of me when I returned?" Kurt answered, "Maybe it's my way of retaliating, or maybe I didn't like feeling that I needed anyone." This led to a deeper exploration of Kurt's past relationship with his punitive father and Kurt's having adopted a similar pattern of behavior with others when he feels let down by them.

THE FOCUS OF ASSESSMENT

Although clinicians draw heavily on what transpires in their interactions with clients in order to understand them, they also try to gather information about the major areas of clients' current and past functioning. A relational assessment encompasses numerous foci that will be described and illustrated below.

CURRENT LIFE SITUATION AND INTERPERSONAL RELATIONSHIPS When clients seek treatment, it usually is customary to try to ascertain what has led to their immediate distress and decision to seek treatment. It is not unusual, however, for clients to be unaware of what is triggering their reactions. It is useful for the clinician to explore the meaningful relationships in a client's current life situation and whether there are any changes, stresses, disruptions, disappointments, rejections, conflicts, or losses that are affecting the client. In the following example, the client sought help for depression but did not initially make the connection between her symptoms and her feelings of disappointment and frustration because of her mother's behavior.

A WOMAN WHO FELT UNAPPRECIATED AND CAST ASIDE Jane, a thirty-six-year-old married woman mother of two school-age children entered treatment when a social worker at the hospital clinic where she was receiving treatment for diabetes urged her to do so. On one of her medical visits after a brief hospitalization following an upsurge of her symptoms that required regulation of her medication, Jane told the worker that she had been anxious and depressed for over a month. She reported being very emotional and unable to sleep, and she could not understand why she was so upset. She described her marriage as fine and her kids as doing well. She said that she missed working but didn't think that leaving her job was at the root of her problems. Initially Jane thought that her mood would pass and that her medical condition might be causing her to be depressed. She became more concerned when she was discharged from the hospital and found that she still felt "down."

   During Jane's initial visit with a therapist, she spoke about the contrast between her feelings of anxiety and depression and the positive state of her life. In probing further about the important people in Jane's life, the therapist learned that Jane's mother was still alive and that Jane had two younger brothers, both of whom were having problems. At the therapist's request, Jane spoke about one brother's serious marital problems and her other brother's substance abuse. She blurted out, "If he (Paul) wants to kill himself, let him. I know I sound awful but he has been a drain on everyone for years." When the therapist commented that Jane obviously had strong feelings about Paul, Jane replied, "I hate him. He has made my mother ill. He's a user and totally self-involved." Jane launched into an account of Paul's long history of problems since he was an adolescent. She said that two months earlier he had overdosed and almost died. "I wish he would have died. It would be easier."

When the therapist asked Jane to explain, she quickly replied, "I can't take my mother! She still thinks that my brother is God's gift to the human race. She can't accept what a loser he is. She spends all of her time worrying about him and trying to do things for him and she expects me to listen to her and watch her make herself sick over him. I need her too. What about my life and me? What do I have to do to get her attention? She's completely wrapped up in him and has nothing left for me. It's so unfair." The therapist responded that Jane seemed to feel pushed aside and nonexistent. She replied, "It's always been that way when Paul is around. All of my life I have tried to do the right thing and to make her happy. I don't know if she thinks my life is so easy and that everything comes to me without any effort. Meanwhile my creep of a brother is a parasite and he gets all of her attention." The therapist commented, "Is it any wonder that you are feeling depressed?"

As the sessions continued, the therapist learned that although it was the situation with Jane's mother that was causing her to feel unappreciated, cast aside, and nonexistent, Jane had left her job due to similar feelings she had about her supervisor. As a nurse, Jane said that she liked working, keeping busy, and being productive but found that she was expected to put in longer hours than she was getting paid for, was working for "a pittance," and was being discouraged from taking the time off that she was due. "To make matters worse, my supervisor gave me a hard time when I asked to change my schedule because of my kid's needing me to take them to school. Then she sent two other nurses who are totally lame on an all-expenses-paid trip to a conference in Seattle that I would have liked to attend. I'm the one that they count on to hold down the fort and my coworkers get to go off and have a good time." Jane said that she felt totally unappreciated and exploited and had decided to take a leave of absence. Although she found that she liked being at home, she thought that she felt more alive when she was working and didn't know what to do. The therapist asked if Jane thought that not working might be contributing to her feeling vulnerable lately. Jane acknowledged that the therapist could be right but added, "What's the point of my working if I'm going to feel unappreciated there too?" The therapist commented that she could see this created a dilemma.

It is noteworthy that, later in the treatment, Jane would accuse the therapist of not caring about her, not appreciating her, and giving other clients preference over her at certain times if the therapist took some time off that interfered with Jane's session time, expected Jane to give notice if she were going to cancel a session because of her busy schedule, or was unable to reschedule one of Jane's sessions because her desired time was taken by another client. Thus, Jane's characteristic reactions also appeared in her relationship with the therapist.

SELF-CONCEPT AND SELF-ESTEEM REGULATION In trying to assess what might be triggering a client's problems and seeking of help, it also is useful for clinicians to consider what has occurred that may have disrupted or challenged a client's self-concept or lowered their self-esteem. In the following example, the client's growing awareness that her marriage was failing prompted her to feel that her world was collapsing.

A PERFECTIONIST WHO FEELS A SENSE OF FAILURE AND HUMILIATION Sarah was a forty-five-year-old employed mother of two twin girls when she entered treatment because "my life is falling apart." By this Sarah meant that she was becoming increasingly frustrated by her husband Al's inability to stop drinking, dwindling income, constant irritability, lack of involvement with their children, and disinterest in her. Sarah cried when she talked about her feelings about Al and her hopes for the future. She and Al had married ten years earlier, and she didn't realize the extent of his alcohol use at that time. She has seen him go "downhill" since the children were born. "He could be anything if he would just try. He could be a good father and spend more time getting clients. He could stop drinking. He says he loves us, but he doesn't try to help himself. If he loved us, wouldn't he try?" The therapist responded, "That's a hard question to answer. Sometimes love isn't enough to stop someone from being self-destructive. Al has been a problem for a long time. What is making things seem worse now?" Crying again, Sarah responded, "I can't help him. Nothing I do works." She went on to say, "What really got to me was that he finally agreed to see someone for treatment and I got the name of a therapist and set up an appointment for him. He didn't show up. He didn't even tell me. I had to find out when the doctor called. I felt so ashamed. I didn't know where my own husband was. I don't know what to do anymore." When the therapist said that Sarah seemed to feel that she should be able to help Al if he couldn't help himself, Sarah asked, "Isn't that my job? I've always prided myself on being able to take care of things. Everyone has always told me that I was a strong person who could do anything she wanted. Most of our friends look up to me and think I have it all together. How little they know. I feel like such a failure."

The two themes of failure and humiliation were prominent in what Sarah spoke about in the sessions that followed. More than anything else, Sarah felt that Al's problems reflected badly on her attractiveness and lovability as a woman, her attempts to have the perfect marriage, and her strength and competence as a helper. On the one hand, she didn't feel attractive in comparison to others and dated this back to feeling "awkward and fat" as a child and adolescent, and to her mother's constant efforts to monitor what Sarah ate and frequent criticisms of her appearance. Alternatively, Sarah was highly intelligent and hardworking and often received praise from her teachers. She was the valedictorian of her high school graduating class, where she had an almost perfect record academically. She developed friendships with girls who confided in her and looked to her for advice and help with their problems. Moreover, Sarah's father often shared his business concerns with her and taught her "the trade," so to speak. As Sarah became older, she used to give him business advice. Wanting to find the perfect husband, Sarah didn't marry Al until she was thirty-five. Although in retrospect it seemed clear that there was ample evidence that he had serious issues at the time of their marriage, Sarah needed to believe that Al would fill the bill in order to make her feel that she was successful in life. During their marriage, she could not face the extent of his difficulties and continued to expect him to change and to become the man of her dreams. As the negative effects of Al's problems escalated, Sarah began to feel desperate and when her attempts to help Al failed, she could no longer sustain her belief that things would get better.

Sarah formed a positive connection to the therapist and never missed a session. Nevertheless, somewhat apologetically, she repeatedly made reference to how difficult it was to come to sessions and how "lousy" she felt before she arrived despite feeling somewhat better when she left. In exploring this with the client, the therapist learned that Sarah felt that the sessions were proof of her "failure," and having to talk about her problems caused her to feel humiliated. Likewise, Sarah had difficulty sharing what she considered to be her "screw-ups" with her children because she wanted the therapist to like and respect her abilities as a parent.

CHARACTERISTIC MOTIVATIONAL AND RELATIONAL PATTERNS The clinician should evaluate what motivates the client generally, the nature of the client's usual ways of relating to others and to the world, and whether these patterns are helpful or problematic. In the following example, a continuation of the previous case, Sarah showed a pattern of relating to men who kept her continually frustrated and left her with feelings of failure.

A WOMAN WHO NEEDED "TO FIX" MEN   In the case of Sarah, it became apparent that she not only had idealized her husband, Al, despite his obvious serious problems at the time of their marriage but had a pattern of admiring men who disappointed her and whom she tried to change. Early in treatment, the therapist learned that of Sarah's ongoing struggles on the job. A salesperson, she worked for a man "who has a great talent for buying merchandise that will sell but who has no people skills or business savvy. If he just listened to me, I could make him more money. I keep telling him but he's stubborn. I think he hears me and then he turns around and does exactly what he always does to screw things up. He hurts it for me. My clients don't want to deal with him. I know I should leave. It's not like he's paying me that well." In response to the therapist's question of why Sarah stayed, she said, "The business could really be fantastic and I just don't understand why he won't do what it would take to improve things. It would be so easy. I don't want to give up, but I get so angry with him. Sometimes he has the nerve to attack me for not working hard enough. I can't believe it. It's so depressing." At one point the therapist commented that it seemed that Sarah felt that she needed to fix her boss. She replied, "I know what I'm doing if he would just listen to me. He could be so successful. I want to help me. He doesn't let me."

Sarah's background also revealed that her father, whom she greatly admired, had made some bad business decisions during her adolescence that had serious consequences for the family's economic well-being and resulted in Sarah's having to go to a state university rather than the better-known private school that she wanted to attend. Several years later, when the business recovered somewhat, Sarah's father asked Sarah's brother to manage the business. Although Sarah had grown up believing in the family myth that he was the "smart one" in the family," he turned out to be "a disaster" and let the business go downhill despite Sarah's efforts to help him. "My father should have put me in charge of the business, but of course he would not ever have done this because I'm not a boy. My brother thought I didn't know anything either." Sarah went on to describe her brother's current financial problems and his stubborn refusal to take her advice, and her distress that she was financially entangled with and dependent on him for income from the business and could not extricate herself. In fact, it appeared that Sarah might have become more independent of her brother by letting him "buy her out," but instead she continued to try to influence him.

Learning about Sarah's idealizing tendencies, along with the resultant disappointment she repeatedly experienced, put the therapist on alert that this pattern might show itself in Sarah's relationship with the therapist.

QUALITY OF EARLY CARETAKING AND INTERPERSONAL EXPERIENCES

The clinician should explore the client's significant early relationships and experiences in order to understand where and how the client's development progressed or became derailed. What were the client's early attachments like? How did the client seem to approach relationships in early childhood and later in life? Were the client's significant caretakers basically attuned to the client and were they idealizable figures? Did they provide sufficient mirroring of the client's capacities, talents, and interests? Did they intrude on the client or use the client to meet their needs and expectations? The answers to these questions not only can help the clinician understand the clients early experiences and their impact on clients' personalities and patterns of relating but also can provide clues to how the transference-countertransference dynamics in the therapeutic dyad might evolve.

The following example shows a man whose long-standing fears of rejection and avoidant pattern (Shilbret 2005; Gubman 2004) that began in early childhood presented a major stumbling block to his coping successfully with his job loss and to making meaningful connections.

A MAN IN RETREAT Marvin, a fifty-five-year-old gay man, entered treatment after being let go from a position that he disliked but had occupied for twenty years. His company gave him six months of salary and health benefits. Initially relieved to be free, he began to feel lost and felt very worried about his financial future as he only had a small amount of savings and would not be able to collect Social Security until he was sixty-two or take any of his meager pension until he was sixty-five. Recently, Marvin had been isolating himself more than usual and had stopped attending church. He spent his time on the Internet and felt terrified of applying for jobs. He was fearful of drinking again but did not want to return to Alcoholics Anonymous because of the bad experiences he had earlier in his sobriety.

A man who did not get along well with others and who shunned taking on much responsibility, Marvin had found a niche in which he felt reasonably well despite his dislike of his work. Born in the South, he was estranged from his parents and two younger siblings. His described his mother as an alcoholic who was physically abusive at times. She would beat him on the backside if he did not meet her ever-changing expectations of him. She also wanted him to be her companion when she drank. and Marvin recalled making her drinks for her when he was old enough to do so. He viewed his father as passive and unavailable. He did not feel close to his brother and sister. From an early age, Marvin described feeling timid and frightened of others. He spent hours alone in his room and had few, if any, friends. His avoidance of relationships with his peers intensified as Marvin struggled with his feelings of sexual attraction to other boys, which he tried to hide. He left home when he went to college and continued his pattern of isolating from others. He was very fearful of being "found out" and remained inactive sexually until he graduated. Marvin anticipated rejection by others and was extremely anxious when he socialized. He had difficulty making and keeping friends. When he did try to reach out, he never felt that others liked him. He was quite judgmental of others and displayed a lack of sensitivity, flexibility, and willingness to compromise in relationships. He had some brief relationships with men when he was in his twenties when his drinking escalated. He entered Alcoholics Anonymous and became sober and moved north, where he found the job he stayed in for twenty years.

In addition to working, Marvin attended concerts and plays, mostly by himself, and volunteered in church-related activities, in which he often experienced dissatisfaction. He fluctuated between trying to reach out to others when he became lonely and depressed and isolating himself when he felt disappointed or rejected. His tedious and frustrating job was nevertheless a focal point of his existence.

In early sessions, Marvin said that he mainly dreaded the idea of having to start over. He was convinced that any job he might find would be boring and unbearable, and he hated the fact that he had to work at all. Although he seemed eager to meet with the therapist, Marvin rarely initiated conversation and waited to be drawn out by the therapist. He seemed to need concrete evidence of the therapist's interest in him. He had difficulty exploring his feelings or reactions and did not make efforts to adopt any of the therapist's suggestions about how he might look for a job. On one occasion, when the therapist questioned him about his seeming "stuck," Marvin answered, "I guess I need a 'kick in the ass' before I make a move."

In the next example, the client's inability to extricate herself from an abusive relationship reflected unmet childhood needs and early family patterns.

A WOMAN WHO LONGED TO FEEL SPECIAL

Ellen, age twenty-nine, entered a women's shelter after fearing that her husband of eight years would try to harm her physically. Although he had been verbally and physically abusive to her episodically for several years, his drinking and threats of violence had increased in recent weeks. Even so, she stayed with him and only left when she found a loaded rifle in the trunk of his car. She had no family or friends that she could turn to for help and sought out a shelter that she had once noticed in a nearby neighborhood.

When Ellen spoke to the counselor at the shelter, she seemed distraught and said she did not know what to do. Speaking of her husband, "He's all I have. I don't know what's happened to him. He's so suspicious of me. He thinks I'm always interested in other men, which is totally untrue. He's the one I have always wanted. I know it doesn't seem possible but he can be wonderful. He was the first man who made me feel special and taken care of. I cold deal with his moods if he just weren't so extreme. He's frightening me."

Significant in Ellen's history was the fact that her mother was a depressed woman who was separated from her husband and totally overwhelmed by her three children. She was emotionally unavailable for nurturing and would occasionally have violent outbursts in which she would hit Ellen with a hairbrush or hanger. Ellen had the responsibility of caring for two of her younger siblings. Ellen's father was a charming traveling salesman who was rarely home but who doted on Ellen and brought her pretty clothes on his occasional visits. She longed for him when he was absent. When she was an adolescent he disappeared, and she later learned that he was killed in an automobile accident. Ellen described herself as a loner who wanted others to pay attention to her but felt insecure. She felt different from other girls and didn't trust them. She was meticulous about how she dressed and tried to be appealing to men. She left home after her mother died of liver disease caused by her drinking. When Ellen was working, she met her husband, who was good-looking and much older than she and who made her feel "like a queen." She described his wanting to be with her all the time, and she found this flattering. She did not recognize the extent of his possessiveness, jealousy, and proneness to violent outbursts, especially when he was drinking. "He's like two different people. I love him when he's not acting crazy and I can't stand him when he's drinking. I just try to wait it out until the man I love returns."

In her early sessions, Ellen was very solicitous of the therapist, often asking her how she was doing at the beginning of each session. She needed a great deal of encouragement to share what she was feeling and often was apologetic if she admitted to being upset or depressed. Sometimes she would seem fearful if the therapist made an unexpected movement toward her. This seemed to reflect a hypervigilance about being attacked suddenly if she let her guard down. Gradually Ellen became more relaxed in sessions, more able to talk about herself openly, and more trusting that the therapist was not going to turn on her as her mother had done.

AFFECT REGULATION AND MENTALIZATION

It is important for clinicians to evaluate selected aspects of clients' internal structure that are necessary to help them interact with others and with the world. A crucial aspect of internal structure is the person's capacity for self-regulation, which includes the capacity to manage emotional arousal through self-soothing behaviors, regulate emotional arousal, respond appropriately to emotional stimuli, and regulate aggressive and sexual impulses. A second important structural component is the capacity for mentalization, which involves the individual's ability to recognize and reflect on his or her own thoughts and feelings, to distinguish inner states from outer reality, to develop empathy and understanding for others, and to become skillful at social interactions.

A MAN AT THE MERCY OF HIS INNER STATES   Victor, a thirty-one-year-old day hospital resident, was trying to gain control of his substance abuse, self-cutting, and self-sabotaging behavior. He had been in outpatient treatment and twelve-step programs several times but had always relapsed. He had trouble being alone and without external structure. In exploring his background, the therapist learned that Victor grew up in a single-family home. His father left when his Victor's mother was pregnant with him and never was heard from subsequently. Consequently, Victor never knew his father. Victor described his mother as anxious, fearful, and self-involved. They received by public assistance and some income from his mother's house cleaning. She drank heavily when Victor was a child and adolescent. Victor described feeling that his mother looked to him to take care of her and did not show much interest in him. He stayed close to home, did not make many friends, and barely passed his courses at school. Victor disliked his mother's frequent boyfriends whom he felt used her. He tended to isolate himself and was not able to tell his mother about his concerns. To regulate his feelings, Victor engaged in self-harming behaviors such as cutting and substance abuse, all in secret from his mother. He reported that only after cutting could he feel relief and fall asleep. As an adolescent, Victor found some female friends with whom he could share his struggles and pain. Unfortunately, they also came from troubled homes, used drugs, and could not help Victor learn more functional ways to regulate his feelings. Victor was able to pass his courses at school and graduated from high school despite his lateness and poor attendance. He continued to live at home and worked at a series of jobs that seemed to end because of Victor's unreliability because of his substance use or his conflicts with coworkers whom he felt did not like him. When his mother died, Victor found a room in a neighbor's house and was able to earn enough money working in supermarkets and other menial jobs to support himself. He had some superficial friendships, and his major enjoyment was going to movies. He often had fantasies about going to college and making something of his life. On several occasions, he actually enrolled in training programs but was unable to complete them. Whenever he tried to stop using drugs and cutting himself, he would begin to feel flooded by his feelings and would grow suspicious of others' motives. Although he tended to feel worse when he was alone, relating to others made him anxious.

It seemed clear to the therapist that a major reason for Victor's ongoing difficulties centered on his problems with self-regulation and mentalization. He seemed to lack the internal structure to help him to self-soothe and to find ways of coping with his inner states. Moreover, from her beginning work with Victor, it became apparent that he had trouble recognizing and verbalizing his feelings. Additionally, Victor was fearful of being taken advantage of by others and often confused his fears with reality. Thus, he often felt at the mercy of what he felt were his coworkers' negative attitudes toward him and was unable to take actions in order to ascertain the true nature of their feelings or to become friendly with them. It became clear that an important part of the work with Victor would be helping him to identify his feelings, to find ways of managing them, and to learn how to check out others' motivations toward him without assuming people were against him.

SIGNIFICANT EARLY EVENTS AND THEIR MEANING

Were there early losses, major disruptions, outright neglect or physical or sexual abuse, or other traumatic events? It is important for clinicians to bear in mind that many clients may not recognize the link between these early experiences and their current problems, or they may minimize or not even remember the traumatic nature of certain events. It may not be timely to push the client to recall the nature of these painful experiences early in treatment before the client has a positive bond and feels safe feels with the therapist.

A MALE SURVIVOR OF PHYSICAL ABUSE   In the earlier case of Kurt, the fifty-five-year-old hospital transportation manager who was threatened with job loss because of his punitive behavior toward his staff, the therapist learned that Kurt grew up with a verbally and physically abusive father, who died when Kurt was nineteen years old. Initially, Kurt reported that he saw himself as strong and independent, hated weakness, and tended to be self-critical. He said that he hated imperfections in himself and became extremely depressed if he made a mistake. Kurt realized that he was under stress but tended to see his punitive behavior at work as appropriate to the situation. He did not recognize that his characteristic way of viewing or dealing with his staff reflected a dysfunctional pattern. Nor did he see any link between his father's attitudes and abusive behavior and his own leanings. In fact, when the therapist explored Kurt's background, Kurt minimized his father's abusive behavior, told the therapist that his father was only occasionally violent, and said that the father never really hurt him. Only as he grew to trust his therapist did Kurt start to report the extent of physical abuse that he had endured. He remembered his father making fun of him, criticizing him continuously, and once hitting him so hard that Kurt dislocated his jaw.

It was only when Kurt and the therapist were able to explore the impact of Kurt's relationship with his father and the latter's violent behavior that he was able to begin to make real progress. He came to a better understanding of how he had internalized his fathers attitude toward him and others, and how he repeated some of his father's behavior when he was frustrated or disappointed. Through his growing positive relationship with the therapist, Kurt began to recognize that although he was a strong person who tried to act as if he did not need anyone, he did have needs for emotional support and validation and felt alone and depressed when his needs were not met.

GENDER, CULTURAL, SEXUAL ORIENTATION, AND OTHER ENVIRONMENTAL FACTORS

It is important for the clinician to appraise the impact of clients' cultural background, gender, sexual orientation, and other types of diversity and unusual life experiences on their usual ways of seeing and relating to themselves and others and the world. It is important to consider how the client's self-concept, identity, relational patterns, values, attitudes toward life, and expectations have been influenced by his or her particular cultural background. To what degree does the client identify with and accept his or her cultural background, gender, or sexual orientation? How have the clients' experiences with disapproval, rejection, stigma, discrimination, and oppression from an early age shaped their internalizations, opportunities, and supports? Because of the significance of these issues, chapter 8 will focus on the treatment process with diverse clients.

6. COMPONENTS OF RELATIONAL TREATMENT

Relational theory views all human behavior as a product of the interaction between individuals and others. Incorporating this perspective into the clinical situation necessitates major changes in the way we envision how clinician and client work together in all phases of the treatment process. Although relational thinking reflects an identifiable core of treatment principles, there are two somewhat different emphases along a continuum of interventions. The early relational theorists emphasized clinicians' holding functions, empathic attunement to the client, and the elimination of countertransference attitudes that might interfere with their empathy with clients. They focused on understanding the nature of clients' developmental arrests and relational patterns, strengthening the self and improving relational patterns through the provision of selfobject experiences and opportunities to develop new forms of relating to others, and modifying internalized bad objects and destructive patterns of interaction. They tended to see transference as reflecting what clients alone bring to treatment while recognizing that the clinician's personality and behavior may trigger certain reactions. Finally, they emphasized clients' contributions to clinicians' countertransference by inducing them to feel certain emotions.

In contrast, more recent relational theorists have stressed the interaction between clinician and client rather than the clinician's holding function. They allow more room for the expression of the clinician's countertransference and subjectivity and encourage more spontaneity and less restraint on the part of the clinician. In viewing each member of the therapeutic dyad as exerting an influence on one another, they advise clinicians to create opportunities for a dialogue with their clients about their mutual impact. They see transference and countertransference as codetermined by client and clinician and as providing the material that can be used to foster client change and growth if managed correctly.

Drawing on both streams of thought, this chapter and the one that follows will consider and illustrate the major general principles that comprise the core of relational intervention. Although they sometimes guide clinicians in somewhat different ways, they can complement one another. This chapter will discuss the importance of collaboration, establishing a therapeutic holding environment, empathic attunement, clinician genuineness, spontaneity, realness, and self-disclosure, recognizing the mutual impact of clinician and client, bridging the subjectivities of clinician and client, therapeutic responsiveness, encouraging new types of relational experiences , and the differential use of interpretation. The chapter will conclude with a brief discussion of ethical and boundary issues that may arise when using a relational approach. Chapter 7 will describe and illustrate transference and countertransference issues, particularly with respect to the management of disruptions and enactments in treatment.

CREATING A COLLABORATIVE PROCESS

In keeping with an emphasis on the intersubjective nature of treatment, most relational clinicians would agree that the establishment of a collaborative process in which both clinician and client are coparticipants in the treatment is essential from the beginning of treatment. A collaborative approach communicates respect and validates clients' own experience and goes a long way in preventing a nontherapeutic interaction in which clients are placed in a diminished position in relationship to clinicians' authority. It is advisable for the clinician to explain to the client that both members of the therapeutic dyad will do the work of the treatment together. Instead of assuming the role of observer and maintaining a passive, distant, and seemingly objective stance as clients talk about their presenting problems and life stories, it is important for clinicians to actively engage with clients in understanding the nature of their concerns and what may be contributing to them. The clinician encourages and helps the client to share what is important, pays careful attention to what client says, accepts what the client thinks and feels, and asks relevant questions. While help-ing clients to explore the meaning of the events and circumstances of their lives, clinicians offer their thinking about what the client expresses. They check out their own impressions with clients in order to arrive at a better grasp of clients' struggles. In so doing, clinician and client coconstruct the client's personal narrative.

ESTABLISHING A THERAPEUTIC HOLDING ENVIRONMENT

Drawing on the importance of the maternal holding environment during the developmental process, many relationally informed clinicians try to cre-ate a therapeutic holding environment that sustains clients. Thus, the treat-ment situation should stabilize clients, enable them to feel safe, assist them in containing and verbalizing their feelings, mobilize their motivation, and facilitate their cooperation with and trust of the clinician.

There are some general features of an optimal therapeutic holding environment, such as consistency, clarity about expectations, empathy, genuineness, acceptance, interest, clear boundaries, and respect for cul-tural and other kinds of diversity. Nevertheless, its components should be individualized and flexible based on an assessment of what the client needs. For example, clients who are sensitive to noise or easily distracted may require a space that is free from impingement. Likewise, those who are frightened of small and enclosed spaces may need to meet in a more open setting, whereas individuals who are demanding of time, erratic in their session attendance, disorganized, or impulsive may benefit from the establishment of clear guidelines and limits. Clients who need to feel reassured of the therapist's availability, realness, and interest may relate more easily if they are given selective personal information about the clinician, while those who have difficulty maintaining a sense of connec-tion to the clinician outside of sessions may benefit from having frequent sessions. Individuals who have difficulty sharing their thoughts and feel-ings may find it useful for the therapist to be active in reaching for and verbalizing what the client is experiencing. Clients who are especially sensitive to intrusion may need the therapist to wait for the client to speak or to ask for feedback. Finally, those clients who are impulsive or self-destructive may require active and protective interventions such as day treatment, twelve-step programs, or other types of external structure (Goldstein 2001).

Creating an optimal therapeutic holding environment may require clinicians to be more real and responsive to some of their clients' requests and needs for selected personal information, additional time, more frequent contact, or concrete evidence of their caring. Being flexible may be difficult when a treatment setting itself adheres to rigid procedures, imposes strict rules and policies, or makes it difficult for clients to gain access. Even if clinicians show more restraint in responding to clients' requests, it is useful for them to convey understanding of the reasons behind such requests without implying that clients are being too demanding or needy.

Another important feature of a therapeutic holding environment, particularly for impulsive clients, is clinicians' ability to help them contain their turbulent feelings and tendencies toward action. In order to do this, it is advisable for clinicians to help clients to get in touch with and verbalize their feelings and to understand their symbolic communications or attempts to put their feelings into actions. Sometimes it may be necessary to set reasonable limits on disruptive, inappropriate, or extreme behavior.

For those clients who experience severe anxiety and feelings of aloneness outside of sessions and who are unable to maintain a sense of connection to the clinician, the use of transitional objects or phenomena may be an indispensable component of a therapeutic holding environment (Wells and Glickauf-Hughes 1986). The clinician may suggest that clients write down their thoughts and feelings or visualize being with the therapist or others who are supportive figures when they are by themselves. The clinician may actually give the client an object such as a book, paperweight, or photograph that can serve as a reminder of the clinician, or the clinician may arrange to talk to clients briefly by telephone at designated times or send them postcards during vacation periods. Sometimes telephone answering devices serve as transitional objects, and clients are reassured by hearing the worker's voice without having to speak to the worker personally. E-mail can be another means by which the client and worker maintain contact with one another in between sessions, as is shown is the following case.

PROVIDING A TRANSITIONAL EXPERIENCE Susan, a thirty-five-year-old, married woman suffered from panic disorder and depressive symptoms that seemed to have their origins in her traumatic history. She revealed having had an ongoing abusive relationship with her mother. Susan reported that her mother ran the household, which included Susan's two younger brothers, like a military camp. Each day was unpredictable in terms of what sort of punishment would be placed upon her and her brothers. As the eldest, Susan said that she tried to protect them, which only made her mother discipline her more harshly. Her mother forced her to stay in a locked, dark closet for many hours at a time. At times she would soil herself and her mother would ridicule her, which resulted in her feeling a profound sense of shame. At times her mother made her attend school with soiled clothing, and her classmates teased her mercilessly.

After working with Susan for a number of months, the male therapist noticed that she was somewhat erratic in her use of her sessions. At times she was productive and hard working, and at other times she seemed distracted and shut down. When her less productive sessions increased in frequency and duration, the therapist wondered aloud with Susan if she were aware of what was occurring between them. She responded that she always had an agenda for the sessions but was increasingly feeling immobilized and unable to follow through on her plan. When the therapist asked if he was doing something to make her feel uneasy, Susan said that she often felt ashamed about talking about her childhood "time and again" and wondered if the therapist was becoming bored or judgmental toward her. She couldn't identify anything that he was doing to make her feel this way. The therapist reassured her that this was not his experience and wondered how the two of them could work together to try and deal with this impasse. Susan thought a moment and asked, "Would you mind if I sent you an e-mail a few days before each session?" She explained that if the therapist knew what Susan wanted to talk about before the session, this might help her to talk more openly. "You can also ask me questions about the email correspondence." Not having done this before, the therapist thought that the plan was worth trying as it might serve to keep Susan focused and somewhat less ashamed. He also thought that it served a transitional function in between sessions. Susan would know that she would be in the therapist's thoughts when he received her e-mail, and the therapist would be in her thoughts when she wrote it.

In subsequent weeks, the e-mail correspondence did seem to help Susan keep a focus in her sessions. It seemed important to her that both she and the therapist bring their printed copies of the e-mail agenda to the session. Typically, the therapist would ask Susan where she wanted to start, based on her e-mail agenda. Although the e-mail helped Susan stay focused, it also served a somewhat defensive function for her when her feelings were charged. She turned to reading her e-mail at these times. This defensive action seemed necessary as Susan would become overwhelmed by the painful memories of her past. It was necessary for the therapist to monitor and help her to regulate her affects.

The treatment proceeded in this manner for several months. Gradually the emails began to raise more loaded issues that Susan seemed to want to deal with in sessions. For example, on one occasion she sent the following e-mail before a session: "I was hoping to sleep better tonight but I just gave [my husband] a call. He's away on a job and he went nuts on the phone. Things aren't going well for him tonight on top of his being extremely tired and sick with a cold. We haven't had a phone call like this in quite a while and I still don't know how to deal with him. Sometimes I don't know if I can stay with him but I am afraid to leave him. I'm not looking forward to the coming weekend. I'm also having a lot of confusing and upsetting memories about my past. I want to be free from my mother but I don't know how to be. I will see you Thursday at 3:00 p.m." It appeared that the e-mail correspondence enabled Susan to keep moving forward at her own pace.

EMPLOYING EMPATHIC ATTUNEMENT

Clinicians' ability to show understanding and demonstrate responsiveness to clients is essential in all phases of the treatment process. Employing empathic attunement is a way that the clinician strives to "to be where the client is." Clinicians try to place themselves in their clients' shoes, so to speak, and to understand what it is like to be the client. A reliance on empathy contrasts with the use of experience-distant comments or theoretically based interpretations that the clinician imposes on a client even if they do not appear to fit with the client's experience. Such interventions tend to place priority on the clinician's view of reality rather than on the client's subjectivity and personal narrative.

Because clients have different needs and ways of viewing themselves and others, being empathic takes many forms and does not always look the same. For example, a socially isolated individual who is fearful of relating to others may need a clinician to show more restraint rather than to expect more closeness. Likewise, empathy with a potentially abusive mother may necessitate that the clinician recognize how out of control the mother feels at times rather than reassuring her that she will not act out.

Although most clinicians are likely to see themselves as reasonably empathic people, this does not mean that it will always be easy for them to respond with empathy. Clinicians have different perceptions, attitudes, values, life experiences, and background from many of their clients, and this may make it difficult for them to be empathic. Likewise, clinicians' theoretical biases or gaps in knowledge about their clients' cultural backgrounds or lifestyle may cause them to misinterpret clients or to misconstrue their motives and behavior. A potential stumbling block to empathy occurs when clients show intense and extreme reactions that may not seem objectively warranted by their life circumstances. Therapists must nevertheless convey that they appreciate what clients think and feel, and resist seeing clients as overly dramatic, minimizing their pain, or pointing out what seem to be extreme reactions or unrealistic expectations and attitudes. Another potential impediment to sustained empathy stems from the intensity of a client's emotions. It is difficult to watch people in pain without feeling overwhelmed or having to take it away, empathizing with a patient's despair while conveying hope, and dealing with the tragic circumstances of peoples' lives. Finally, although similarities between therapist and client can foster mutual empathy, it can be anxiety producing and taxing when therapist and client are experiencing similar life events at the same time, as is shown in the following example.

ANXIETY ABOUT AGING PARENTS Eileen was a fifty-five-year-old recently retired teacher who entered treatment because of generalized anxiety and depression. She worried about her health and aging, her parents' eventual physical deterioration and death, and being alone. Never marrying or having a long-term romantic relationship, she lived by herself and socialized with a few close friends. Her parents were in their early eighties and lived in a condominium complex in Florida. Eileen spoke to her mother several times a week and visited them dutifully three times a year. She had one married brother who lived in a nearby state.

Eileen rarely dated when she was younger and was never eager to marry, thinking she would settle down eventually. When she turned fifty, she became highly anxious and depressed and ruminated about all of the terrible things that could potentially happen as well as her lost opportunities. She hated her job with the Board of Education because of its increasing demands and couldn't wait to retire. She rarely went on vacations, only spent money on necessities, and tended to have trouble doing nice things for herself, except for attending cultural events, lest she be punished if she enjoyed herself too much. Not allowing too much pleasure was the way that she bargained with God not to make something really bad happen.

Eileen's childhood memories were of being in a protective family who were highly anxious themselves. They frequently admonished Eileen and her brother about the dangers of the outside world. Both parents lacked a sense of adventure or fun. They seemed burdened with survival. They did not encourage Eileen or her brother to make friends or engage in outside activities. Although Eileen described her parents as devoted and responsible, she felt that neither of them was comfortable with talking about or expressing feelings or displaying overt signs of affection. A lonely child and adolescent, Eileen recalled being unable to share her concerns with her parents for fear that she would upset them. She sometimes felt that she was crazy and that no one would understand her. From an early age, she liked to have structure and developed routines and superstitions that provided this. She went to college while living at home and eventually moved to her own apartment, not far from her parents. Eileen experienced her parents' move to Florida as difficult but eventually adjusted, maintaining frequent contact with them.

The therapist was five years older than the client and had an eighty-six-year-old mother who lived alone in another city. The therapist felt good about herself and enjoyed her life. Although she was aware of concerns about her own and her mother's aging, she was not prone to worrying. In the early part of her treatment of Eileen, the therapist felt able to listen to her seemingly endless accounts of her fears, angry tirades, depressive ruminations, and expressions of hopelessness without becoming overwhelmed by them. The therapist was able to use her closeness in age to Eileen, their common life-stage experiences, and her awareness of some of the sources of her own manageable concerns to empathically connect with Eileen's subjective experience.

After about a year of treatment, the September 11 terrorist attack on the World Trade Center occurred. In the weeks that followed, Eileen was terrified and enraged. The therapist was not immune from severe anxiety and distress during this period but nevertheless was sufficiently composed to be there for her patients who were profoundly affected. She was able to listen to their fears, deal with their sense of loss, grief, and rage, share their concerns, offer some suggestions about how to deal with their anxieties, and explore what the attacks had triggered without being flooded with emotion, on the one hand, or having to cut off her feelings, on the other. In her work with Eileen, however, the therapist was aware of feeling agitated as Eileen filled the sessions with nightmarish but plausible scenarios of how the terrorists could attack in the future, and vivid accounts of the photographs and films of the event. Not wanting to inhibit the patient, the therapist did not comment on her own anxiety or offer interpretations about Eileen's reactions. She had difficulty listening to Eileen, however, and was preoccupied during their sessions. After several weeks, in desperation, the therapist asked Eileen why she thought she was going into such graphic detail. Eileen suddenly smiled, saying, "I'm glad it gets to you. I don't know why but it makes me feel better." It was only then that the therapist began to recognize that Eileen wanted to actually see the therapist's anxiety in a palpable way in order to reassure herself that she was not crazy or alone in her terror. Likewise, she finally understood what now seemed so obvious—that by obsessively recounting the terror of the event and its potential aftermath, Eileen was trying to regain some control of a world gone out of control. When the therapist was able to convey her new understanding to Eileen and to eventually link her response to this situation to Eileen's early childhood experiences, she became calmer. Exploring how her early coping patterns helped her survive but also hampered her coping became an important focus of the ensuing work.

About a year later, Eileen returned from a visit to Florida where she experienced the devastating multihurricane season of 2004. She was agitated and depressed and filled her sessions with graphic details of her parents' helplessness, physical incapacities, housing problems, and fear during the hurricanes and after. She described how they would have died of neglect if she had not been there. Moreover, she gave vivid, hair-raising accounts of how health professionals and other so-called service people were totally incompetent. Although Eileen had returned, she felt that her worst nightmare was coming true, and she did not know what she was going to do in the near future to protect her parents. She knew that they were going to die soon, but she felt that was secondary to thinking that they would be powerless if they needed help.

In the month prior to these events, the therapist's concerns about her now eighty-eight-year-old mother had escalated. Her mother seemed to be complaining more about her various aches and pains and more withdrawn socially. Three of the therapist's close friends, as well as other patients, were struggling with the physical and mental deterioration of their parents and their need for increased caretaking. This problem seemed to be of epidemic proportions. Although the therapist had compartmentalized her concerns about her own mother's health to a significant degree, she found herself having more frequent visions of having to interrupt her practice and teaching in order to attend to her mother's needs.

In the session with Eileen after she returned from Florida, the therapist became anxious by Eileen's account of her parents' and her own harrowing experiences. Uncharacteristically, she was fidgety and had trouble concentrating on what Eileen was saying. Although she recognized what Eileen was stirring, she was not able to regain her internal equilibrium until after the session was over. In the session itself, she tried to conceal her discomfort, forgetting what she knew so well about Eileen—that she often needed to know that the therapist was feeling her anxiety and distress. Later, when the therapist had time to process what had occurred, she realized the depth of her own concerns about the future. She thought of disclosing her anxiety about her mother to the patient but rejected the idea in this instance because she thought that it would shift the focus away from Eileen to the therapist. Instead, she decided that it was important for her to share her sense of just how frightening the Florida experience was that she focus on the reality of Eileen's concerns and to comment on her feelings of loss of control and of being crazy and alone. When the therapist was able to bring up these issues with Eileen in a subsequent session, the client became somewhat calmer.

Clinicians sometimes become concerned that being empathic implies going along or colluding with a client who may be seeing things in a distorted way or engaging in destructive behavior. It may be more important for clients to experience clinicians' willingness to enter their worlds and see things from their perspective rather than to be confronted too quickly with their problematic attitudes or behavior. Nevertheless trying to understand clients and accepting their feelings is not the same as agreeing with the client. It is possible for clinicians to show that they understand but to have different perspective on what is occurring without pushing the correctness of their point of view, as is shown in the following example.

BEING EMPATHIC WHILE SHARING A DIFFERENT PERSPECTIVE   Ken, a reluctant client, entered treatment after he and his wife separated. He said that he wanted to show her that he could change and become more in tune with his emotions and more sensitive to her. Although he attended sessions regularly, he seemed to have some minimal curiosity about himself and his feelings. His history revealed that he was raised in a staunchly conservative, military family with his father, who was dominant and controlling. He described never being able to disagree with his father and said that he only developed his own interests after he went to college. He attended college in a distant state and had little contact with his parents after his graduation.

As he became somewhat more comfortable with the therapist, Ken spoke about conflicts centered on masculinity, assertion, passivity, and aggression. On one occasion, he described some very stereotypical views of gay men and his homophobic reactions to a coworker. He disclosed to the therapist for the first time that he had had quite a tender relationship with his maternal grandmother for many years when he was a young child. She was an artist, and her work and creative energy fascinated him. He had a memory of his grandmother teaching him how to paint when she visited their family home. His father came upon the two of them and exclaimed, "Painting is a girl thing! It's not for boys." He immediately insisted that Ken get outside and play football with the neighborhood boys.

The therapist experienced a conflict. He empathized with how frightened Ken had been of his father and recognized that his father's attitudes and behavior may have made Ken turn away from his grandmother and from his own softer, more artistic side. At the same time, the therapist wanted to question Ken's homophobia and stereotypes about gay men, not because the therapist felt judgmental about these attitudes but because he thought it was important not to go along with Ken's father's views that likely had been detrimental to Ken. The therapist understood that Ken's inability to be in touch with his own feelings was likely related to these series of interactions with his domineering father throughout his childhood. In this instance, the therapist said, "I understand how confused and angry you must have been when your father interrupted your special moment between you and your grandmother." Ken acknowledged that but immediately said that he was glad his father sent him outside because "I didn't want to be too 'girly' or become a 'fag.'" The therapist responded, "I can understand that but many people, including me, don't think of creative activities or painting as being either too 'girly' or 'gay.' It would be too bad if you had to reject a part of yourself that you liked because of a stereotype that your father had." Ken reflected on what the therapist said and commented that he supposed that therapists did need to be accepting of all kinds of people. The therapist responded, "You still think that your father was right?" Ken replied that he hadn't really thought much about it. "He was my Dad. I was afraid of him, I wouldn't have dared to question him." Seeing that Ken was not where the therapist was about this subject, he simply agreed. and Ken moved on to further discussion about other conflict he was experiencing in his work environment.

BEYOND EMPATHY

The clinician's ability to convey that he or she understands the client and his or her efforts to contain the client's feelings and impulses may not be sufficient to "hold" certain clients, who exhibit behaviors that are potentially self-sabotaging, dangerous, or destructive. Sometimes it may be necessary for the therapist to point out or set limits on problematic behavior. This is best accomplished when clinician engage collaboratively in problem-solving efforts with clients about what will enable them to manage their anxiety, impulsiveness, or erratic and self-destructive behavior. This type of approach "can be a new experience for the patient with a person who appropriately cares and protects" (Adler 1985:212). It is particularly important with clients who have backgrounds of deprivation and neglect where the clinician's passivity in the face of a client's out-of-control or otherwise destructive behavior can signal a repetition of the inadequacies of their early caretakers. Nevertheless, any limits that are set should be established thoughtfully rather than as a consequence of the worker's anger or because of his or her own anxiety or preferences. The unilateral establishment of strict rules should be avoided. For example, some clients who abuse drugs, alcohol, or food or who engage in self-mutilation and other forms of destructive behavior may not be able to maintain total abstinence or refrain from their usual behavior as a prerequisite for treatment. Refraining from making hard-and-fast rules does not mean that the clinician does not act. The clinician's timing in placing expectations for ceasing and desisting such actions is important. The clinician continues to address the behavior by keeping it in focus, exploring its current triggers or underlying causes, identifying the gratification obtained from it and resistance to giving it up, and helping the client find other ways of managing their urgent feeling states. In the following example, the therapist became concerned about the client's plan to engage in self-destructive behavior and felt it was necessary to intervene.

DISCUSSING A CLIENT'S SELF-DESTRUCTIVE BEHAVIOR Lawrence, a thirty-six-year-old lawyer, was in treatment for a number of issues, ranging from marital difficulties, poor work performance, depression, and a sexual addiction history spanning most of his adult life. He came into treatment when his wife discovered a bill that showed a sizable amount due for telephone sex. He disclosed to her that he was addicted to pornography. In his initial session, Lawrence told the male therapist about his profound sexual addiction. Working from a home office, he was often unproductive during work hours as he would spend excessive amounts of time on his personal computer searching and viewing pornographic sites. He also was involved with chat rooms in which he and others would create elaborate sexual scenarios, and he admitted that he was drawn to the creation of sadomasochistic scenes with other participants. He masturbated compulsively at times. Last, he also disclosed that he had been with approximately thirty prostitutes over the last five years.

Lawrence had joined Sexual and Love Addicts Anonymous (SLAA) approximately one year before coming to therapy, and his wife assumed that he was no longer sexually acting out. At times he attended meetings regularly, and at other times he would avoid his twelve-step sponsor and the meetings. Members of SLAA make their own self-appraisal about how they define the destructive nature of their addiction. Lawrence, who tended to think in all-or-nothing terms, had decided that the only sexual activity he would allow himself would be his intimate relationship with his wife. He considered any other sexual behavior, including masturbation, to be crossing his line of sobriety. He discerned that he should define masturbation as part of his addiction as he noted that his pattern was that masturbation led to other acting out sexual behaviors. Lawrence had been successful in staying "sober" from his addiction for one three month period. Beyond that, his pattern would be to refrain from sexual acting out for short periods and then he would often find a "rationale" for acting out. This would range from having a fight with his wife to a missed business opportunity to rewarding himself for excessive work. Clearly, he was struggling to maintain his goals about his addiction.

As with many others in SLAA, Lawrence's paternal grandfather sexually abused him for many years, spanning his latency. He spent considerable time in his therapy exploring the impact of the trauma history on his sexual behavior, and he recognized many links—his insight was helpful, but his behavior change was slower. Some six months into his therapy, Lawrence reported that he was worried about the upcoming weekend as his wife was going to be out of town. This was a time in which he tended to act out considerably. He predicted that he would probably cruise the strip to pick up a prostitute, which he anticipated with a great deal of sexual excitement. He also reported feeling unsafe at times, and he thought this contributed to the excitement. He made a direct link to the anticipated excitement that he experienced as a young boy when he knew his parents would leave him in the care of his paternal grandfather.

The therapist asked Lawrence about his safety with prostitutes, and he admitted that he liked to have sex with them in somewhat public places. He felt excitement about being seen by others; he recalled feeling tremendous tension and excitement when his grandfather would stimulate him sexually, especially if there was a chance they would be caught. He also said that he knew that he could completely damage his law career if he was ever caught with a prostitute. The therapist also learned that Lawrence did not protect himself from sexually transmitted diseases.

The therapist was worried about the self-destructive nature of Lawrence's anticipated liaison with a prostitute. It was illegal, unsafe from a health standpoint, could wreck his career, and could contribute to the demise of his marriage if discovered. He shared his concern with Lawrence and wondered if there were less dangerous behaviors in which he could engage during his wife's absence. The client reminded the therapist of his "bottom line" by saying that he could not masturbate and stay within the confines of his commitment to himself at SLAA. The therapist quietly said that that seemed irrelevant if he was going to seek out a prostitute. He also said, "I am very worried about you and want you to reconsider what you are going to do." Surprised, Lawrence seemed affected by the therapist's concern and said something like "I guess I can alter my bottom line if it means I am not chancing my own self-destruction." The therapist agreed with him. Lawrence did maintain his sobriety during his wife's absence, but, more important, this incident seemed to mark a turning point in Lawrence's recognition that he could choose not to be self-destructive.

GENUINENESS, REALNESS, SPONTANEITY, AND SELF-DISCLOSURE

Displaying genuineness, realness, and spontaneity in the therapeutic relationship can be extremely beneficial. These personal qualities encourage a bond of mutual identification that permits the therapeutic work to go forward. Researchers on psychotherapeutic outcome confirm that when the therapist demonstrates kindness, understanding, and warmth, the therapeutic outcome is usually more positive (Whiston and Sexton 1993).

Likewise, as chapter 2 notes, there are times when it may be appropriate, if not necessary, for clinicians to self-disclose. There are three main types of therapist self-disclosure:

1. The therapist's verbal or behavioral sharing of thoughts, feelings, attitudes, interests, tastes, values, life experiences, and factual information about himself or herself or others in the therapist's life.
2. The therapist's revealing of thoughts and feelings about what is occurring in the treatment process, the rationale for certain

interventions, dilemmas the therapist experiences, and aspects of therapist's personality.

3. The therapist's sharing of his or her countertransference reactions and contributions to the therapist-patient interaction, particularly in dealing with disruptions and enactments as will be discussed in chapter 7.

When used in an attuned fashion, therapist self-disclosure can have many good outcomes. It can enable clients to feel that their needs are understood, to risk relating, to diminish their feelings of shame and aloneness, to explore their experiences, to feel validated in their very existence, and to explore the meaning of their patterns of relating. It also can serve to demystify the therapeutic process. In the following example, drawn from the work with Eileen, the retired teacher presented earlier who was very worried about her aging and deteriorating parents, the client's questioning resulted in some disclosures by the therapist that had positive consequences.

REVEALING PERSONAL INFORMATION WHEN QUESTIONED Eileen was frantic when she returned from visiting her parents in Florida. She filled the sessions with horror stories about the poor quality of health care that her parents received and escalated in her panic about the future. Feeling desperate, she asked in a challenging voice, "How do you expect me to live my life with all this happening and with all that is going to happen to them and to me?" The therapist responded, "I hear your desperation. I wish I had the answer. You are asking a question we all have to deal with at our age. It's not easy. Some days it's quite frightening and depressing. The film star, Bette Davis, once said that getting older is not for sissies." Eileen commented that she appreciated the therapist's honesty and her not trying to convince Eileen that she was seeing things too negatively. "It makes me feel crazy when friends tell me that I have to think positively." Then Eileen uncharacteristically asked a personal question, prefacing it with "You don't have to answer, but I was wondering if your parents are still alive?" The therapist replied, "My mother is eighty-eight and lives by herself. My father died about five years ago." Eileen responded, "So you know what I'm going through. That's a relief." The therapist said, "I know to a degree, but I think you are really suffering a lot right now. Your relationship with your parents has been so important to you. It's very frightening to you to think of their deteriorating and your losing them. It makes everything seem out of control." Surprisingly, Eileen (referring to her need for control) said, "Well you know how I get when I feel that way." "Yes, I do, but perhaps there's another way that you could regain some control." The therapist and client then talked about what Eileen might do realistically to ease her parents' situation and make her feel that she was helping them. Soon after, with the therapist's encouragement, Eileen contacted a private geriatric care manager agency in Florida in order to see what services they could provide and had a serious talk with her brother about his visiting Florida more often.

Despite the usefulness of therapist self-disclosure in many situations, like any intervention, an unattuned self-disclosure can result in a rupture in the therapeutic relationship that requires repair as will be discussed in more detail in chapter 7. The following example illustrates a case in which the therapist's decision to reveal personal information resulted in the client feeling let down and that the treatment was no longer for her. It also suggests that although the therapist thought he was considering the client's needs, some of his own needs likely were involved in the self-disclosure.

THE DOWNSIDE OF A SELF-DISCLOSURE Anne, a thirty-year-old nurse, sought help for depression. She felt overwhelmed by her patients and tended to overwork to the point of exhaustion. A parentified child, Anne had a long history of taking care of others at the expense of her own needs. She formed a strong bond to the therapist and looked forward to her sessions with him. On one occasion, the therapist had to cancel a session abruptly and later disclosed to the client that he had cancelled his previous appointment because he had to travel to attend the funeral of his brother. The therapist's guilt about his sudden absence and the fact that Anne was particularly sensitive to his availability made him decide to share the reasons behind the cancellation. After the disclosure, Anne seemed somewhat preoccupied and distant in the session. She usually was more focused, but instead she appeared distracted and somewhat sullen. The therapist listened for some minutes and then commented, "It seems to me that your demeanor shifted when I told you of my brother's death." Anne replied, "What do you expect? I guess I will have to take care of you, too." The therapist was taken aback by her somewhat angry response. He acknowledged somewhat defensively that his disclosure might have been perceived as an invitation for support but that he had other people in his life with whom he could share his feelings, and that he did not need her to take care of him. Anne looked startled. Realizing that he was making the situation worse, the therapist then apologized. "I should have realized that my saying what I did might have felt like a burden." Anne replied, "Maybe I'm being a selfish bitch. Of course I'm sorry about your brother but I just want my therapy to be for me. I realize how much energy I have spent always taking care of people. I don't want to have to worry about you."

Anne went on to say that she had made a lot of efforts not to know the details of the therapist's professional or personal life. She knew that the therapist was a social work professor and an experienced clinician, but she had consciously not searched out other details about the therapist as a person. She said that she had fought the urge to "Google you" as she didn't want to know what his academic interests or publications might be. She reminded the therapist that in their first session she had told him that she did not want to know anything about his accomplishments or personal life. In fact, the therapist had forgotten about that statement. In thinking about what had transpired between them, the therapist recognized that perhaps there was more to his unattuned self-disclosure than he had originally thought. It was possible that, finding Anne a rather sympathetic person, he did want her to know that his brother had died and was looking to her to take care of him. This realization helped him to understand that one of Anne's issues they had not discussed was how to regulate the degree to which she "took care of" others to whom she was close rather than her more "all-or-nothing" approach to her relationships.

There are other kinds of disclosures about the therapist in addition to the three main types mentioned above. For example, some disclosures are unplanned and inadvertent, for example, when the therapist and client have accidental out-of-the-office contact, or when others share personal information about the therapist to the client. These contacts can be thought of as strange encounters of the extratherapeutic kind. Likewise, events in the therapist's life, such as pregnancy or sudden illness, may interfere with treatment and necessitate the disclosures of various types. In the following example, the personal information about the therapist that the client learned accidentally had a negative impact on the client and necessitated special attention.

AN UNFORESEEN AND INTRUSIVE DISCLOSURE Janet, a thirty-eight-year-old woman who had been in treatment for some time following the break-up of a five-year-relationship with a man she had hoped to marry, overhead a conversation between the therapist and a colleague (one of his suite-mates) in the shared hallway space in their psychotherapy offices. The colleague inquired about the therapist's wife's health, using her first name. Unaware that Janet was in the waiting area, the therapist responded that he was quite concerned as his wife was taking considerable time to recover from a nasty virus. The two therapists exchanged some conversation about their upcoming vacations and agreed that they would enjoy the reprieve from the unrelenting winter weather that these would bring.

Janet coughed in the waiting area, cueing the therapist that she was there. Departing from her usual bubbly, seductive self, Janet was sullen and quiet at the start of the session. When the therapist asked what was going on, she angrily blurted out, "I knew you were probably married, but you didn't have to rub my nose in it. You are mean. Don't you know that I am really attracted to you?" The therapist had been aware of her developing an "eroticized" transference and had been wondering how and when he would be able to speak with her about it in a collaborative way.

Janet vented for some time, saying that she didn't appreciate knowing that the therapist had a wife waiting for him at home and that he was concerned about her health. At the time, Janet was living alone and longed for a committed relationship. More troubling for her was overhearing the therapist's comment about looking forward to his upcoming winter holiday. She assumed that he would be glad to not have to deal with her when he was away. She sarcastically said, "I hope your 'better half' recovers by the time you go away."

Feeling angry and defensive, the therapist was able to internally process what felt like an unwelcome intrusion in his world. He told Janet, "I understand that hearing this conversation gave you a lot of real information about me that upset you. I'm sorry that it happened as it did. We need to understand how this is going to affect our work together. I have been aware that you have strong positive feelings toward me, and we also need to talk about what that means for our work. My concern for my wife and my looking forward to vacation does not change my belief that I can be of help to you or negate my enjoyment of our work together." Janet was silent. The therapist commented that she looked sad. "I always seem to come up empty. It's very painful." The therapist responded that he knew she felt very alone right now, but that one of the goals of therapy was to help her to find and sustain the kind of relationship that she needed and wanted. "It's true that I can't be that person, but it doesn't mean that I don't care about you." Janet eventually commented that she supposed the therapist was the sort of person who cared about others both inside and outside of therapy sessions. "I think

I have made some progress since I've been coming here." The therapist responded that he thought so too."

Although some writers (Goldstein 1994) have advocated the use of self-disclosure selectively and in keeping with an assessment of the client's needs, other writers, such as Hoffman (1991), Aron (1992, 1996), Ehrenberg (1995), Maroda (1994, 1999), and Renik (1995) consider therapist self-disclosure as an essential part of all therapeutic work. It is a complicated issue and decision whether clinicians should show more personal restraint or be selective in their disclosures in order not to impinge on a client in a nontherapeutic way, or instead allow their personalities freer reign. Slochower (2005) has contrasted some of the assumptions of the "holding" versus the "interactive" model of intervention. She concludes that there are clients for whom the therapist's spontaneity or self-disclosure may be threatening, and instances where the clinician's interventions need to be guided by an assessment of the client's needs, which is more characteristic of the holding model. In contrast, other clients are more able to consider and assimilate the idea of the clinician as a separate person and can benefit considerably from a more interactive approach.

RECOGNIZING THE MUTUAL IMPACT OF CLINICIAN AND CLIENT

Similar to the developmental process, all therapeutic interactions are influenced by both clinician and client. Thus, the clinician is never a totally neutral or objective observer of the client and is always both an observer and a participant who shapes the process. Clinicians are real people whose personalities, values, background, expectations, biases, theoretical orientations, and behavior in treatment exert an influence on how they view clients, their empathic attunement to them, and the nature of client–clinician interactions. Likewise, client characteristics and behavior influence the clinician. It is a fallacy to believe that clinicians can eliminate the potential influence of what they bring to the treatment situation or what they experience in reaction to clients. Although the clinician's self-awareness or participation in supervision may help to lessen nontherapeutic attitudes and interactions, even those who are self-aware do not always recognize how their personalities and biases, for example, may be influencing their perceptions of and work with clients. Because of these considerations, it is advisable for clinicians to actively consider the ongoing impact of the personalities of both client and clinician on one another. Clinicians cannot perform this monitoring alone, however, and need clients' assistance.

BRIDGING THE SUBJECTIVITIES OF CLINICIAN AND CLIENT

In order to recognize the mutual impact of clinician and client on one another, it is usually necessary to engage with the client in a dialogue about differences that may exist between clinician and client. This type of discussion, which also may involve clinicians' self-disclosure, may be necessary especially when the clinician and client are of a different gender, sexual orientation, culture, religion, ethnicity, or racial group and share different life experiences, values, and views of the world, as will be discussed in chapter 8. It can bring important issues that are affecting both participants in the therapeutic dyad into the open. It also can allow for greater mutual understanding, eliminate areas of dissonance in the treatment, and pave the way to more positive engagement and interactions. It is not always easy, however, to know when it is preferable for clinicians to show more of who they are, or instead, to remain in the background.

In addition to talking about differences between clinician and client, it also is useful to acknowledge similarities. However, clinicians need to be cautious in thinking they have a full understanding of the client's experience as a result of a similar background. A shared worldview is helpful in developing an alliance, and the clinician needs to always ask for specific details of the client so as not presume some aspect of the client without asking. Similarities can also lead to mutual blind spots and collusions.

DEALING WITH RELIGIOUS SIMILARITIES AND DIFFERENCES Tom, a middle-aged, married, high school teacher, presented for therapy when he began having trouble managing his anger with students in his classroom. It became apparent that many of his difficulties had their roots in his early childhood experiences. His history revealed that he was raised in a strict, Roman Catholic home in which his parents structured daily evening prayers as a family, including the recitation of five decades of the Rosary (a prayer that would take approximately twenty to thirty minutes to complete). In one session, Tom recounted his days at a private, Catholic boarding school and the discipline that he and other students received at the hands of the clerics who were the teachers in the school. Talking about the hypocrisy of the faculty, he noted that the clerics did not behave in a very Christian manner. "I hope you don't think I am being too hard on them. I don't know what your religious background is." The therapist said that he understood the client's feelings and that what he described was not unfamiliar to him.

"I imagine you then had to go to confession to one of them and ask for forgiveness for having angry thoughts towards them?" Tom seemed surprised and relieved by the therapist's comment. He said, "Yes, how crazy was that? They were the ones with the anger problems but I had to confess to them." He then asked directly if the therapist was a Roman Catholic. The therapist responded that he had been raised in a Catholic family and had attended a parochial school, with the teaching staff being nuns. He then added, "I also experienced some contradictions." The therapist went on to share a story about his childhood in which the "privacy" of the confessional was somewhat farcical. "Each month our entire school would be taken to the adjoining church to go to confession. Our parish priest was an aging, benign but decidedly hard-of-hearing priest. We had to speak loudly while in the confessional booth. The priest would bark out 'I can't hear you. Speak up!'" Tom saw the irony and said, "That's funny. Every other kid in line could hear you." Both therapist and client chuckled, and each shared a couple more stories about similar experiences in which the clerics did not practice what they preached. They also acknowledged that each had good role models and experiences as well in that system, but it was real that there were many flaws. This shared experience of similar backgrounds resulted in mutual empathy and strengthened the therapeutic bond.

As the treatment progressed, Tom became aware of how his experience of being silenced and/or punished for inconsequential behavior by the priests was contributing to his rigid standards and his anger toward his own students. The therapist was able to playfully suggest that perhaps he was angry that his students didn't have to come to him to confess their transgressions.

THERAPEUTIC RESPONSIVENESS

The emphasis on the experiential nature of treatment in addition to its role in developing insight has focused attention on clinicians' use of themselves in meeting clients' needs at times in treatment. Clinicians' responsiveness can take many forms and generally is guided by what therapists believe will foster the therapeutic relationship and the change process. The clinician does not deliberately set out to reparent the client but does interact with the client in growth-promoting ways that the client may not have experienced previously. The therapist's ability to be a new kind of object also shows the client that there is a world of potentially more gratifying relationships than the client had experienced previously. This helps the client to take risks in developing relationships outside of the treatment that can serve to reinforce new ways of relating to others and perceiving the self.

The provision of support and encouragement has certainly been a part of most treatment methods at times, but self-psychology introduced the importance of the clinician serving as an actual selfobject in a variety of ways that enable clients to strengthen their self-structures through the process of transmuting internalization. Many clients who come for help have not experienced validation of their feelings and experiences, have lacked idealizable adults in their lives, or have never shared a sense of likeness with significant others. In order to provide new types of experiences, it often is important for the clinician to provide a range of selfobject functions.

In addition to providing acknowledgment and affirmation of as well as resonance with the client's feelings, it also is especially useful for the clinician to search out, identify, validate, and work with clients' strengths and talents. It is not always easy to do this when clients are beleaguered by severe personality pathology. At the very least, however, the fact that they have sought help is a strength upon which to build. Likewise, it is useful to acknowledge the fact that even those who display longstanding and severe problems may have shown remarkable resiliency in surviving difficult circumstances, and that many of their problematic attitudes and behaviors may have helped them to survive.

ENCOURAGING NEW TYPES OF RELATIONAL EXPERIENCES

At certain points in treatment, it is beneficial for the clinician to encourage clients in their quest for more mature selfobjects and new types of relationships in the world outside of treatment. Likewise, it is advisable for clinicians to support clients' efforts to seek out new opportunities, to develop their interests, to expand their activities, to find new employment, or to try out new behaviors in relationships.

DIFFERENTIAL USE OF INTERPRETATION

Clinicians go beyond the provision of support and encouragement in treatment. They often make comments that help clients understand the link between their current problems and past frustrated needs or relational patterns. Thus, with Sarah, a woman client who was described in chapter 5, her self-concept and self-esteem hinged on having the "perfect" marriage and job. She felt humiliated and a sense of failure when she was unable to help him stop drinking or get her employer to do the "right" thing. The therapist might say, "You have prided yourself on being strong and competent, and it is very difficult for you feel good about yourself if you can't 'fix' those close to you who seem to need your help. It feels intolerable to you when your husband does not live up to your ideal. It makes you feel like you have failed. Perhaps this is because you were made to feel responsible for others from a very early age at the same time that your needs and abilities were ignored by your parents and siblings no matter how hard you tried?" With Mark, a male client who emigrated with his family from a Communist country (also described in chapter 5), his generalized anxiety seemed related to his traumatic past. The therapist might say, "Perhaps you have not recognized how much your current anxiety is related to the constant fear that something terrible might happen to you and your family when you were a child, and to your strong feelings of responsibility to take care of your sister?" With Jane, a diabetic woman client described in chapter 5 who became very depressed when her brother's problems escalated, making him the center of her mother's attention and taxing her energy, the therapist might say, "You seem to be feeling pushed aside and totally unappreciated once again. Perhaps this is reminding you of how unappreciated you felt when you were younger? It seems to result in your feeling enraged at the unfairness treatment you have received in your life and powerless to do anything about it." The purpose of these interpretations is to help clients recognize that their reactions stem from earlier frustrating interactions with others.

There are many clients who are chronically or repeatedly depressed. Some have trouble feeling good for very long, if at all. They may exhibit self-defeating and self-destructive behavior or be unable to make good choices in their relationships and work life. Some display entrenched negative attitudes about themselves and have difficulty experiencing others, as good objects. It sometimes seems as if these clients are stuck or are clinging to their negative views of themselves and others, or to their penchant for entering into frustrating interactions and difficult situations no matter how much empathy or support they receive, or how much success or achievement they obtain.

Often it is advisable for clinicians to draw attention to clients' difficulties in freeing themselves from their attachment to "bad" internal objects that dominate their behavior. Clients may not be aware of this dynamic or may accept its presence but be unable to extricate themselves from these powerful introjects because, were they to do so, they would feel totally alone or extremely guilty. The client acts as if he or she would rather stay attached to their internal bad objects than form more satisfying relationships with others or adopt more positive views of themselves. Interpretations of this dynamic often are resisted by clients because they are experienced as attacks on their ties to internal objects whom they feel they need consciously or unconsciously. Such interpretations need to be offered in ways that do not blame the client for his or her pathology. For example, with a woman client who had a history of physical abuse who is having difficulty leaving an abusive relationship with her husband, the therapist might say, "It is understandably hard for you to make a move. Your mother was all you had even though it was necessary for you to feel that you would be taken care of at all. Perhaps this is why it is hard for you to leave your husband? You feel you will be totally alone, and a part of you feels that you must stay in the marriage in order to get your needs met." Moreover, clients need to feel that clinicians understand their need to avoid taking any risks or making any changes. For example, with a male client who is having difficulty mobilizing himself to find a new job after having been let go from a previous position, the therapist might say, "I know that it is important to you to protect yourself from being disappointed again, and perhaps this is a reason you are finding it difficult to look for a job? At the same, you are running out of money to support yourself and getting more depressed. It's a dilemma. What do you think might help you to take a step forward that does not feel too threatening right now?"

In order to be effective, the interpretations of the presence of so-called bad objects should come after the clinician has pointed out the ways in which they are operating in clients' lives. The clinician also must help the client to understand the link between his or her current feelings and behavior and the ways in which he or she was responded to and the people with whom the client identified in his or her early life. This interpretive emphasis must be accompanied by the clinician's provision of sufficient "holding," help in clients' developing more positive internalizations, and encouragement in risking new behaviors.

BOUNDARY AND ETHICAL CONSIDERATIONS

The relational emphases on the clinician's use of self to respond selectively to clients' needs in order to foster their development and on the clinician's spontaneity, genuineness, and self-disclosure contrast with more traditional psychodynamic models that have advocated therapist restraint in gratifying clients and revealing who they are in the clinical situation. Being more real to the client creates new challenges for therapists. First, there is not a clear road map for when and with whom to be more revealing and/or gratifying so that more uncertainty is introduced into the clinical situation. Being more open and responsive also requires that clinicians risk being more transparent to their clients. This can be threatening, and many therapists may prefer the privacy of a therapeutic model that tells them to remain anonymous and neutral. Likewise, being more real may also alter the nature of power in the therapeutic situation so that the therapist and client exist on a more equal basis. Some therapists prefer a position of being the authority.

A second challenge involves the clinician's ability to do what is beneficial for the client and to act in the client' best interests rather than to indulge his or her own needs. This does not mean that clinicians cannot derive pleasure from their interactions with clients. It does mean that it is necessary for clinicians to consider when their actions are good for clients or for themselves. It is not always possible to know the answer to this question with certainty, and clinicians will inevitably make mistakes. Previously, however, errors have been made when therapists have been too withholding, frustrating, or neutral with clients who needed a different kind of responsiveness. Thus, more traditional therapeutic models may have led to errors of omission.

A third challenge involves the issue of how to maintain appropriate therapeutic boundaries and ethics at the same time that clinicians feel freer to express who they are and to meet certain client needs in the clinical situation. When does therapist self-disclosure become too stimulating, close, or seductive? When does meeting client needs selectively encourage a non-therapeutic dependency or powerlessness? When do therapists' needs for clients' applause, idealization, intimacy, or even affection cause therapists to use clients for their own purposes? It cannot be overstated that the exercise of self-awareness and the use of supervision and consultation are important ways that clinicians can protect themselves and their clients.

7. TRANSFERENCE AND COUNTERTRANSFERENCE: DISRUPTIONS AND ENACTMENTS

Beginning with Freud, psychoanalytic clinicians recognized that both clients and clinicians bring conflicts and relational patterns based on early childhood experiences to the therapeutic relationship. Traditional psychoanalytic theory viewed transference as emanating from the client and countertransference as beginning with the clinician. Relational theorists have expanded our understanding of these two concepts. They have alerted us to the presence of two major types of transference, the selfobject transferences and the repetitive transferences. Each type of transference raises somewhat different issues and calls for different responses from the clinician. Likewise, they view countertransference reactions and their management differently (Hanna 1998). Because relational theorists view both clinician and client as exerting a mutual impact on one other in the here-and-now, they reconceptualize transference as being codetermined by both clinician and client and as containing both past and current elements (Aron 1996). For example, the client's so-called transference to the therapist may stem from his or her accurate reading of the clinician rather than from a distortion of the therapist's personality and participation. Although clients may attempt to repeat their past early relationships or seek responsiveness to their frustrated selfobject needs in the therapeutic relationship, the clinician invariably plays a part in stimulating, intensifying, or blocking the client's reactions. Likewise, the clinician may actually resemble and act in a similar manner as the parent or need clients to act in certain ways for the benefit of the clinician. Needless to say, clinicians may not always be aware of their impact on the client or may fail to acknowledge the reality of a client's perceptions, tending to see the client's reactions as stemming only from what they alone are bringing to the treatment relationship. In relational treatment, the ways in which the clinician understands and addresses these *transferences* in the here-and-now interaction in the treatment relationship play a significant role in bringing about client change.

This chapter will discuss and illustrate the nature of both the selfobject and repetitive transference and the nature of countertransference. It will pay special attention to the ways in which disruptions of and enactments in the transference occur and are managed.

THE SELFOBJECT TRANSFERENCES

Kohut discovered the selfobject transferences, which reflect the revival of frustrated early mirroring, idealization, and alter-ego or twinship selfobject needs in the new, more empathic and nonjudgmental context of treatment. Wolf (1988), a collaborator of Kohut, expanded the types of selfobject transferences to include the transference of creativity and the adversarial transference. Both authors thought that these transferences generally emerge naturally in treatment when clinicians are empathically attuned to and responsive to clients. They represent clients' efforts to get their archaic needs met, and thus treatment provides clients with a "second chance" to complete their development. Tolpin (2002) enlarged upon the concept of selfobject transferences and wrote about them as leading-edge transferences because they reflect the client's efforts to reach for health. She concurred with Kohut's view that clinicians should welcome any signs of these reactions and allow them to flourish instead of prematurely discouraging them.

Like Freud, Kohut thought that the clinician's countertransference reactions potentially interfered with treatment. He advised therapists to be self-scrutinizing about their countertransference reactions and to regulate and eliminate them so that they do not result in misattunement or outright mistakes. Potentially problematic countertransference can result from the therapist's conscious and unconscious attitudes and reactions to clients that arise from the therapist's personality, cultural background, values, theoretical beliefs, or need to express certain emotional needs in the treatment relationship.

RECONCEPTUALIZING AND OVERCOMING RESISTANCE

Kohut believed that many clients may have difficulty or may "resist" developing a selfobject transference or becoming emotionally involved in treatment because of their fears of being frustrated, disappointed, or retraumatized. This may be true especially for clients who have suffered in childhood. It is important for clinicians to recognize that this so-called resistance is an understandable outcome of clients' past disturbing, if not traumatic, experiences (see chapter 3). Individuals who experience chronic feelings of rage due to the severe and repeated assaults they experienced in early childhood may show their so-called resistance by acting in a provocative manner that taxes the therapist's empathic abilities. Overcoming clients' so-called resistance requires that clinicians accept where clients are, move at their pace, convey verbally empathic understanding of clients' fears and need to protect themselves, and withstand clients' behavior without retaliating or withdrawing. Some clients, however, also may require concrete evidence that their needs are understood and demonstrations of the therapist's active caring, genuineness, and responsiveness. In the following example, the therapist initially felt defensive when her client challenged her but recognized that the woman client, who had been mistreated in childhood by her mother, used anger to protect herself.

AN ANGRY AND CHALLENGING WOMAN   Karen, a thirty-eight-year-old Korean American woman, entered treatment because of her increasing depression about her health problems, what she described as her husband's "stupidity" and "insensitivity" to her, unhappiness with her job, and her difficulty becoming pregnant. She had severe arthritis that caused her considerable pain and had been trying to become pregnant without success. Although she felt desperate to have a child, she was enraged at her husband, Max, for not making her feel important and for ignoring her needs. She was not sure that she still loved him but did not want to divorce him and raise a child on her own. The couple had seen numerous couple therapists without experiencing much success in improving their relationship. Karen felt that she had sacrificed in order to marry as she turned down a high-paying position at a prestigious company in another city in order to be with Max. "He repaid me by inviting his first wife to the wedding" and by putting higher priority on the needs of his daughter from his first marriage than he did on his life with Karen. "He just wants me to fit in to his life and doesn't want to make any compromises. He's so stubborn. I can't stand him."

Exploring Karen's background revealed that she had grown up in a small southern town after her parents emigrated from Korea. Although the circumstances of their having left were somewhat vague, it seemed that Karen's parents enjoyed considerable wealth in Korea but were forced to leave. Although her father eventually was able to earn a comfortable income in the United States, the parents never regained their financial and social position. Karen's mother was bitter about her life, depressed about her separation from her family and friends, and chronically angry with her husband, whom she blamed for their situation and for neglect of her because of his long working hours. Accustomed to having household help in Korea, she was disinterested in her home and in caring for Karen and her three younger siblings (two brothers and a sister). According to Karen, in addition to her mother's emotional unavailability, she was very critical and would scream at and hit Karen if the child displeased her in any way. Karen felt that although her mother was erratic in her treatment of Karen's brothers, her mother paid somewhat more attention to them than to her, often catering to their needs. She developed a rivalry with her sister. Karen turned to her father, a kindly man, for some nurturing. Although he was responsive to her, he was seldom home and died when she was nineteen, when Karen was in college.

Karen was different from her peers and tended to stay by herself. She never felt successful in making friends or dating. "I have no use for people who want to use me or who just want sex." In fact, she tended to have a dim view of most people's motives, citing how her younger brothers had treated women and how more recently they had "ripped off" her mother. She had little that was good to say about her sister, who was married and lived nearby but who was very jealous of Karen and treated her badly.

As an adolescent, Karen devoted herself to school. She was a good student and drove herself to achieve. She dated occasionally but tended to make her work her life. When she reached her midthirties, she began to panic about never marrying and being able to have children and decided to try "to find a husband." She met Max on a vacation. Born in Europe, he seemed older and more mature than other men she had dated. "I wanted to make it work."

In the beginning of treatment, Karen vented her anger at everyone in her life. If the therapist asked a question to try to clarify what Karen was saying, Karen would respond curtly with an angry edge to her voice. "Don't you get it? Aren't you listening?" If the therapist commented that Karen seemed angry, she would make statements like, "Can't I be angry?" or "I hope you are not one of those therapists who tell me that I'm too angry.

What good does that do?" Alternatively, if the therapist made what she felt was an empathic comment, Karen would say, "I don't need your sympathy. I need solutions." The therapist felt somewhat taken aback by the strength of Karen's challenges and was at a loss to know what to say. She got hold of herself, however, and began to think about why Karen might be expressing herself in such an angry and challenging manner and why she held such a dim view of others. She speculated that although Karen spoke of her past with anger, that she must have felt very hurt and alone as a child and adolescent and decided that she could only count on herself. Despite wanting to find someone whom she could count on and who would make her feel important, it was likely that Karen believed that no one would ever be there for her and protected herself from disappointment by pushing people away. The therapist also recognized that although she had been making appropriate comments, it was possible that she had been feeling defensive and thus not engaged with the client in seeing life through her eyes. When the therapist began to share her thoughts about these dynamics with Karen, Karen gradually began to soften and to become more revealing. For example, on one occasion when Karen challenged the therapist, she replied, "I guess my comment makes it seem as if I am not really hearing you and that I am not interested. I can see that understandably this would make you feel frustrated because you have had this experience so often in your life." Or the therapist would comment," You are so convinced that people will let you down that perhaps it is hard to give me a chance, particularly if I don't seem to get you 100 percent. You may be protecting yourself from beginning to trust me only to feel disappointed. If I seem to fail you, it strengthens your conviction that I can't be trusted." In commenting on Karen's anger and challenging comments, the therapist would say, "I wonder if it is not easier for you to show your anger rather than letting people see how hurt and alone you feel. I think you want to be able to trust me but are fearful that you won't be able to count on me. If I say something that doesn't seem quite right, it scares you and you get angry." The therapist repeated these types of interventions on numerous occasions. One time, Karen responded that several people, including her sister, had told her that she pushes people away with her anger. "I just think people don't care enough to want to get to know me better." Soon after, when Karen spoke about not being able to forgive Max for his insistence on inviting his wife to the couple's wedding, a subject that she mentioned repeatedly and almost obsessively, the therapist said, "It was pretty stupid for Max to do that because it made you feel he was putting her before you, but his behavior nevertheless seemed to mean to you that he did not really love you, a feeling you have had a lot in your life." Instead of challenging the therapist, Karen sighed and replied, "I think he loves me when it's convenient for him. I thought my father loved me but he was never there. He was involved in his work and let my mother treat me badly. I don't understand how he could just look the other way." The therapist responded, "I guess you felt you never came first with anyone." Karen said, "Yes. You know, in Korea, it is only the first wife who gets respect." The therapist responded, "That's important. It adds another dimension to understanding your feelings about Max's feelings for you." This theme of never coming first repeated itself throughout subsequent phases of Karen's treatment and also appeared in the transference itself at a later point. What was important, however, was that the therapist's efforts to empathically relate to the fears that were behind Karen's angry challenges of her gradually enabled her become more emotionally engaged in the treatment and to develop an idealizing transference.

RECOGNIZING AND REPAIRING DISRUPTIONS IN THE TRANSFERENCE

Once clients form a selfobject transference, treatment does not proceed smoothly as disruptions, obstacles, and impasses occur even in the most successful situations. In the classical and ego psychological psychoanalytic models, disruptions or impasses were thought to be the result of the client's unconscious resistances and defenses. Thus, it was thought that they resided in the client. The therapist was admonished to remain neutral, abstinent, and anonymous in the therapeutic relationship and to employ interpretation in order to overcome the resistance and gain insight into the childhood origins of clients' conflicts.

It is not only clients' resistance and defenses that cause disruptions in treatment. The nature of the selfobject transferences themselves makes them vulnerable to disruption when the therapist fails to live up to a client's expectations, misunderstands or misinterprets the client's needs, or does not respond sufficiently to the client's needs and communications. Moreover, the potential for such disturbances are built into the therapeutic process because the treatment has certain constraints that potentially frustrate the client. For example, the therapist is not always available, each session is time-limited, vacations and illness occur, and interruptions, such as emergency telephone calls, take place. Likewise, the clinician is only human and sometimes gets tired or sick, has difficulty concentrating, fails to understand the client at times, or does not always respond sensitively. Moreover, the therapist is not able to embody all the ideal or perfect characteristics that clients may seek.

When there is a disruption in the treatment relationship, the client may show a range of reactions, including silence, anger, disappointment, loss, feelings of injury, de-idealization, depletion, and fragmentation. There may be missed appointments, lateness to sessions, or threats to leave treatment. Continuing tension and lack of harmony in the relationship may derail the therapeutic work and result in a stalemate. Consequently, the therapist must quickly recognize and repair the disruptions that occur as part of the treatment process. When such disruptions are repaired, the client regains a feeling of well-being and the treatment resumes its proper course.

There is another reason why it is important to repair the disruptions that occur. Repeated disruption-restoration sequences are part of the work of the treatment. They present clients with instances in which they experience and come to accept human limitations, disappointments, and failures that are nontraumatic because of the clinician's nondefensive and empathic attitudes and interventions. For clients who have had few, if any, interactions of this nature with significant others, the therapeutic relationship can serve as a powerful new opportunity that enables them to solidify their sense of self and interpersonal relationships over time.

It is crucial that the atmosphere of the treatment and the clinician's overall ability to be empathic and responsive be "good enough" to provide a stable backdrop in which temporary and nontraumatic disruptions can be overcome. If the disappointments in or frustrations by the clinician are too profound or frequent or the therapist is not sufficiently understanding and responsive most of the time, it will be more difficult to repair the disruptions.

The clinician can follow ten steps to repair a disruption that has occurred.

1. The therapist acknowledges to the client that there is a disruption or impasse in the therapeutic relationship.
2. The therapist and client explore the client's perception of the therapist's possible role in causing the disruption.
3. The therapist helps the client to verbalize feelings of disappointment in, rejection by, or anger at the therapist.
4. The therapist empathizes with the client's point of view and acknowledges having played a role in triggering the client's reactions.

5. Therapist and client explore what the disruption or impasse means to the client.
6. The therapist may or may not offer reasons for empathic failure.
7. The therapist explores what can be done to rectify the empathic failure that has occurred and to repair the relationship.
8. The therapist links clients' understandable reactions to the therapist to their past experiences with significant others. It is important, however, for the therapist not to move into this step or the next one before having sufficiently acknowledged the client's perception of the therapist's actual role in precipitating the disruption.
9. The therapist may link clients' current reactions and past experiences to their ongoing reactions to others in their lives.
10. Therapists engage in self-reflection and/or supervision to understand the reasons for their possible empathic failures.

An indispensable feature of this approach is the clinician's ability to understand the reasons for the client's reactions even if they seem extreme and unwarranted and to accept the validity of the client's subjective experience even if it is at variance with the therapist's intentions or perceptions. The therapist refrains from confronting patients with the seemingly distorted or overly intense nature of their responses. This does not mean that therapists cannot share their own perceptions of the situation or their reasons for their behavior. The purpose of such explanations, however, is to clarify where and how misunderstandings and misinterpretations may have taken place rather than to try to convince the client that the therapist is "right" and the client is "wrong." It is not always easy to implement this approach to dealing with disruptions and impasses. Well-meaning and empathic therapists may nevertheless make inadvertent and unintentional errors or show lapses in empathy even while thinking they are doing the right thing. In some instances they may staunchly defend their point of view and actions if the client challenges them or seems to display negative reactions to their interventions. "There is a ubiquitous resistance to the acknowledgement that the truth we believe about ourselves is no more (though no less) real than the patient's view of us" (Schwaber 1983:389).

In the following example, the therapist recognized and attempted to repair a disruption that occurred with a client when the therapist did not fully appreciate the client's fragility and the extreme nature of the client's idealization of him. In this case the disruption led the client to become grandiose and almost delusional.

A PROFOUND REACTION TO THE DISRUPTION OF AN IDEALIZING TRANSFERENCE

Dr. M had seen Jerry for approximately three months in individual therapy in an outpatient mental health clinic in a general hospital setting. Jerry had presented for treatment at the insistence of his wife, who suggested that he needed to become less self-centered and more in touch with his feelings. The clinician saw Jerry as having narcissistic traits but did not think that Jerry had a narcissistic personality disorder. Although Jerry was skeptical about treatment, he made an unusually quick attachment to the therapist in which he appeared to idealize him, relating to him as an expert authority who would help save his marriage.

Significant in Jerry's history was his father's sudden death when Jerry was nine years old. He continued to live with his mother. Jerry described her as preoccupied, depressed, and placing many burdens on him. He tended to be a loner and spent much of his childhood and adolescence riding his bicycle when he was not in school.

Dr. M also led a long-term, insight-oriented therapy group in the clinic, and he and his coleader had two openings for the group. Although he had started with Jerry in individual therapy, Dr. M suggested to Jerry that he would be a good candidate for the group as his presenting concerns (or those of his wife) were related to difficulties in interpersonal relationships and lack of self-awareness. Jerry seemed excited about the prospect. A consequence of Jerry's participation in the group, however, was that he could not continue in individual treatment with Dr. M because the clinic policy prohibited a client being in individual and group therapy with the same therapist. When the therapist raised this with Jerry, he continued to be enthusiastic about joining the group.

When Jerry joined the ongoing group, Dr. M was startled and dismayed at the way in which Jerry portrayed himself and spoke about Dr. M. Jerry told the group members that Dr. M had invited him into the group so he could be of assistance to the coleaders in managing the group's interactions. He went on to say that he considered his individual treatment a complete success, the credit for which belonged to Dr. M. Jerry continued to speak at some length about the many attributes and strengths that Dr. M possessed. The other group members seemed surprised and put off by Jerry's view of himself as a consultant to the coleaders and by his extreme idealization of the therapist. One participant playfully suggested that he had noticed a few flaws in Dr. M. The coleaders and other group members did share in the humor of the comment. Jerry, however, became quite distraught and angry. He was unable to hear any critique of the therapist.

He started to monopolize the group process by giving an extensive and quasi-delusional account of the clinician's expertise and his own role as an "assistant" to the leaders. Dr. M's coleader gently attempted to have Jerry talk more directly about his feelings about joining the group, but Jerry seemed fixed on the idea that he was there only to assist Dr. M. When the group session ended, Dr. M asked Jerry to wait for him so that they could talk about how he was feeling.

The process was painful and somewhat frightening for the group members, who understood that Jerry was unrealistic in his self-appraisal and his view of Dr. M to the point of seeming to be out of touch with reality. After the group, the coleaders discussed Jerry's behavior in the group and what it meant. Dr. M realized that he had made a mistake in urging Jerry to join the group and to stop individual therapy with him. In doing this, the therapist had inadvertently taken an action that caused Jerry to feel rejected. The therapist had underestimated Jerry's fragility and the desperate nature of his idealizing transference. Dr. M and his coleader recognized that Jerry needed to continue in individual therapy with Dr. M and to withdraw from the group. Dr. M felt that Jerry clearly showed indications of being somewhat delusional, and the clinicians recognized this as a transitory state as a result of his feelings of rejection and his anger at the other group member for questioning Dr. M.'s clinical skills.

When Dr. M. sought Jerry out in the waiting room after the group meeting, he said that he could see that Jerry felt very stressed in the group and that, if it was all right with him, Dr. M. would like to reinstate their individual therapy and postpone his participation in the group. Immediately, Jerry seemed relieved and appeared calmer and more realistic. He agreed to resume treatment with Dr. M.

In reflecting on what he now realized was a mistake in his work with Jerry, Dr. M. wondered if there were more to his suggesting that Jerry attend group therapy than his belief that this modality would be good for him. The therapist recognized that he had not felt fully engaged with Jerry, whom he thought lacked insight and was not overtly emotionally involved in the treatment. Consequently, Dr. M's suggestion that Jerry join the group did reflect a desire not to continue with him, or at least the feeling that it did not matter to Jerry whether Dr. M continued with him or not. Thus, it is possible that Dr. M felt narcissistically injured by Jerry.

In their next meeting, Dr. M acknowledged his error in prematurely placing Jerry in the group, and with some effort Jerry was able to express his feelings of disappointment and rejection. Dr. M apologized for not realizing how important the individual therapy was to Jerry and asked him to give him another chance. He decided, however, not to disclose his countertransference to Jerry because he felt this might produce further injury. In subsequent sessions, Jerry brightened up. His idealization of Dr. M continued for some time. Some months later, the therapist was able to help Jerry connect his feelings of rejection to the death of his father and his mother's preoccupation when Jerry was a child.

THE REPETITIVE TRANSFERENCE

In the second type of transference, the repetitive transference, clients repeat old early relational patterns in treatment because they are stuck or bound in scripts of the past. Concurrently, they may wish to free themselves and to have different kinds of relational experiences with "new" objects. These repetitive transferences have the power of *inducing* the clinician to experience feelings and to behave in ways that cause there to be a *reenactment* of the client's past (see chapter 3). Sometimes these *enactments* reflect early trauma. In these instances, the enactment may be made more complicated because a major aspect of the client's early experience may be dissociated and not subject to conscious recall.

In a relational perspective, the concept of enactment has to be expanded in order to accommodate the fact that clients are not always solely responsible for an enactment that may take place. Clinicians bring their own needs and past to the treatment situation. Mutual enactments are an inevitable part of the treatment process (Renik 1995). Even when they occur, however, the outcome can be positive if the clinician and client are able to reflect on and process the meaning of the enactment in a growth-promoting way. Sometimes, however, clinicians may stimulate an interaction or become so pulled into a repetitive pathological pattern that they cannot extricate themselves. The result may be a collusion or actualization of a client's deeply entrenched manner of relating or negative expectations. Although in some instances it may be necessary for clinicians to play a role in an enactment before extricating themselves and the client, a collusion about which the therapist is unaware will prevent therapist and client from exploring what is transpiring. Likewise it will obstruct the therapist's ability to relate to the client in a new and more positive way.

In understand and managing enactments, it is important to consider the concept of countertransference from a different perspective (Hanna

1998). Rather than eliminating countertransference, the totalistic view suggested the importance of accepting and using countertransference (Hanna 1993a). It encompassed what Winnicott termed objective countertransference, which refers to natural or quite justifiable reactions of the therapist to extreme aspects of the client's behavior, and concordant identification, in which the therapist identifies with the main emotion that the client is feeling at a given time, or with the feeling that the client has put into the therapist by means of projective identification (Racker 1957). For example, the therapist's empathic immersion in the client's story may lead him or her to experience the client's rage. Or the therapist's feelings of anger may stem from the client's use of projective identification, in which the client projects his or her aggressive, often disavowed, anger into the therapist. The latter is experienced as a hostile enemy who can be justifiably hated and controlled. In complementary identification, the therapist takes on a role in response to the client's behavior. He or she may begin to feel like a harsh and controlling figure while the client perceives the therapist as being like the client's authoritarian parent.

The main treatment implications of the totalistic conception of countertransference are that the therapist must contain the client's projective identifications in his or her mind without acting on them. Therapists then use what is occurring in the treatment relationship or their feelings to understand the nature of the client's relational patterns as they appear in or are enacted in the transference–countertransference dynamics.

Because of the intersubjective nature of the clinician–client interaction, therapists cannot always understand the nature of their countertransference without learning about the client's perceptions. Moreover, it is neither possible nor desirable for therapists to eliminate their reactions completely because this would deny them a subjective existence. Instead, it is advisable for therapists to actively consider the ongoing impact of the personalities of both the client and the therapist on the treatment process and to help the client to think about both participants as separate people.

RECOGNIZING AND MANAGING ENACTMENTS

It is advisable for clinicians to identify enactments as they are occurring, extricate themselves from being the "old" object, and, in so doing, provide the client with a "new" kind of object or relational experience. Additionally, the clinician helps the client to identify and understand the reasons behind these enactments. These activities are a major way that treatment enables clients to relinquish the old patterns and develop new and better forms of relating to others (Aron 1996; Cooper and Levit 2005). Indicators that the client may be utilizing projective identification or enacting earlier relational configurations in the treatment appear in the clinician's strong or repetitive reactions to the client, in the client's seemingly distorted views of the clinician, and in the clinician's sometimes unusual ways of responding to the client. For example, therapists may experience feelings of resentment, helplessness, inadequacy, or boredom. They may feel perplexed by the client's accusations that the clinician is angry and critical, act cautiously lest they do something to upset the client, refrain from implementing usual policies, or make special efforts to reach a client.

There are different ways of addressing the client's tendency toward the use of projective identification and enactment. The clinician who is alert to the nature of his or her countertransference reactions may simply attempt to contain the turbulent nature of the client's inner life and distortions, withstand the client's attacks without counterattacking, and refrain from replicating pathological interactions. Alternatively, the clinician may try to help the client to examine, understand, and own his or her feelings and relational patterns by drawing attention to and interpreting what is occurring in the client–worker interaction.

There are eight steps in recognizing and managing enactments.

1. The therapist actively monitors the relational dynamics in treatment, especially if there is a seeming impasse or difficulty in the relationship.
2. The therapist comments on the relational dynamics that are present in order to make what is occurring in the relationship more apparent.
3. The therapist invites the client to explore what is contributing to what is occurring between client and therapist.
4. The therapist is self-scrutinizing and acknowledges how he or she may be contributing to what is occurring. The therapist may or may not disclose what he or she is bringing to the interaction.
5. The therapist explains that what may be occurring between client and therapist may not only be related to what is occurring in the "here and now" but also may be repeating the "there and then" or important experiences that the client has had with significant others.

6. The therapist may link what is occurring in the treatment to what occurs in other relationships in the client's current life.

7. The therapist comments on the reasons that the client may keep repeating the past and why it is difficult for the client to experience, engage in, or take in "new" types of relationships.

8. The therapist is alert to repetitions of the relational dynamics in the clinician–client relationship, tries to avoid being the "old" object, and engages in the steps outlined above.

A MUTUAL ENACTMENT   In the following example, George and his therapist became aware of a complementary projective identification pattern after the two experienced a rupture in the treatment relationship. Although the mutual enactment had escalated, the therapist was able to repair the rupture and to use what was occurring in the clinician–client interaction to help both members of the therapeutic dyad focus on important issues.

The therapist, a middle-aged man, had recently moved into a home office, conducting his private practice out of a separate but adjoined structure to his family home. The client, George, was a depressed, anxious man who had been in treatment with the therapist for approximately one year at the time of the change in office space. George was raised in a highly controlling family in which his father was hypercritical of him and often berated George for a range of characteristics, including his ineptitude at mechanical or other "traditionally" male activities.

Shortly after the move to the new office, George mentioned to the therapist that the outer office door was sticking somewhat and that he should shave some of the frame to ease the door's sticking points. Acknowledging briefly that this was something that did require attention, the therapist did not place high priority on fixing the door. Lacking in carpentry skills, he avoided getting to the task. When George arrived the following week, he sarcastically said, "So, I see that you haven't fixed it yet." Once again, the therapist acknowledged that the door was in need of repair. George then went on to say that he noticed the bathroom faucet was leaking a bit and that this was wasteful of water. He added that he also noticed that some paint had been splattered on the carpet in the waiting room area and that it looked messy. The therapist was aware of feeling defensive and angry at the critique coming from George, but he simply acknowledged that George was correct in his observations.

The following week, George commented that the door was operating a bit better but then asked the therapist if he thought he had taken enough off of the frame. He went on to say that the door would probably swell in humid weather and that they were headed toward the summer. The therapist felt very angry. When George went back to the (yet unrepaired) water faucet and the paint splatters, the therapist could no longer contain himself. He abruptly said to George that he wasn't sure what this had to do with his therapy and asked him why he was not focusing on his own issues. Surprised, George looked like the therapist had hit him and became sullen. All he could say was, "I'm just trying to be helpful." Suddenly, he began to cry quietly. The therapist felt mortified at what had occurred. He realized the extent to which George's critical observations had caused him to feel assaulted. He had lost his objectivity and ability to empathize with George. He saw how his abrupt, angry comment reflected a counterattack or retaliation that had deeply wounded George. In feeling criticized himself, the therapist had become the critical father toward George, and George became frightened and quiet.

The therapist commented that he knew his comment had upset George and he was very sorry for what he had said. "Sometimes therapy helps us understand important issues, and I think that if we try to explore what has recently occurred between us, it can be of help in your treatment." George stopped crying and said that he knew he had been acting very critical of the therapist and didn't know why. He said he hadn't meant to be critical. The therapist replied that he hadn't meant to be critical either but that both of them had become caught in an interaction that probably resembled past experiences each of them had had in their lives, adding, "You are not the only one who had a critical father." Surprised, George then said that he knew what is was like to be criticized about these sorts of things. He recounted a story in which his father had berated him in front of neighborhood children because George had built one of the "worst tree forts in the history of the world." The therapist empathized with George and finally realized that George's behavior was an enactment of a complementary projective identification. With his suggestions and critique, George was treating the therapist in the same manner that George's father had treated him, but in so doing, George also was acting toward the therapist the way the therapist's father had treated the therapist, making the therapist vulnerable to the mutual enactment. The therapist thought it was noteworthy that he had allowed the client's criticisms to build up, making him feel inadequate, and was unable to either fix the problems in the office or speak up to the client.

The therapist was able to use this incident to learn more about how George's father's harsh treatment of him had led him to be harsh with others and with himself. This opened the door to the therapist and George beginning to work on gradually lessening the demands he placed on himself, which in turn reduced his feelings of failure and depressive phenomenology. Thus, the mutual enactment, which could have had a disastrous effect, actually furthered the therapeutic process. It also led to the therapist's gaining greater awareness of a vulnerability that he had in relations to a critical client who was able to trigger dynamics from his own past.

Many authors (Hoffmann 1983; Ehrenberg 1995; Renik 1995; Maroda 1999) advocate the use of countertransference disclosure, that is, the revealing of feelings that the clinician has about the client or in interaction with the client. They argue that this intervention opens up the discussion of potentially frightening and disruptive feelings, clarifies the nature of enactments, shows the client that the therapist understands the client's inner world, and enables the client to experience the therapist as genuine and truthful. In discussing, Maroda (1999:99) argues that the only way that the therapist has to complete the cycle of affective communication and to show the client that he or she has gotten the message is to disclose the strong affects that the client is inducing in the therapist. She further suggests that the therapist's truthfulness will help the client to be more truthful, and that when revealing strong countertransference feelings, one should distinguish between what the therapist feels and how the therapist behaves since the goal is to provide new kinds of experiences for the client. In the previous example, the therapist might have shared with George that the therapist was becoming angry and defensive in response to George's critical observations, and that something was occurring in their interaction that was important to understand with respect to what each of them was contributing. Ideally this would have led George to reflect on his behavior and the reasons for it and what it might be saying about his relational patterns and internalized view of himself. It also might have led the therapist to share aspects of his own past that made him vulnerable to the client and how this helped him to understand what the client had experienced earlier in his life.

There are some problems and issues associated with countertransference self-disclosure. Even Maroda (1999) cautions therapists not to disclose strong feelings at times when they feel on the verge of being out of control and expresses caution about revealing erotic countertransference because it is too stimulating and threatening generally. Moreover, it becomes difficult to understand the nature of the mutual enactment if the therapist's feelings about the client are interfering with his or her therapeutic role. Even when countertransference disclosure is carried out in a sensitive and tactful manner, the risk exists that clients may experience these revelations as assaultive, particularly at early points in treatment, and may cause disruptions. For example, as the parents did earlier in a client's life, the therapist may burden the client or may communicate that the therapist expects the client to provide mirroring and cater to the therapist's needs or may seduce the client emotionally only to frustrate and reject the client. Likewise, there is a danger for therapists who work with particularly withdrawn, self-absorbed, or devaluing clients who have difficulty relating and deny the therapist's separate existence or value to sometimes feel resentful that they do not exist as separate or are not appreciated for who they are. This can lead to unattuned self-disclosures of difference and separateness rather than sameness; these may invade the clients' space, may interfere with the process of idealization, or may demand too much closeness that can create severe disruptions in the treatment. Aron (1991:42) acknowledges that insisting that the client engage in a discussion of the therapist's personality may be experienced as intrusive and disruptive and constitute an impingement stemming from the therapist's own narcissistic needs. It may run the risk of shifting the focus from the client to the therapist, and thus the timing of such interventions is crucial.

8. MULTICULTURAL ISSUES

Relational theories offer a broad perspective from which to consider race, ethnicity, culture, and other diversity factors that are intertwined with personal and interpersonal dynamics. The relational model's emphasis on the client's and clinician's subjectivities and the coconstruction of new relational patterns based on a mutually created therapeutic space add new dimensions to clinical social work practice with vulnerable and oppressed populations. This chapter addresses how the diverse subjectivities of both client and therapist influence one another; how race, ethnicity, culture, and other diversity considerations shape the shared therapeutic space; and finally, how the nature of therapeutic action looks in a multicultural practice from a relational point of view. To date, there is only a small group of psychodynamic authors who write about cross-cultural concerns. This group includes Caucasian authors (Altman 1995, 2000; Ringel, 2000, 2001, 2002, 2005; Roland 1998), African American authors (Leary 1995, 1997, 2000; Holmes 1992), and Latino authors (Perez-Foster 1996). The work of these writers and clinicians is discussed throughout this chapter.

EARLIER CONTRIBUTIONS AND NEW PERSPECTIVES

Previous psychodynamic theories such as drive theory, ego psychology, and object relations theories were organized around Western notions, privileging individuality and autonomy over dependence and affiliation, and a nuclear family structure over group and community. In cultures in which family and community affiliations and interdependence are the normative modes of relating, and continue beyond childhood and throughout life, these psychodynamic models have been viewed as irrelevant (Perez-Foster 1996). In addition, only few psychoanalytic authors considered the influence of race, ethnicity, and culture as important factors in the process of development, internalization, identification, and self-other engagement.

One dilemma that has been raised in the literature in regard to clients of color is the intersection between cultural group characteristics and individual uniqueness. Psychodynamic theories have tended to ignore sociocultural factors in their focus on individual dynamics, whereas multicultural and feminist theories have erred in the opposite direction, by privileging culture, race, and ethnicity over individual differences. Chodorow (1999) contributes to this discourse, suggesting that each paradigm complements the other, integrating individual variations within their environmental context. She notes that the psychoanalytic perspective can be helpful in examining individual differences and uniqueness within the culture.

As Chodorow suggests, it is important to appreciate the impact of culture as well as individual differences based on history and personality. Cultural biases may occur whether the client and therapist come from the same or from different cultures. Same-culture clinicians may assume that they share common characteristics with the client, or identify with the client based on their seeming similarities, but fail to attend to individual differences between the client and themselves. Clinicians who come from a different community from that of their clients may carry conscious and unconscious stereotypes about minorities that color their perceptions of their clients but that fail to consider individual differences (Perez-Foster 1996).

With their investigation of the coconstructed verbal and nonverbal engagement between client and clinician, relational theories raise new questions. These questions concern the therapist's, as well as the client's subjectivities, their mutual perceptions of one another, and the ways in which both influence each other through the racial, social, economic, and cultural contexts they are embedded in. The relational approach is especially significant in a context where many client-therapist dyads bring diverse histories, points of views, and assumptions, and where both may carry unconscious perceptions and biases toward the other's minority group affiliation.

THE IMPACT OF THE CLIENT'S AND CLINICIAN'S SUBJECTIVITIES

Both client and therapist bring their histories, identifications, and attitudes toward diversity to the clinical encounter. Developmental experiences, values, and social and institutional structures shape their perceptions of one another. Holmes (1992:1) suggests that these issues may include "white therapist guilt, black therapist over-identification with the downtrodden, and warded off aggression in patients and therapists." Holmes adds that it is the therapist's job to elaborate on broader meanings than race that clients of color may bring, including developmental and transferential dynamics. Leary (2000:658) comments that "race and ethnicity have been largely emphasized as pertaining to people of color, rather than as dynamic constellations with relevance to all persons."

The client's expectations of the therapist may also be culturally, ethnically, and racially based. For example, Roland (1998) discusses the Japanese client's perception of the therapist as a teacher and authority figure who is meant to provide advice and solve problems. Leary (2000) describes an African American client who is disappointed that Leary, an African American therapist, does not seem to conform to African American cultural standards in her choice of profession and husband.

Race, ethnicity, and culture may also become complex transference and countertransference constructions. Holmes, an African American psychoanalyst, writes about an African American patient who projects her internalized racism onto Holmes and is upset that she has been assigned to a black therapist (Holmes 1992). Finally, Altman (2000) examines his own countertransference response to an African American client whose checks keep bouncing. He acknowledges being fearful that if he demands payment, his client will view him as a "greedy Jew," at the same time that he views his client as an untrustworthy black man.

CONSIDERING THE CLIENT'S SUBJECTIVITY   In relational practice, the client' subjective perception of the clinician becomes an important area of investigation, not only as distortions colored by the client's previous experiences, but as potentially valid and accurate perceptions of the therapist's attitudes. The client's observation that the therapist may be biased, is not well attuned, or is condescending to the client may therefore be based on the client's accurate perception of the therapist. The client's observations of the therapist's response to their diversity affiliations may also be linked to social, political, and economic realities that are inseparable from personal and interpersonal factors. Clients who come from minority groups frequently experience political, economic, and other institutionally based discrimination that may be evoked through the person of the therapist (Leary 2000). In relational practice, these themes are not static but subject to ongoing mutual negotiations, both "within persons as well as complex negotiation between persons" (Leary 2000:649).

For example, an African American client's experiences with prejudice and oppression may influence his or her negative perceptions of a white therapist, but the client's internalization of racism can contribute to developing a positive, idealizing transference toward a white therapist and a negative, dismissive transference toward an African American therapist. As mentioned previously, Holmes (1992) writes about an African American client who was disappointed when Holmes was assigned to work with her, as she perceived her as less accomplished than her white colleagues. Similarly, while working in a low-fee mental health clinic, an experienced white social worker was assigned a Haitian client who was terrified of her African American intake therapist and was greatly relieved when she was transferred. The client's fear seemed related to her personal experience of abuse and neglect with her own black Haitian family. These examples suggest that clients' diversity-based perceptions are intertwined with developmental experiences as well as transference and countertransference paradigms. Although it is important that the therapist be culturally competent and aware of the dynamics of racism and oppression, they should also be responsive to the unique developmental experiences each client brings with them, and to the transference dynamics that may encompass personal, interpersonal, and larger social and cultural agendas of the wider culture in which the client and therapist live.

The meaning that clients give to a therapist's gender, ethnicity, race, sexual orientation, and other types of diversity may elicit and bring forward transference dynamics that appear to be based on socially constructed perceptions of race, ethnicity, and gender. They also may have other meanings that are unique to the client's developmental experiences. Because of one of the author's (SR) multiple identifications as a woman, a white woman, a Jew, an Israeli, and an immigrant, minority clients have responded to her in a variety of ways based on their previous experiences. Several clients identified with her outsider status as a Jew and as an immigrant, whereas others saw her as a representative of the mainstream culture that had oppressed and discriminated against them and their community. One African

American gay client viewed her immigrant status as sign of incompetence, and her perceived heterosexual orientation as a sign of her potential biases against him, projecting his own internalized racism and homophobia onto her. Rather than focus only on his experiences with a racist, homophobic society, however, the client and the therapist examined his developmental experiences within his family of origin and within the gay community at large. Their mutual inquiry revealed that painfully, his feelings of rejection originated within his African American family. Moreover, racism was present in his own gay community. These investigations showed the complexity of oppression that is present internally, interpersonally, even in a client's close community and within society at large, and how it may manifest itself between client and therapist.

Thus, the client's diversity-based subjectivity is a complex mixture of developmental and sociocultural forces, and the therapist should not lose sight of either dimension. Client and therapist should also engage with mutual investigation as to how their own identity is influencing one another, and how mutual meanings are negotiated between them.

THE THERAPIST'S SUBJECTIVITY   In addition to the client' subjectivity, the therapist's subjectivity is an important factor in a relational practice. What therapists feel and how they respond to the client have in the past either been discarded as interfering with the therapeutic process (Freud 1912) or seen as a projection of the client's affects onto the therapist (Klein 1952). Sandler (1976) later formulated the notion of role responsiveness, suggesting that the therapist responds to the client's transference with either complementary or a concordant (same) countertransference. Current relational writers added the notion of the therapist's subjectivity, constructed not only based on the client's disowned affects, but also rooted in the therapist's own history and experiences. Several authors suggest that therapists grapple with the meanings of their own legacy in regard to race, or other marginalized identities in this culture. Altman (2000), Harris (2007), and Suchet (2004), among others, suggest that it is important for a white therapist to examine his or her white identity and its relation to racism in this country. Harris (2007) notes that whiteness, by its own erasure of identifiable identity, and its cocoonlike protection within a privileged world, negates its link to racism and oppression. She recalls the decontextualized artifacts that her grandfather brought to her own childhood home in Canada, taken from indigenous peoples in Canada, objects that lost their religious and symbolic meaning and became generic decorative articles. From an adult view, she now recognizes the "whited out" conflicts represented in these seemingly innocent decorative objects, and the act of buying them, or rather "shoplifting" them.

The process of therapists' self-reflection upon their own links to racism and oppression may be a complex one. We all have multiple identities. Although one of our identities may derive from an oppressive community, we may have other experiences in which we were oppressed and victimized. For example, a clinician may be white, but also a woman, Jewish, and an immigrant. Whatever her main identity at the time, she may have faced both positive and difficult experiences. It is important to examine how each of our identifications shape us and shape our view of and responses to our minority clients.

AN AFRICAN AMERICAN CLIENT AND A WHITE THERAPIST   An African American male client was late to many sessions and missed several others with his white therapist. When this pattern continued for a period of months, the therapist found herself in a dilemma. She wanted to confront the client about his behavior but was reluctant to do so. She did not want him to perceive her as a representative of the oppressive white culture. Nor did she want to enact the negative interactions that he had described to her many times before. Eventually, she started to wonder whether she and the client were enacting a scenario in which the client acted as the therapist's oppressor and forced her to experience his own experience of being devalued, manipulated, and disregarded as an African American male living in a racist society.

Increasingly, the therapist's view of the client as an African American man who experienced discrimination and poverty, and her guilt at her own feelings of frustration and anger, conflicted with her experience of being victimized by the client through his own inconsiderate behavior. A breakthrough occurred when the therapist finally confronted the client on his behavior and shared her feelings of frustration about having to wait for him "to show up." As the therapist communicated her thoughts that the client did not seem to value their mutual therapeutic work, the client began to cry. He recalled how he himself would wait for his estranged father to come to scheduled visits, never knowing if he would show up or not.

The therapist's eventual willingness to grapple with the complexity of her own feelings, and to go beyond differences in race, ethnicity, and skin color, allowed the client to discover more complex meaning hidden in his own developmental history, which contributed to a deeper understanding of what had occurred between them. Therapists' ability to reflect on their subjective responses is essential in a relational practice with diverse clients. These reflections are typically a multifaceted process that may include the therapist's experiences and identifications with otherness and oppression, and their responses to the client that are shaped by the client's transference, their subjective experiences, and their professional training.

A COMPLICATED COUNTERTRANSFERENCE   A Jewish therapist found herself experiencing a complicated countertransference response with an adolescent gay male client who idealized Hitler and identified with him. As a professional, she understood the client's identification with a powerful yet tortured figure that he both identified with and aspired to be. She rationalized that for the client, Hitler was a symbol rather than the real historical figure who inflicted tremendous sufferings on her people. But she also identified as a Jew whose relatives were murdered in the Holocaust, and she experienced fear and anxiety about her client's own homicidal or perhaps suicidal urges, and revulsion at his choice of an ego ideal. The therapist's identification with her cultural heritage drove her to try help her client to create some distance from this dangerous identification by providing him with a book by Victor Frankel, but she also realized that it was important for her to investigate and acknowledge her own sense of an "inner monster," and for both of them to allow space in the treatment to process his complex feelings.

Thus, it is important for relational therapists to reflect upon their own multicultural identity and its meaning within broader sociocultural context, and their developmental experiences, as well as to be aware how these identifications intersect with their countertransference responses to particular minority clients with whom they work.

THE THERAPEUTIC SPACE: THE MUTUAL IMPACT OF CLIENT AND CLINICIAN

The mutual impact of both the client's and the clinician's subjectivities upon each other is an important factor in their shared therapeutic space. The client–therapist impact upon one another can contribute to the construction of new and transformative internal patterns between self and other. The working-through process may optimally result in the construction of more adaptive patterns of interactions. The mutual impact of client and therapist can also trigger old and destructive paradigms based on oppressed and marginalized racial and cultural identities. In this relationally shared space, the dynamics of power, impasses, and enactments are viewed as opportunities for change and growth, rather than as therapeutic failures.

POWER DYNAMICS BETWEEN CLIENT AND CLINICIAN Power is an important dynamic, especially in practice with clients who come from oppressed communities. Although the social work literature emphasizes the egalitarian relationship between client and clinician, the therapeutic relationship is asymmetrical, with the clinician seen as the expert, the one who determines the "rules" of the interaction, and the one who holds the power and the expertise. The therapist's position as an authority may work well with some cultural groups. For example, there is an extensive literature that suggests that Asian clients may prefer an authoritarian relationship with therapists because of their own hierarchical culture, and therefore they expect therapists to solve problems and to provide solutions (Ringel 2001, 2005; Roland 1998). African American clients, however, may experience the relationship with a white therapist as perpetuating old and oppressive paradigms. The converse may be true for African American therapists who work with white clients (Leary 1997). Moreover, therapists themselves may feel racial guilt when treating African American clients that causes them to make special allowances, as suggested by Altman (2000). In some cultures, sharing personal information with an outsider is seen as unacceptable, and cross-cultural clinicians may find themselves having to renegotiate traditional notional of therapeutic frame and clinical boundaries, as the following example shows.

TRYING TO ENTER THE CLIENT'S WORLD A white social work graduate student spent the summer in Jamaica, working with a Jamaican woman and her family. She discovered that in order to be accepted by her client she needed to visit her at home, eat her food, and meet with her friends, in other words, to become part of the family, so that the client would trust her with intimate information and her struggle with family conflicts. The student found it difficult, however, to navigate between her two identities—that of the friend and that of the professional—and had to find inventive ways to share her professional observations and expertise so that these would be heard and accepted by her Jamaican client.

Sometimes clients may prefer to talk with someone outside the community who can provide confidentiality if the issues they grapple with risk their ostracism by their community.

THE USEFULNESS OF AN OUTSIDER A graduate student worked with a torture victim from Rwanda. Although the client spoke poor English, and she and the student had difficulty understanding each other, the client felt more comfortable with the student because she was an outsider who, she believed, would not judge or reject her, as her Rwandan community would have done if they had known that she had been repeatedly raped by Hutu militants. She seemed to prefer a therapeutic relationship whereby the social work intern would listen to her narrative and provide her with advice and validation.

IMPASSES AND ENACTMENTS

As described in previous chapters, more recent relational perspectives view the therapist as both an old and a new object (Cooper and Levitt 2005). The therapist's role is more active and engaged, helping the client to experience and enact more adaptive relational patterns. To that end, the therapist becomes a participant in the client's familiar but dysfunctional interactive dynamics, and these enactments may then be processed between client and therapist so that the client can start to engage in more successful interactions.

Enactments that occur in multicultural practice have a special dimension. They arise when both client and therapist fall into old roles in which each takes on a position related to diversity inequities present in either's experience and in society at large. Clients may pull therapists to enact familiar relationships based on their minority status, and the therapist may respond because of his or her own personal history and experience as a member of a majority group, or as member of an oppressed minority.

A TRANSFERENCE INVOLVING THE CLINICIAN'S "MINORITY" AND "MAJORITY" STATUS A transgender client identified the therapist's Jewish heritage, including the discrimination, pogroms, and Holocaust that the Jewish community experienced, with his own marginalized experience as a transgender individual in straight Christian society. On the other hand, the therapist also represented the majority culture that the client believed a held rigid and oppressive view of people like himself. He alternated between idealization and identification with the therapist's heritage, and disappointment and anger in what he experienced as her biased attitudes. This client's transference mirrored the therapist's countertransference, as she found herself feeling deep empathy for and identification with him, as well as resentment and frustration. Thus, they fell into respective roles to those he experienced with his parents, siblings, coworkers, supervisors, and social institutions. At times, the client perceived the therapist as representing the oppressive forces that had rejected and marginalized him. Concurrently, the therapist struggled between the desire to contradict his perceptions and her recognition that the client needed to perceive her in this particular way in order to work through his own feelings of rage, sadness, and frustration. During these enactments, the client became the author's oppressor, and the author the victim that was reduced to a restricted, confined role from which the client would not allow her to venture.

THE TRANSITIONAL SPACE OR THE THIRD SPACE

As discussed in chapter 3, the concept of the third has been important in relational treatment. More recently, it has been utilized to understand how culture, race, and ethnicity that both client and therapist bring with them influence the treatment, and how the interaction between client and therapist is transformed into a new, third dimension.

Mattei (2008) suggests that the "ethnic third" should always be kept in mind as an at times unverbalized dimension in the treatment. The therapist should reflect on the impact of race, ethnicity, class, and culture on his or her own history and point of view, and on his or her countertransference with a particular client. It is also important to engage in the transformative process that occurs between clients and therapists as each of them brings his or her own subjectivity to bear upon the other, and a new, third dimension evolves based on this interaction.

CREATING A "THIRD" IN THE TREATMENT PROCESS A young African American lesbian woman entered treatment in order to make sense of her relationship with a cold and rejecting older girlfriend. The client was initially extremely uncomfortable in discussing the details of her relationship, perhaps anxious regarding how the white, seemingly straight therapist might judge her. The client became more open and revealing about sexual and sadomasochistic aspects of her relationships as the therapist became more familiar and trusted. The client, however, experienced herself as shy and as easily embarrassed by her need to be loved and cared for. Concurrently, the therapist initially viewed the client as a masculine, somewhat intimidating woman who grew up in a culture that was completely foreign to the therapist.

The client reported an early history of growing up in a single-parent family, where her mother was overworked and she had to care for younger siblings, reflecting the reality of many African American clients. Although her socioeconomic and familial background was not unusual, the client's ability to transcend her difficult history and become a well-educated professional on her own was quite remarkable. In her personal relationships, however, she still pursued the love and attention she did not get from her mother.

As they came to understand each other better, client and therapist developed a pattern of playing a game of hide and seek whereby the therapist would recognize the client's need to be seen and recognized, and the client, feeling exposed and embarrassed, would start to laugh and hide her face like a little girl. This pattern was predicated on the client's history as a poor African American girl growing up in a single-parent family, but also on her unique personality and interactions with the therapist. This new pattern helped the client to better understand her interpersonal difficulties, and her pursuit of emotionally unavailable women who distracted her from her own disowned needs and desires.

In a relational perspective, it is advisable for therapists to reflect on how race, ethnicity, and culture contribute to particular role responsiveness that the dyad is engaged in, or contribute to an unusual behavior in the clinician with a particular client that may be related to cultural as well as personal factors.

THERAPEUTIC ACTION

From a relational stance, therapeutic action includes the clinician's use of self in a more transparent, participatory way that may involve self-disclosure of the therapist's state of mind, mistakes, and the creation of new verbal and nonverbal experiences within the therapeutic space (Stern et al. 1998). Holding, affect regulation, and mentalization are modes of therapeutic action that take on particular meanings when diversity issues are attended to in the client–therapist encounter.

THE CLINICIAN'S SELF DISCLOSURE As previous chapters have discussed, the contemporary relational clinician has become a more active participant in the therapeutic interaction and is more disclosing, transparent, and participatory. This stance may not be useful with clients from certain cultural groups. For example, in some non-Western cultures, including Asian society, self-disclosure would not be necessary or even welcome. Roland (1998) discusses his work with Japanese clients who look to the therapist for advice and problem solving but prefer to maintain formal boundaries and are not comfortable knowing the therapist's personal experience or personal identity. Generally, the decision about whether or not to self-disclose should be based on the individual's needs rather than his or her cultural background. For example, there are clients of color who may benefit from the therapist's self-disclosure, and others who may find it intrusive or irrelevant. Clients bring their own unique experience, developmental issues, and subjective needs that the therapist must evaluate, along with their affiliation with an oppressed or a minority group, as the following two vignettes illustrate.

THE DECISION NOT TO SELF-DISCLOSE In the treatment of a previously dis cussed transgender client, the therapist thought that rather than disclosing her subjective attitudes and feelings, it was more important to allow the client to displace his anger at and disappointment in her as a representative of a rejecting and oppressive majority culture. The therapy could then focus on his painful experiences and examine their impact on his sense of self, and difficulties in establishing trust and forming intimate relationships. The therapist believed that contributing her actual subjective perspective at that time would have been experienced as intrusive and as a violation of the client's therapeutic space.

Similarly, the African American young gay man who viewed the therapist as a representative of a marginalizing straight mainstream culture, as well as a devalued immigrant, needed her help in investigating the links between his biases and his own history of rejections and disappointments. Disclosing her subjective reactions might have shifted the focus away from these important clinical issues.

COCONSTRUCTION OF MENTALIZATION AND REFLECTIVE FUNCTIONING As discussed in previous chapters, mentalization is the ability to reflect upon and verbally articulate states of mind, including thoughts and emotional experiences.

It also includes the capacity to understand others' states of mind and to be empathic. The therapist's role is to help clients identify their thoughts and feelings and communicate them, as well as to gain insight into others' inner states of mind, and their own impact on others. Race, ethnicity, culture, and other diversity factors shape the interactive process of reflective functioning between client and clinician. The therapist may encourage and help clients to reflect on and articulate the place of cultural history in their lives, how it shaped their affective experience and their interactions with others, and how it shaped their thinking processes. The relational process between client and clinician may also contribute to the client's understanding of his or her impact on others, and the client's perceptions of others may influence his or her own, and the differences between his or her cultural perspectives and those of others.

IMPROVING THE CAPACITY FOR EMPATHY   With an African American male client, the therapist and the client reflected on his family history of being sharecroppers in the South, his place as a first-generation college student in his family, the burden he experienced regarding his parents' expectations for him to succeed and excel, and his feelings of guilt and failure when he left his Ivy League university to pursue an acting career. His parents wanted him to become a lawyer, or even a civil servant. The client gained a better understanding for why it was so important for his family to see him attending an elite university, and to describe him to their friends in terms of his achievements, which reflected on their own success in American society. This understanding helped him to gain deeper understanding and empathy for what they had been through, and to view their need to use him as a "trophy" rather than accept him for who he was with greater equanimity.

This client also gained a better understanding for his difficulties at the university, where he experienced himself as a member of a small minority, an African American from a lower economic background, and as a gay man among the majority of wealthy white heterosexual students. He recognized that his anger, resentment, and withdrawal from social relationships prevented him from forming potential friendships with classmates who wanted to get to know him. He reflected that rather than viewing him as inferior, other students might have found him interesting and intriguing, and capable of enriching their own narrow life experience. As the counseling process developed, he started to appreciate that he was using these apparent differences from others to protect himself from feeling inferior and experiencing rejection, a familiar childhood experience that was no longer true. He started to experience more empathy for others who, despite their apparent privilege, may have experienced their own pain and difficulties.

PROVIDING HOLDING, CONTAINMENT, AND AFFECT REGULATION The concepts of holding (Winnicott) and containment (Bion) emerge from object relations theories. These concepts refer to the clinician's function of providing an affective containment for the client's feelings, and a holding environment, similar to the maternal environment that provides safety and security. Within this environment, the client can engage in exploratory behaviors, take new risks, and practice new behaviors. The construct of affect regulation elaborates on these earlier relational constructs, suggesting that the function of holding, regulating, and containing is mutual and bidirectional (Beebe and Lachmann 2002). Both client and therapist regulate and symbolically hold one another as they coconstruct a shared therapeutic space and develop a unique pattern of mutual regulation that can be unconscious and nonverbal. Race, ethnicity, culture, and other diversity factors add layers of external and internal meaning to the understanding of holding and containment.

HOLDING AND CONTAINMENT IN A CULTURAL CONTEXT A young Muslim woman, a daughter of immigrants from Bangladesh, entered treatment because she experienced internal conflicts regarding her identity. She struggled with her desire to please her parents and be a "good Muslim girl," and her identification and wish to be part of the American culture. Moreover, she wanted to have an independent, assertive, and feminist sense of self. This internal struggle found expression in her relationship with men, where she found herself complying with their demands and having a difficult time making her needs heard and asserting her own choices. Although the therapist helped her examine this dilemma and validated both sides of her struggle, providing a safe space to investigate and express her conflicting identifications and wishes, the therapist recognized that there was an overarching social and cultural context that needed to be included and acknowledged.

Complicating her internal and interpersonal split, the client reported that she had grown up in poverty, witnessing her father's efforts to provide for the family, and encountering frequent instances of discrimination because of her dark skin color, religion, and immigrant identity. She reported her feelings of alienation among her mostly white, wealthy high school peers, and in her private college, where she was accepted with a full scholarship. Both the client and the author recognized that her experience with injustice had led her to choose a profession in which she helped to organize other marginalized, excluded communities. Holding the client meant including all the different levels of her experience, within her traditional Muslim Bangladeshi family, among her poor Bangladeshi community, as a woman in American society, and as an immigrant daughter. It also raised the question of how this client was holding the therapist, a Jewish immigrant from Israel, who may have shared some of her struggles but was also on the other side of the religious and political fence. As the client let the therapist know that she felt recognized and understood by her, and appreciated the therapist's efforts to understand her experience on multiple levels, the therapist wondered how the client experienced the therapist's own religious and cultural subjectivity. Although both client and therapist were recognizing and regulating one another as women and immigrants, the client also needed the therapist to hold her with less mutuality and intrusion. She needed a safe space where she could experience and communicate her painful conflicts. The client reflected on her earlier experiences of poverty and invisibility, and her decision, despite, or maybe because of, traditional upbringing, to become a rebel, an outrageous punk girl who wore tattoos and cut her arms. She slowly shared her desperate need to be in a relationship, and her inability to assert her voice and wishes, despite her feminist beliefs and decision to fight for justice in more public arenas.

This vignette shows that holding, containment, and mutual regulation of affect become more nuanced and complex when racial, ethnic, cultural, religious, political, and other diversity issues are attended to within the internal and the interpersonal, and that a multiplicity of identities, both those of the client and those of the therapist, need to be recognized, expressed, and held by both client and clinician.

CONCLUSION

The concepts and vignettes provided in this chapter suggest that only broad relational principles can be drawn regarding multicultural practice, without losing the richness and uniqueness of each individual client. Each client is embedded in a social and cultural context, and each brings his or her own unique identity and complex set of experiences. Although identity may be rooted in the client's experience of oppression and vulnerability, other identities may represent their identification with the oppressor, or with successful aspects of their experience. Therapists as well bring a multiplicity of experiences and identifications that interact with the client's experiences in complex ways. Self-observation, curiosity, freshness, and creativity, therefore, are some of the important qualities that relational clinicians bring with them to the multicultural encounter.

It is important to be aware of how the client's marginalized identity and the therapist's own heritage of oppression or marginalization shape and influence one another. From a relational perspective, each client–therapist dyad is unique, and both clinician and client coconstruct a therapeutic space based on their individual histories and experience. Impasses and enactment may have a specific meaning based on the cross-cultural prism that both client and therapist cocreate, in which developmental experiences and larger sociocultural dynamics mix and intersect.

Finally, therapeutic action with vulnerable populations holds unique meanings. When evaluating the efficacy of self-disclosure, the nature of therapeutic holding, and the process of self-reflection and mentalization, relational clinicians should keep in mind the client's unique cultural experiences and the communal history in which his or her subjectivity is embedded. It is important to honor both these aspects of the client's experience, as well as the clinician's personal and cultural heritage.

9. RELATIONAL PRINCIPLES IN BRIEF TREATMENT

Economic conditions and the ever-increasing influence of managed health care led many therapists and theoreticians to look for abbreviated models of psychotherapy. The very nature of clinical social work practice often necessitates brief contact with clients. For example, social workers who conduct clinical work in hospital, medical, and mental health settings often only see clients when they are in-patients in the system. As length of stays tends to be short, there is increasing need for social workers to utilize models of brief intervention.

Safran (2002:171) comments that "brief psychotherapy has its origins in Ferenczi and Rank's (1924) pioneering attempt to counter the trend toward longer analyses that was emerging at the time." It was not until the 1970s and beyond, however, that theorists put forth numerous short-term psychotherapy approaches. Although there has been a longstanding tradition of short-term dynamic therapy, the brief therapy literature has been somewhat slower than the long-term treatment literature in moving toward relational principles. Few short-term models have integrated relational principles.

This chapter describes and illustrates a relational short-term therapy model that can be used in clinical social work with individuals. Chapter 10 will discuss relational treatment in both short-term and ongoing work with couples, families, and groups. In contrast to other short-term social work models that do not integrate dynamic theories, a relational short-term treatment model focus emphasizes the importance of a client's interpersonal relationships, is consistent with clinical social work's person-in-situation perspective, and emphasizes the clinician–client relationship in the treatment process. Although there is some variability as to "how many sessions" constitutes brief therapy, the working definition of brief therapy in this chapter ranges from six to thirty sessions, with a definitive end point (termination) being decided at the outset of clinical treatment. After providing a chronological summary of short-term treatment, the chapter more fully describes and illustrates the components of one model, brief relational therapy, that is being studied extensively, particularly at Beth Israel Medical Center in Boston. Its main contributors are J. Christopher Muran (2002) and Jeremy D. Safran (2002, 2005).

A CHRONOLOGY OF BRIEF THERAPY

There is a myriad of literature that elaborates brief treatment models for psychotherapy. An often-verbalized critique of these models relates to the limited applicability of the models to a wide range of clients (Ringstrom 1995). They tend to require highly motivated clients who can tolerate quick and deep interpretations without extreme anxiety or other negative effects. Although many of the models discuss the importance of finding a focus for the brief treatment (often of an interpersonal nature), they tend to be one-person psychology approaches to brief treatment.

For example, James Mann (1973, 1991) developed a model called Time Limited Psychotherapy (TLP), utilizing ego psychology constructs. He stated that the "single goal of TLP is to diminish as much as possible the patient's negative self-image (1991:21). He did not describe specific inclusion criteria, but, like most short-term theorists, he ruled out severely disturbed clients (those suffering from either mental illness or personality disorders). He thought that clients and therapists should focus on a central issue in treatment that they aggressively explore. Mann's model is unique in that he rigidly adheres to a time limit of twelve sessions, conducted on a weekly basis. In fact, he suggested that the issue of time limits should be utilized to understand the entire process of treatment. He also advised that setting a definitive termination date propels clients to shift in their affective experience. He thought that a "satisfactory termination is one in which the patient leaves treatment feeling sad. … Sadness in place of depression allows for separation without self-injury" (36).

Messer and Warren (1995) wrote that proponents of brief treatment such as David Malan (1963), Habib Davanloo (1978, 1980) and Peter Sifneos (1992) all maintained allegiance to a drive/structural understanding of the model of the mind. These authors developed their models of brief therapy while staying consistent with drive theory's metapsychological assumptions. They noted that an "impulse (I) or feeling (F) leads to a defense (D), which, when unsuccessful, results in anxiety (A)" (Messer and Warren 1995:70). These authors recognized that current problems or conflicts are repetitions of some earlier constellation of factors from one's origin family, and they advocated a treatment focus that integrates the impulse/defense/anxiety model described above.

More specifically, in Peter Sifneos's text, *Short Term Anxiety-Provoking Psychotherapy*, he summarized his many years of research of brief therapy. Here, he cited characteristics of potential clients, namely, that the client should have had at least one positive relationship with a caretaker in her earlier life. Additionally, the client should show high flexibility and be fairly intelligent and psychologically minded (1992:20). He thought that there should be a particular focus for the treatment. Sifneos was somewhat unique in his approach in that he emphasized the interpretation of clients' oedipal concerns, which aroused considerable anxiety. He considered the anxiety central to the process as he assumed that the client would want relief from the anxiety; this wish would thus propel the client to change aspects of their behavior.

Malan (1976) and Davanloo (1978, 1980) both embedded their short-term models in a triangle of conflict—"that is, the impulse-defense-anxiety triangle" (Ringstrom 1995). They saw clients' problems as involving intrapsychic conflict that is highly defended against. In their technique, clinicians become very active in interpretation of the client's core conflict and thus must be able to tolerate confrontation of core and longstanding intrapersonal and interpersonal issues. The client is expected to be able to articulate highly charged transference feelings about the clinician.

Hans Strupp and Jeffrey Binder published a text called *Psychotherapy in a New Key: A Guide to Time-Limited Dynamic Psychotherapy* (1984) They suggested that their working assumptions of short-term therapy represent a traditional psychoanalytic point of view (21). As such, they emphasized that clients will develop a transference relationship that is viewed as a constellation of neurotic conflicts that have their roots in childhood patterns of conflict. Their focus on the transference relationship is embedded in the working principle that a client's problems are rooted in disturbed or dysfunctional interpersonal relationships. They suggested that the therapist is a "more or less uninvolved technical expert whose task (analogous to that of a surgeon) is to penetrate the defenses in order to gain access to the major conflict lying beyond' (23). The focus of the process of the twenty-five to thirty sessions is then to understand and interpret the transference neurosis of the client. Change occurs when the client is able to gain insight into the connections of current maladaptive interpersonal relationships with their historical antecedents.

Binder and Strupp further developed their model of brief treatment when they later conceptualized interpersonal problems as reflecting cyclical maladaptive patterns (1991:140). They described that clients unconsciously cast themselves and others in complementary roles that contribute to their overall interpersonal style and character formation. These four categories of formation are:

- Acts of self—the patients' feelings, thoughts, wishes, and behaviors of an interpersonal nature
- Expectations of others' reactions—either the conscious, preconscious, or unconscious expectations of how others will respond to their actions
- Acts of others toward self—the patients' observation of or perception of how others interact with them
- Acts of self toward self (introject)—how the patients treat themselves when they are managing interpersonal exchanges

In *Time-Limited Dynamic Psychotherapy*, Hanna Levenson utilized the cyclical maladaptive patterns noted above. She said that she departed from Binder and Strupp somewhat in her focus in treatment. In contrast to conceptualizing insight as the main vehicle of change, Levenson emphasized her attempts to have clients change patterns by offering a new (corrective) interpersonal relationship in the therapeutic relationship (1995:40).

Simon Budman and Alan Gurman further added to brief therapy literature in their text, *Theory and Practice of Brief Therapy*. They encouraged clinicians to broaden the potential foci of brief treatment by assessing what they termed the interpersonal-developmental-existential (I-D-E) domain. These authors suggested that their approach was neither exclusively symptom-based nor exclusively intrapsychic or interpersonal. Rather, they wrote that their amalgam was based upon a range of evolving principles of couple, family, existential, attachment, and human potential theories, among others (1988:27–28).

Budman and Gurman paid a great deal of attention to the precipitant and timing of the client's decision to enter treatment. The foci that they emphasized are related to the I-D-E domain. They explored whether the client had experienced any form of loss, developmental dysnchrony, or interpersonal conflict. If a clear focus did not emerge in these three domains, they explored the symptom picture of the client to see if they could find a major focus there. Lastly, if the clinician could not find a focus in any of the above, then the exploration became more focused on the client's character structure. The focus for brief treatment arises out of one of these five domains. Once a focus is formulated, the client and therapist work tenaciously to discuss this thematic area in depth.

Although the literature contains other authors and/or forms of brief psychotherapy, the contributions discussed so far have been fundamental in the historical development of brief therapy models. The following two models are more relational in their emphasis.

BRIEF RELATIONAL THERAPY (BETH ISRAEL MODEL)

As noted above, Christopher Muran (2002) and Jeremy Safran (2002) developed a model of relational brief therapy, implementing psychotherapy research in the specific areas of treatment alliance and the process of change. A paper written by Safran, Muran, Samstag, and Winston (2005) describes the results of a two-step research project that compared the outcomes of three types of short-term treatment:

■ Short-term dynamic psychotherapy (STDP)—also previously known as brief adaptive psychotherapy. The authors suggested that this model is similar to the Binder and Strupp (1984, 1991) model described above. There is a very heavy emphasis on understanding, interpreting, and working through the transference relationship.
■ Cognitive-behavioral therapy—a manualized treatment approach based upon treatment approaches of Beck et al. (1979) and adaptation of other cognitive therapies. The patients' core belief systems, automatic thoughts, and dysfunctional attitudes are challenged and modified.
■ Brief relational therapy—the focus of the remainder of this chapter.

The research initially focused on building a treatment alliance with personality disordered clients and then evolved to aspects of the treatment alliance and change in brief therapy models. Safran reported that brief relational therapy is as effective as the other two forms of brief treatment noted above when working with personality disorders. He also found that clinicians using brief relational therapy principles had significantly fewer dropouts in therapy than did either the cognitive-behavioral model or the short-term dynamic therapy model (2002:172). Focusing on the relationship is particularly important for social work practice as often social workers need to engage mandated clients into a clinical process—a less authoritative working relationship furthers the clinical work.

Muran suggests that the brief relational therapy model "integrates principles from interpersonal-relational and humanistic psychotherapies as well as contemporary theories on cognition and emotion" (2002:119). It recognizes that all individuals have multiple selves in their identity, and that everyone lives in a world of changing and multiple constructions of self. The change process arises from two intersecting ideas. Clients need to be "thrown off balance emotionally" or "decentered" in order to precipitate an expanding awareness or insight of self and other processes. Second, clinicians need to offer a new relational experience in the treatment process in order to challenge the individual's maladaptive relational schema. Utilizing a brief model necessitates that clinician and client share a strong working alliance and can formulate goals from an intersubjective framework. Social workers using a brief model recognize that the treatment will be particularly relevant for specific identifiable issues. Although the assessment of the client will unfold over time and the social worker is open to a shifting understanding of the client, the presenting concerns of the client command attention. Some clients may involve themselves in different courses of brief therapy, at different times, over their adult lives. Thus, the treatment addresses certain relational patterns in the client's current life situation and does not aim for "complete" character change.

Safran (2002) outlines the main principles of his brief model as follows:

■ The model is considered a two-person psychology, as there is a collaborative exploration of the symmetrical contributions of client and clinician to the interaction. The clinician understands the subjectivity of her perceptions.

■ The ongoing focus of the work is based upon a here-and-now analysis of the clinical relationship. He recommends that the clinician think out loud about what one is experiencing.

■ The model emphasizes intense exploration of the subtleties of the clients' experiences as these unfold in enactments.

■ The clinician is cautious about suggesting that these enactments are always transference phenomena, and he does not assume that these enactments can be generalized to other interpersonal relationships of the clients.

- Clinicians utilize self-disclosure often in the process (172–173).
- Clinicians recognize that each session may provide unique opportunities — what was true in one session may not be true in another and what was true at one moment may not be true in the next (182).

This model of brief therapy discourages the identification of a core conflict or maladaptive relational pattern at the outset of treatment. Contrary to other models of short-term treatment, this approach recognizes that the clinicians cannot be so "objective" in the early phase of assessment that they can make such an assessment. Safran et al. (2005) suggested that case formulation does not happen initially in treatment but rather happens when enactments are understood and processed in the treatment relationship. As such, the clinician encourages the client to be patient with the process and to allow it to unfold within the therapeutic dyad. The therapist recognizes that understanding is only partial in the beginning at best, and that awareness or insight on the clients' part is achieved mostly through an ongoing cycle of enactments, deconstruction of the enactments, and understanding of the process of the enactments (Safran 2002:175).

The following example shows the unintended consequences of applying some of these principles.

EXAMINING A PROBLEMATIC CLIENT–CLINICIAN INTERACTION IN BRIEF RELATIONAL THERAPY The male therapist agreed to see a thirty-eight-year-old professional man, David, who called him after his wife encouraged him to do so. David mentioned on the telephone that his wife was a therapist in an adjoining community, and that the therapist had taught her when she was a M.S.W. student twelve years earlier. The therapist did not currently know the wife and asked if the client felt there would be any conflict within him about seeing the therapist, in view of his having been the wife's professor. David replied that this was indeed why he sought therapy, as his wife had spoken positively about the therapist. He added that he was anxious to start treatment to try to feel less depressed and to better manage his free-floating and almost continuous anxiety.

The client's health insurance allowed up to twenty psychotherapy visits in each calendar year, and David suggested that he did not want long-term therapy. He had previously been engaged in treatment and hoped that these twenty sessions would suffice to ameliorate his anxiety and depression. Although the therapist did not identify himself as a "relational" therapist to the client, he did have this framework in his thinking as the work began. The therapist encouraged David to bring issues of current importance to him to the sessions and said that they would see what unfolded between them as David started to explore his current relationships and patterns with family, work, and friends. Probably because of his previous therapy experiences, David spent the first two sessions essentially giving his developmental history. The therapist was curious about this, as he had not asked David to do so but nonetheless found his narrative to be interesting and informative. The therapist did formulate some beginning ideas about David's difficulties but did not share these with the client. He felt that it was important for the therapist and the client to coconstruct the assessment in collaboration with one another.

At the beginning of his third session, David asked if the therapist would give him a summary of his assessment and what the goals of his treatment would be. The therapist empathized with David's wish to have a structured plan in place but also let him know that it might be more useful for them to explore issues as they arose. The therapist indicated that he and the client would understand David's problems better and formulate goals as they worked together. David seemed to agree and went on to talk about some work-related issue. He described feeling that he was doing more than his share of the work in his office and that he was attempting to remedy this situation by being more assertive with his coworkers.

Arriving fifteen minutes late to his next session, David announced that he would be stopping therapy after this session. The therapist told him that he was puzzled and somewhat saddened to hear this as he thought they had made a good beginning. The therapist asked if they could discuss the reasons for the client's decision together and said that he was open to hearing any concerns or critique so that he could better understand David's needs. David had not overtly shown frustration or anger with the therapist previously but then angrily told him that he didn't want to work this out together — rather he wanted the therapist to tell him what was wrong with him and what he could do to change it. He reiterated that he needed to have specific goals for the therapy and that he couldn't stand all of this business of "letting things unfold." The therapist replied that he could see that his approach was contributing to David's anger but again said that he thought it was important for he and the client to try to understand how and why their interaction was troubling David. This comment seemed to make David more enraged.

Although the site of this tension was clearly in the treatment relationship, the therapist also knew that David had experienced his father as somewhat disinterested in his activities. The therapist wondered if a part of David's reaction was being activated from his history, but he did not interpret this to him. Rather, he stayed focused on his interaction with the client.

David then caustically said that the therapist apparently didn't practice what he preached. He went on to say that his wife had chastised him for not having specific goals in his therapy. She said that the therapist had always impressed upon her and her colleagues (when she was his student) that it was essential to be goal-directed and to keep the focus with clients who would "resist" the process. Of course, the therapist imagined that he probably did say such things in classes many years earlier. He then told David that he had "blown it" with him because although he had attempted to be collaborative with him, he did not realize that David expected a different approach and thought the therapist was not doing what he should be doing. The therapist further acknowledged that he had made it difficult for David to verbalize his sentiments because the therapist had been so insistent that things should unfold. The therapist also said that he could understand the pressure David might be getting from his wife but that he thought it was important for David and him to continue in their work together.

David became less angry and said that he thought the therapist didn't care much about his progress because of his laissez-faire approach. His previous therapist was very structured, and David wondered why the therapist was not directing him to talk about certain parts of his history or current relationships. The therapist apologized for missing what David needed from him. As the therapist encouraged David to verbalize his frustrations, David began to feel better about the therapist and the treatment continued. A theme that emerged was David's feelings of being lost without structure and uncared about when he did not receive positive feedback from others. Thus, although one might say that one aspect of the relational thrust of the treatment frustrated the client, exploring what the interaction between therapist and client meant, in keeping with relational principles, helped to illuminate a core issue that David experienced in other relationships.

This vignette also illustrates another important guiding point of brief relational therapy: keeping a focus on the present moment in the therapy. Safran (2002) comments that focusing on the present moment may seem antithetical to a time-limited treatment. Clinicians sometimes worry that the present focus treatment will not sufficiently prepare the client with "insight" or tools to take home with them to manage other dilemmas or difficult interactions. The brief relational therapist encourages a collaborative effort that focuses on the process of the interaction (in contrast to following the content). Although this is a traditional social work principle, it is important for the relational therapist to directly encourage the client to identify his or her internal processes as they unfold in therapy and also in outside relationships. It is important to demonstrate this process of introspection and also to encourage this with clients. Fonagy et al. (2002) refer to this capacity as the capacity for mentalization. Clients are encouraged to reflect on their own internal states while simultaneously imagining what might be going on in the other person's mind. This skill can be actively built by focusing on the present moment between the client and clinician, as the following example shows.

HELPING A CLIENT TO REFLECT ON HER INNER STATES AFTER A DISRUPTION The male therapist began working with Kari, a twenty-six-year-old graduate student who was studying anthropology. She confided that she was somewhat worried about her marijuana use and wondered if it was affecting her progress on her master's thesis work. Kari identified that she wanted to work on this issue but was reluctant to have the therapist actively "monitor" the amount of and help her reflect on the reasons for her usage. It was important to her that she be the one to initiate discussion about her drug usage.

A rupture occurred in the therapeutic relationship when Kari told the therapist in an animated way how she had managed a difficult interpersonal relationship with one of her friends. She had felt good about being assertive and said that she had been able to do this, even when she was "stoned." The therapist had previously heard that her marijuana use tended to make her passive and commented that Kari seemed pleased with her assertiveness, despite her been stoned. The therapist mistakenly had taken license to reflect back to her the context of her assertion, thinking she had raised the issue of marijuana herself. As Kari continued to talk about interpersonal relationships with a range of friends, the therapist noticed a considerable shift in her affective expression. Although previously animated, she was developing a monotonous tone in her conversation, and she seemed increasingly distant as the session progressed.

As the therapist searched for what changed the process (the content was essentially the same), he realized that Kari's tone had changed after he made his comment about her being stoned when she was assertive. He reflected to her that his experience of the session had shifted, and that he was finding her current manner of expressing her thoughts to be somewhat flat and detached. She initially denied this, but when the therapist encouraged her to reflect on her inner experience, Kari did acknowledge that she felt deflated. The therapist imagined with her that his comment about her assertiveness, even when stoned, must have felt like a criticism. He said that he could imagine that she heard that comment as his being parental and judgmental. He added that this was not his intention. Kari did say that she felt betrayed when the therapist commented about her drug use because she thought they had agreed that he would not actively pursue that theme unless she initiated the discussion. She did not think she had invited a discussion about her marijuana use — rather, she thought she was talking about her ability to be assertive. As the therapist and client further deconstructed their interaction, the therapist noted how the process of reflecting on and mentalizing Kari's current inner experience indeed was instructive to understanding what had occurred in the therapeutic relationship.

Safran (2002:177) notes that "one of the implicit goals of BRT is that patients develop a heightened awareness of the present moment through identification with the therapist's stance." The possibility of trying to actively utilize the process of even what seems like minute interactions between the therapeutic dyad offers a tremendous growth for both to be continuously aware of how one's internal world is affecting a range of thoughts, behaviors, and feelings. This ability to deconstruct present moments is a relationship skill that well serves the client (and the clinician), as the following example describes.

DECONSTRUCTING A CONFLICTUAL INTERACTION Mrs. A., a sixty-five-year-old married woman, entered treatment to deal with the death of her younger and "cherished" brother. She was the older of two children and was raised in a father-dominated home in which she felt like she was treated as a second-class citizen. According to the client, her father valued and spoiled her brother, who was eight years her junior. The mother tended to be passive and unable to protect Mrs. A. from the critical voice of her father. Mrs. A. was unaware of her tendency to idealize her brother; she was more aware of her ambivalence toward her deceased father.

During a session in which Mrs. A. was describing the last pain-filled days of her cancer-stricken brother, the therapist was aware that the client was having a hard time catching her breath. She appeared to be in a defensive mode with her shoulders hunched, was quite uncomfortable, and seemed to increasingly withdraw. She had been talking about her role in administering morphine to her dying brother and had shamefully acknowledged that she thought about giving him extra medication to "speed the process" of his death. As she articulated this, the therapist also became aware of inhaling deeply as if to protect himself from thinking that Mrs. A. had accelerated her brother's death. He was aware of her idealization of her brother but had not yet started to discuss her ambivalent feelings toward him.

In that moment, the therapist made a comment that some might read as an "experience distant" interpretation stemming from a nonrelational theoretical frame. He said, "I can imagine there were times when you would have had murderous feelings toward him throughout your life." Thinking he had gone too far, he was not all that surprised when Mrs. A. became defensive and denied that she ever felt that way. At this point, the therapist became aware of the client's body posture and his own. Each was rigid, with their shoulder blades held high, and seemed to reflect their mutual efforts to control their respective breathing. As the therapist relaxed his own posture and shared with Mrs. A. that he was going to have a sore neck and back if he kept this up much longer, she looked at him quizzically and asked him what he was talking about. He commented on his experience of inhaling deeply during their conversation and wondered if she was aware of having done the same. Mrs. A. became aware of her body stance as well. She started to gently chuckle, sharing that she often thinks she is going to develop a permanent shrug if she doesn't learn how to express her feelings more readily. She went on to describe that she often feels neck pain and headaches because she is often unaware that she is constantly holding her breath in potentially conflictual interactions. The therapist asked her if she thought they were headed for a conflict and she said, "Of course we will have conflict—it happens everywhere." He agreed with her that this was likely so but wondered if they could use their own responses in the moment to talk about her reactions to the therapist's comment about her feelings toward her brother, which may have upset her. Gradually, Mrs. A. began to acknowledge her ambivalence toward him. The therapist thought that the focus on their "joint holding of our breath" as a sign of avoiding conflict or anticipated punishment enabled the client to become in touch with her true feelings. The therapist's modeling to her the benefits of using physical signs to access one's internal states assisted her in doing the same. Interestingly, in her next session, she reported that her chiropractor had commented to her that she seemed less tight in her shoulders and neck.

Like other short-term approaches, brief relational therapy sets and adheres to a definitive end point of treatment. The number of sessions may vary, but it is important to maintain consistency with the agreed-upon date of termination of therapy. It also endeavors to help clients understand the meaning of the termination process. Safran (2002:177) suggests that two main issues emerge for most clients as they approach termination of the therapy. Brief relational therapy, however, emphasizes the importance of "thinking of human existence as entailing an ongoing dialectical tension for the need for agency and the need for relatedness." Thus, in the termination phase it is useful for therapist and client to recognize the two tensions of the need for self-definition or autonomy in contrast to the need for relatedness in a mutually satisfying intersubjective relationship. The relational focus on the ongoing collaborative relationship of the therapy relationship provides clients with opportunities for addressing this dialectic in the treatment.

Safran (2002) suggests that one needs to remind clients of the termination, throughout the treatment, and to explore in depth the clients' feelings about this. In addition, the therapist needs to be monitoring her or his own reactions to the impending termination date. By raising the issue periodically, the client has a number of opportunities to bring latent material to consciousness and to talk through these feelings with the therapist. As noted above, it is useful to focus on the process of issues in a here-and-now orientation, highlighting the real interaction between client and therapist.

Often clients will need to explore disappointment, frustration, or anger about not getting what they initially wanted from therapy. Many clients will have idealized expectations of the therapy process or this particular therapist. Most need to recognize their disappointment that ultimately there is no one person who totally understands them or who is able to somehow take away all of their psychic pain. Safran suggests that two predominant reactions may emerge concerning this issue. Dependent, "false-self" clients may deny their frustration with the ending process and may need assistance in legitimizing their angry or disappointed feelings. Conversely, clients who adopt a more aggressive stance toward the therapist may be defending against the felt vulnerability that is activated during the termination. In either instance, it is advisable for therapists to demonstrate that they can withstand the aggression of the client and will not abandon or retaliate (Winnicott 1971).

Other clients need to be assisted in working through their trust issues when they realize that the termination date will stay firm. Therapists can empathize with the loss of the relationship and also demonstrate that they understand why it is difficult to invest in the therapy relationship, considering its brief nature. Again, it is useful to try and develop mutuality with the client that fosters the skills of mentalization and demonstrating the benefits of being tuned in to one's internal world. Rather than assuming the work centers on the maintenance of this relationship, it is most beneficial for the clients to recognize that they are developing mindfulness skills that will influence their interactions with others in their interpersonal realms. Safran (1999) suggests that it is helpful for therapists to openly acknowledge their limitations in meeting the clients' needs so that the clients develop a more complex understanding of what relationships can and cannot do for any individual.

A TERMINATION PROCESS WITH A COUPLE DEALING WITH LOSS A middle-aged working-class couple requested several sessions to help them deal with the aftermath of the decision of their transgender female to male child to have top surgery (breast removal). Their fundamentalist Christian church group had given them a great deal of solace and support from, and they wanted to "move on" in their lives. The therapist contracted for ten sessions. He understood their issues as involving loss.

The treatment issues were particularly poignant for the couple as each had to come face to face with the reality that they could not recapture the idealized relationship with their former daughter. The parents had worked many hours in their-low paying jobs to insure that their daughter would be able to obtain a college education. However, they blamed the liberal "politics" of the college environment in shaping their daughter's view about identity.

Having worked with numerous transgender clients in individual therapy, the therapist frequently drew parallels between those former clients' experiences and what this couple imagined their transgendered child was experiencing. He was able to offer the couple important information about transgender persons that helped them with their own process. They did not have this opportunity with their own child, as they had been dramatically cut off from her/his life and he did not return their calls, e-mails, or any other form of communication.

Despite the ongoing focus on the couple's grief, during the termination, the father became increasingly hostile toward the therapist, saying that he seemed to condone the daughter/son's behavior. The therapist agreed that he was obviously not feeling this particular loss but that he did feel that he was empathizing with the acute grief of each of the parents. He continued to focus on the couple's grief, recognizing the complexity of "losing" a child, but also recognizing that their child was still alive—and that they had no opportunity to know this child because of the emotional cut-off. Moreover, their memories were of their daughter, and they had little information about their transgender child, now identified as a male. The therapist tried to engage them in a process in which they could share the pain of such an unfinished loss (this is a term the mother coined and used often) with him. Their anger, particularly the husband's, was intense and continued unabated.

In the next to last session, the increasingly frustrated therapist tried to remind himself that there was a novel opportunity in each session and in each interaction to help the couple, but admittedly, his tolerance for their intense reactions was lessening. Both husband and wife had been "praying" that their child would reverse his decision and become reidentified as a female. It appeared as if they were defensively attempting to undo the cause of their grief and that this path was not going to help them resolve their loss or help them come to terms with their new child. The therapist had occasionally wondered with them if their son would at some future point be able to have a relationship with them. The couple spoke about their intention of continuing to put invitations out to their son. They seemed to understand that they needed to be welcoming to him and his new identity while also understanding of his need for acceptance and autonomy. They oscillated between wanting to give up completely and wanting to continue to try and offer a supportive connection to him.

The therapist recognized that he was the target of projected aggression as he had not helped the couple to find a way to "convince" their son to revert to his female identity. At one point, the mother blurted out that she wished she would have died—that that would be an easier place from which to move forward. The therapist somewhat impulsively said that he wasn't so sure that would be easier. He quickly added that he had had a death of one of his children and didn't think that he had ever fully recovered from it. The therapist immediately recognized his self-disclosure was not intended to help the couple but served as retaliation against them. He regretted being so revealing and blunt.

Indeed, the clients seemed stunned and quickly offered their condolences. This was near the end of the session, and the therapist was uncertain if they would return for the final session. Indeed, they did come back, and each seemed to be in a somewhat different emotional space. Although still grieving the loss of their "daughter," each said that they understood that they still had a child. Moreover, they said that they had not given up hope that one day they would have the opportunity to build a more satisfying relationship with their transgender child. They were able to talk about the shame they experienced for wishing their child dead, even if it was said out of their own agonizing grief. The therapist apologized for the bluntness of his self-disclosure, but the couple said that they appreciated it. It seemed to have made them realize the finality of an actual death in contrast to their situation. It does seem plausible that the disclosure created a moment of interaction that shook their defensive structure in a positive way. In terms of relational theory, it is likely that the immediacy of the heightened affect in the room with a clarifying (albeit perhaps aggressive) comment from the therapist did considerably shift the dynamic of this couple system.

CONCLUSION

As noted above, it appears as if the brief therapy field is now beginning to articulate principles of relational theory in time-limited frameworks. The brief relational theory being researched at Beth Israel and other potential sites does offer principles and understandings that make the theory truly two-person oriented. While other brief theories offer some valuable modifications to longer-term treatments, the work of Safran, Muran, and others will further assist our application of brief models to our social work fields of clinical service.

10. COUPLE, FAMILY, AND GROUP TREATMENT

This chapter explores the influence of relational theory on "multiple-person" modalities, including couple, family, and group. Wachtel (2008) makes the point that family therapists have not historically made a great distinction between one- or two-person psychologies. He suggests that this differentiation had less meaning for family therapists as these clinicians always directly observed the influence of individuals on one another so that the focus was always interpersonal or relational. Thus, working within the multiperson modality naturally lends itself to relational thinking, and Wachtel suggests that relational theory has been influential in these modalities in that the relational "therapist inevitably becomes part of the system that she is observing" (74). The position of the therapist as a partner working within the system is a key component of couple, family, and group relational principles. The following assumptions guide the work with couples, families, and groups in a relational model.

■ The Western view that a "healthy" self is autonomous, separate, and independent is replaced with a more relational view of self that strives for mutuality.
■ Clients are encouraged to strive for interdependence in their relationships with significant others.
■ There is an equitable sharing of power between the couple, family, or group and the clinician.

■ Intimate relationships are enhanced when clients view themselves as co-creating strengths and deficiencies in their systems. All affect and dynamics are created by everyone in the system.

■ The clinician is viewed as an active participant in the therapeutic work.

■ The clinician's use of self-disclosure is encouraged so as to further the understanding of the process issues of the couple, family, or group and to further the progress of the client system.

This chapter first discusses relational principles with couples and families and then considers the impact of relational views on group treatment.

CLINICAL WORK WITH COUPLES AND FAMILIES:
A RELATIONAL APPROACH

Social workers have a long tradition of providing couple therapy, drawing on many different models. Although there is not an integrated relational approach to couple and family therapy, an object relations framework has had a major impact on these modalities (Bader and Pearson 1988, Lachkar 1992; Lupenitz 1988; Miehls 1993, 1996; Scharff and Savege Scharff 1991; Sharpe 2000; Walsh 2003). In addition, there is considerable literature that describes couple work with trauma survivors (Basham and Miehls 2004; Johnson 2002; Miehls 1997), an important focus of relational treatment. Some authors who have explored countertransference reactions in couple therapy have written from the standpoint of intersubjectivity in couple therapy (Goldstein 1997; Miehls 1995, 1999; Siegel 1997; Trop 1997).

Reflecting a relational stance, the couple or family therapist has many direct opportunities to model different ways of interaction and communication to the troubled couple. DeYoung (2003:65) discusses her view of empathy and couple work when she questions, "What better place for the active-self-reflexive use of empathy than in work with a couple or with several family members?" She suggests that modeling an empathic stance gives the individual members of the couple dyad the opportunity to witness the positive benefits of listening in an empathic way. Miehls (1993) also suggests that modeling of empathy can further the beginning empathic stance of narcissistically oriented couple systems.

Although couples are often embroiled in polarized positions, it is important for each partner to recognize that there is not "one truth" in the room—rather, there is room for multiple viewpoints and perspectives. The therapist empathizes with multiple perspectives without forming an unbalanced alliance with one family member or another. In this way, the relational approach encourages the cocreation of a personal narrative. Moreover, working collaboratively toward consensus becomes a new working model of couple interaction. DeYoung (2003:65) suggests, "This is what listening looks like. This is what being heard feels like. When there's empathy in this room, everything gets safer, doesn't it? Wouldn't you like to try it?"

Another important relational principle is having each family member come to understand that no one person in the system can be wholly responsible for the system's strengths and/or problem areas. Bergman and Surrey (1997:270) suggest that "acknowledging the importance of mutual responsibility for the relationship can be a very new and fresh level of thinking for many people." When the relational clinician continuously questions the assumption that one person is the "cause" of the difficulty, the family members come face to face with the mutual responsibility for the systemic problems. Equally, if the clinician contributes to some misunderstanding in the therapeutic process, it is important to acknowledge the error and to model a corrective experience.

USING A THERAPIST'S MISTAKE AS A CORRECTIVE EXPERIENCE John and Carol, a middle-aged "empty-nest" couple, initiated couple therapy to determine if they would stay together. Their last child of four had left for college the previous year, and the couple increasingly felt distant from one another. The therapist contracted with them to meet for ten sessions to explore the relative strengths and dissatisfactions of the marriage. At the beginning of the fifth session, Carol announced that this would be her last session—she abruptly said that John could continue if he chose to do because the therapist clearly was "on his side." The therapist was surprised because he had perceived his working alliance with the couple to be relatively strong. He also thought that the couple was beginning to understand some of the core relational patterns that led to their dissatisfaction and distancing. In the previous session, Carol had even said that they might be able to remain together. The therapist also was surprised that Carol had picked up on his unspoken countertransference response. Indeed, the therapist did experience Carol as quite controlling and had been encouraging John to more actively express his suppressed anger to her in a direct way. The therapist observed him to be passive-aggressive in his interactions with Carol.

When Carol said she was leaving treatment, the therapist commented that he was glad that the couple was bringing up their concerns. John did acknowledge that he felt the therapist's support. Carol did not seem surprised when the therapist shared that he had experienced some frustration with her during the sessions. She commented that "you think I am controlling and that I am responsible for our problems." The therapist admitted that this did capture his basic response to her, but he quickly pointed out that he had also suggested that John was passive-aggressive toward her. John and Carol each confirmed that the therapist had never articulated this directly. Each was aware that the therapist had tried to encourage John to speak up more in the couple interaction, but each also experienced this as the therapist "siding with him." This exchange opened up further dialogue about the couple–therapist interactions. The therapist admitted that he had become drawn into rescuing John without trying to better understand the metacommunication or affect behind Carol's assertive and/or controlling behavior. She clearly felt more understood, as the therapist was able to empathize with her frustration with John's passivity. The therapist also apologized to them for his blind spot and said that he would reflect on why he had become so frustrated with Carol's interpersonal style. After this exchange the couple continued their therapy until the agreed upon termination date.

Walls (2004:109) emphasizes that the relational couple clinician should support the use of self-disclosure and mutuality in the clinical encounter. She says, "If, in our job as couple therapists, we ask our clients to take risks with each other and us, to be more open and more vulnerable, then we ourselves cannot hold back in these endeavors. ... We are asked not to work 'on' our clients' problems, but to work 'in' them—to bring ourselves to the therapy more fully, to be authentic in our presence, and to strive for mutuality in the process."

THERAPIST SELF-DISCLOSURE WITH A MIXED-RACE COUPLE   In working with a mixed-race couple (male partner is African American and female partner is white), there was a confluence of factors related to race, class, and gender that necessitated authentic disclosure from the white male clinician. Married for six years, the couple presented for therapy suggesting that the therapy was a last-ditch effort to "save the marriage" before they split up. They were having increasingly volatile arguments; they denied any physical altercation between the two of them, but each acknowledged a history of childhood physical abuse at the hands of parents.

Judy was proud of her work accomplishments and had achieved advanced education and certification so that she was employed as a certified accountant in a large accounting firm. She grew up in a lower-class, chaotic family in which both of her parents were alcoholic. She also had been a substance abuser but had been clean and sober for ten years. Kevin worked as a mechanic in a large auto dealership. He was one of many service staff and had a white supervisor. He also was involved with a twelve-step program to maintain his sobriety from alcohol addiction. In fact, the couple had met at a twelve-step meeting.

In a particularly heated exchange, Judy complained to the clinician that Kevin had stayed at work late one night recently. He had not called her, and she had to scramble at the last minute so that she could arrange for childcare. She was scheduled to have a business dinner in which her partner expected her "to court" a corporate client. Kevin claimed that he had forgotten about Judy's work commitment and wanted to accept the overtime work, as he was so rarely given the opportunity. Judy retorted, saying that his extra earnings wouldn't go too far with all of their debt, and that her potential for earnings far surpassed his ability to earn extra income. Kevin appeared sullen. Judy taunted him to reply and he angrily said, "She doesn't get it!"

The clinician intervened, suggesting that he could understand how it might be difficult for Kevin to recognize that Judy was earning so much more than he was earning at present. They could each acknowledge that this was a point of contention between them. The therapist shared with them that he had also felt some discomfort when his partner earned more income than he did, early in their marriage. He added that he had also been raised in a culture in which the "man was expected to be the major breadwinner" and that he had to challenge this societal injunction. The couple, particularly Kevin, seemed interested in the therapist's disclosure, especially when the therapist also shared that he had changed his earning capacity over the years. The therapist asked Kevin if he felt some restrictions on his earning potential, as a black working-class man. He became teary and commented that neither his wife, Judy, nor the therapist had any idea about what it was like to live as a black man in a white middle-class area. He said that he was the brunt of "wise"cracks (racist remarks) on a daily basis, often from white work associates or customers. When he began to cry, the therapist simply said that he was sorry that Kevin had such daily experiences; Judy was able to echo this and suggested that she would be more sensitive to future discussions about finances between the couple. She initially started to say that she understood how racist society was. When the therapist commended her for trying to empathize, he also said that Kevin had a point—that she and the therapist might not be able to completely understand what it is like to live as a black man in our society.

The therapist thought it was important for him to model authenticity and culturally responsive interventions. It also seemed useful for Kevin to realize that he did not lose any part of his masculinity by showing his frustrations and sadness by shedding tears. Additionally, the therapist attempted to equalize power in the room and to honestly acknowledge the chronic nature of racism. As the treatment proceeded, the couple began to reflect on how their views of male/female responsibilities had been socially constructed in their respective families of origin and in society generally. As an interracial married couple, their internalized messages of race also needed to be unearthed. Each carried the stereotype that black men are "lazy"; it was important to recognize that Kevin's less advanced educational status was at least partially attributed to his functioning in a blue-collar position, and that he had actually achieved a great deal considering institutional and societal racism.

Furthermore, it was very important to recognize that Kevin's contribution to the household went far beyond his earnings from his job. Each member of the couple acknowledged that he did more child care and instrumental tasks in the household than Judy was completing. The therapist noted that Kevin and Judy were pioneers in a number of ways—they had forged an interracial couple relationship, they had challenged stereotypical gender roles in terms of wage-earning capacity, and they were modeling a different sort of "black" masculinity to their biracial sons.

Relational family therapists recognize that power within a system is best utilized when family members can move from a "power-over" model to a "power-to" model. A number of the Stone Center writers (Adams 2004; Bergman and Surrey 1997; Jordan 1995; Surrey 1991), articulating their concept of a relational-cultural model, suggest that a "power-over" model of negotiating conflict "is based in a competitive, zero-sum game worldview, in which another's gain is my loss" (Fishbane 2001:278). These authors recognize that most individuals have a difficult time staying connected while dealing with conflict. Understanding that it is part of the human condition to seek connection but still fear vulnerability in the connection, Adams (2004:165) suggests that "it is only through our courage to risk and our capacity to acknowledge both our yearnings for connection and our fears that the grip of shame can be loosened enough to create the potential for a healing connection." In other words, anger and conflict become relational events with each family member striving for connection without feeling too much vulnerability. Old relational scripts often become enacted as individuals re-institute rigid boundaries that protect the "autonomous self." In relational theory, these boundaries are seen as opportunities or points of "meeting and communicating" (Fishbane 2001:275). The issues of wish for connection, the fear of vulnerability, the "power-over" model, and the establishment of rigid boundaries are all evident in the following example.

WORK WITH A HIGHLY CONFLICTED FAMILY Elaine, age thirty-six, Susan, age thirty-four, and Gerry, age thirty-one, were three siblings whose father had died two months earlier after a protracted illness. Accomplished profession-als, they lived in various parts of Massachusetts; the sisters lived in western Massachusetts and Gerry in Cambridge. Elaine contacted the therapist, saying that she was worried that she and her siblings were going to become estranged from one other. Their mother had died ten years earlier. Elaine suggested that she and her siblings were having conflict over the "estate," and that she was hopeful that a few family sessions could assist them to resolve their conflicts.

All three agreed to meet for a two-hour session for the initial consultation. The therapist immediately witnessed the anger among the siblings. Though Gerry was the youngest, he seemed to try to exert his point of view quite aggressively, whereas Elaine appealed to her two younger siblings that they needed to safeguard their relationships with each other as "we are the only family we have." In contrast, Susan seemed distant from each of her siblings and suggested that she just wanted to get on with her life with her husband and children. Neither Gerry nor Elaine was in committed relationships at this point in time. They overtly expressed conflict about who would inherit certain pieces of art that their parents had collected. Although their father's will specified an "equal" split of the financial aspects of the estate, he had not made provision for the disbursement of original paintings or antiques. Each sibling was vying for certain pieces of particular sentimental value, and they seemed deadlocked in the power struggle.

The therapist worked with the family for twelve hours over six weeks. They were able to come to some compromise about the disbursement of the paintings, only after each dealt with his or her resentments about child-hood issues. Gerry had always felt that he was the sole recipient of their father's rage. As the "boy" of the family, he perceived that he was held more accountable to the father's perfectionist standards. He angrily told his sisters that they were able to easily escape their father's wrath, simply by the virtue of being female. Though Elaine had shown the most initiative to be conciliatory in the system, she became very agitated with this characterization of having gotten off easy in the family. She dramatically disclosed that their father had sexually abused her over the course of three years. Susan, the middle sibling, expressed extreme shame that she had gotten off easy, clearly being identified in the family's early history as the father's favorite. She had not been sexually abused or physically abused as her siblings had, and she experienced a great deal of survivor guilt.

The therapist helped the siblings to talk about their wishes to stay connected and fear that they would lose their sense of hard-earned emotional separation from the "pathology" of the system. They were able to revisit key childhood events and to clarify their perceptions of what had transpired. In their retelling of various family events, from their own eyes, there was a great deal of relational space opened up among them—witnessing their shared narratives as opposed to their competitive, "victim" stance that each had brought to the therapy relationship.

In this instance, the clinician did not use self-disclosure to facilitate the therapy process. Rather, he developed working alliances with each individual and helped each to articulate a wish for connection (without being "revictimized"). In addition, he tried to empower each individual as opposed to allowing them to assert power over one another. The family creatively designed a plan in which each would take favorite art and/or furniture into their respective homes for a one-year time period. They then would switch pieces, and this very plan contributed to their ongoing sense of shared "positive" family values and experiences—something that their mother had also cultivated within them as a sibling unit.

CLINICAL WORK WITH GROUPS: A RELATIONAL APPROACH

Grossmark (2007:193) notes that although many relational therapists conduct group psychotherapy, few have applied relational theory to the practice of group therapy. This is perhaps an artifact of the notion that much of group theory focuses on the technique and process of insight-oriented group psychotherapy. The experience of clinical social workers is somewhat different, however, because social workers clinicians facilitate myriad groups ranging from psycho-educational to supportive to didactic to psychotherapeutic, with a diverse clientele from different socioeconomic levels. Social workers lead groups that are formed around community medical, educational, and mental health needs. For example, social workers may lead a group in a medical setting in which the purpose of the group is to offer support for individuals whose partners have received a terminal cancer diagnosis or HIV. This sort of group often combines a psycho-educational approach with strong supportive elements. Some interpersonal issues may be addressed in such a group. In a school setting, social workers may run "identity" development groups for adolescents or a bereavement group for children who have lost a parent through death. A further example may be a social worker running a support group for the chronically mentally ill client in a mental health day-treatment setting. Of course, social workers also initiate and lead psychotherapy groups. Regardless of the type of group, social workers utilize relational theory principles in the following general ways.

■ They create a working climate in the group in which group members experience a holding environment within which to explore relationships.
■ They emphasize that interpersonal reactions are always importantly based in relationships. The focus of the group highlights the fundamental and crucial importance of relationships in our development.
■ They emphasize that understanding "here-and-now" interactions of the group members is crucial to achieving success in goal attainment in the group.
■ They become participant observers in the group, noting their own responses and sharing their responses as appropriate.
■ They judiciously use self-disclosure in group settings to enhance the achievement of the goals of the group.
■ They promote direct and honest feedback among group members about their feelings toward each other and the leader.
■ They recognize that all interpersonal interactions are intersubjective in nature; clients and clinicians all bring their subjectivities into the group process.

Here too, empathy is a key ingredient in the relational group process. The clinician does not function as the authority who stays removed from the process of the group. Rather, Fedele (2004:174) comments that "the experience of mutual empathy in this relational space allows members to examine and modify relational images rooted in the past and replayed in the present." A "not-knowing" approach in the group process is valuable. Billow (2003:118) notes that "the therapist conveys the reality that he or she is not all-knowing but human, and consequently, also must live through unavoidably confusing and emotionally disturbing intervals of group life, and needs and benefits from the containing by other group members." All groups develop their own "personality," and even a didactic, psycho-educational group can be overly structured or programmed. At times, the social worker needs to drop her agenda and attend to the interpersonal process in the group, regardless of the goals of the group.

Relational social work group clinicians experience the group's insistence that they coparticipate in the life of the group in contrast to being a "neutral facilitator" only. Billow (2003:51) comments: "When the group therapist utilizes him or herself in an open, spontaneous manner, the therapist may be producing more obvious disclosures, or different types of disclosures, than those that are also inevitable in traditional individual or group technique." A relational group leader recognizes that some sharing of autobiographical material in the group will enhance connection among all members, including the social worker. From an intersubjective point of view, the "group experience is one where we are drawn into a profound union with others … out of which reciprocity and relationships emerge" (Gordon 1991:44). The willingness of the social worker to be vulnerable often propels what relational-cultural clinicians term a move from disconnection to stronger, deeper interpersonal connections (Fedele 2004).

COPARTICIPATING OR REMAINING OUTSIDE THE GROUP The group therapist had conducted a number of short-term groups in which the focus centered on the identification and resolution of shame dynamics within the members' intrapsychic and interpersonal worlds. (Often individuals who grew up in alcohol-based or violent families, or have experienced some form of childhood trauma, have a high preponderance of shame to work though in their identities.) The therapist and his coleader were accustomed to offering didactic information about self and shame dynamics in combination with experiential exercises that stirred affect. (Identifying and articulating shame-based affect often leads to a lessening of depression-related symptoms of the clients.) In one group, an insightful woman challenged the therapist about why he was not doing a family "shame" timeline in which group participants track their memories of when they witnessed others in their families' being shamed or experienced being shamed themselves. The therapist was immediately struck by how he and his coleader had been staying on the outside of the group. Rather than participating in the exercises themselves, they were circulating among the group members as each completed her timeline and offering support, empathy, or clarification. The group member's challenge helped the coleaders to become more involved in the experience of the group. Both decided that they would do a timeline of their families as well.

Rachman (1990:134) aptly discusses the potential vulnerability of social workers when working with adolescent groups. He suggests that the "trial by fire" that adolescents impose on group leaders can contribute to anxiety within the leader, but it is important to allow adolescents to witness how the leader deals with "emotional reactions in an interpersonal context, the capacity to deal with confrontation, and the value of vulnerability and openness in the relationship." Here again, the relational social worker recognizes the value of self-disclosure (Cohen and Schermer 2001; Dies 1973; Schulte 2000).

AN INEXPERIENCED THERAPIST'S SELF-DISCLOSURE WITH AN ADOLESCENT GROUP ON THE VERGE OF BEING OUT OF CONTROL A junior social worker was on the staff of an in-patient mental health residential unit that housed behaviorally acting-out adolescent young men between the ages of fourteen and eighteen. They were a tough and aggressive group. The social worker co-led a "problem-solving" group with a more experienced staff member who helped him to feel some comfort and safety in the group. On one occasion, the coworker was away in order to take care of personal business, and the younger worker found himself facing the group of ten adolescents on his own. His inexperience and fear caused him to become highly ineffective. Within five minutes, the young guys were clearly out of control; they were swearing, threatening each other, make sexually provocative comments, and decidedly not at all that interested in learning how to problem-solve.

The social worker was aware that he had relied on his coworker to be the disciplinarian and authority in previous groups and felt somewhat helpless and frightened by the affect in the room. In desperation, he appealed to the group's sense of rationality. He simply said that he wasn't sure what to do but knew he was frightened in the group. This caught their attention. He went on to say that he was new at this group leader "thing" and that he had relied on Mr. X (his coleader) to carry the group before. He repeated that he didn't know how to get the group to work together but was feeling pretty anxious about the group degenerating into a physical fight. He reminded them that any psychical altercation immediately would put the antagonists at risk of losing all ward privileges and hoped they could all avoid that. Some group members heckled him and laughed.

His self-disclosure about being frightened, however, led two of the more senior group members also to suggest that they should go easy on the worker, who was new, after all. Although his disclosure was antithetical to his training at the time, it was clearly the right thing to do in the moment. His intuition brought the situation to a place of authenticity. The self-disclosure prompted a respect from the acting out members and fortunately, the group moved forward with its agenda. It is possible that the intervention worked as the young men could unconsciously (or perhaps consciously) respect the honest expression of the clinician's internal feeling world. It felt authentic. Many of these young men had experienced trauma as children and they likely responded to the honesty of the moment. Ferenczi (1932, 1933) noted that "individuals who have suffered childhood traumas that center on parental deception, unresponsiveness, and emotional neglect are especially needy for authentic emotional interaction with a parental figure" (cited in Rachman 1990:135).

A final point about relational group processes stems from the work of the Stone Center theorists (Jordan, Surrey, Walker). These authors and many others who form the relational-cultural model of theorists are currently suggesting that mutuality is a powerful human force that promotes connection. For example, Tantillo (2000) describes relational principles in work with women who suffer from bulimia nervosa. Gagerman (2004) explicitly discusses the benefits of focusing on mutuality for women's development. As noted previously, all individuals strive for some point of connection with others, but the wish for connection is often met with some resultant fear that we will be hurt if we allow ourselves to be vulnerable to others. Tantillo (2000:104) says, "The group leader helps members move from disconnections toward increased connection by developing the real here and now relationships with her and other members in an authentic, mutually validating, and empathic way." In fact, it is important in all social work relational groups to purposefully encourage group members to continuously be monitoring their reactions in terms of when participants want to engage, disengage, or re-engage with other members. It is crucial to develop and track the awareness of one's ability to stay emotionally connected with others. Gagerman (2004) makes the point that relational theorists now have some evidence of the power of relationships when studying contemporary neurobiological theory. Not only are early attachment experiences crucial for healthy brain development leading to satisfying relationships but contemporary relational group experiences can also contribute to a change process that furthers individual satisfaction in the relational world.

CONCLUSION

This chapter has focused on the application of relational theory to multimodal modalities. Although the work in couple, family, and group therapy is inherently interpersonal, the attitude and training of the clinician is crucial to optimize the benefits of contemporary relational theory. As outlined above, these tenets include the role of clinician as participant and cocreator in the process. Second, the client systems are understood to move toward change with authentic interactions, including self-disclosure and use of intersubjective exchanges with the clinician. The work rests on the view that all humans strive for connection but need to be helped to diffuse defensive structures when people become frightened of their increased vulnerability. Regardless of the "type" of couple, family, or group theory that is utilized by the clinician, the essential components of social work relational theory as outlined in this book lead to a deeper understanding of the change process for couples, families, and groups of all kinds.

11. THE TEACHING AND LEARNING PROCESS: IN THE CLASSROOM AND SUPERVISION

This chapter discusses how the principles of relational theories affect both teaching and learning in the classroom and supervision. It explores the perspectives of the student and supervisee when classroom instructors or supervisors incorporate relational constructs into their teaching strategies. It describes the process in which students engage when they begin to think "relationally" about their clinical work. The shift to relational thinking often challenges some of students' and trainees' preconceived ideas and stereotypes about clinical social work practice as well as the ways in which they may have been trained.

Although students come to our graduate programs in social work to learn about contemporary theories and practice principles, their ideas about what transpires in the helping process may reflect traditional or modernist views. This is manifested by their thinking that they will act as "experts" with their clients, remain objective, and stay emotionally detached from the work. Anxious about having to deal with real-life problems with their clients, they tend to yearn for formulas about how to intervene (Miehls and Moffatt 2000). Alternatively, some students have developed a belief system that social work practice will necessitate Herculean efforts on their part, and that their professional task is to "rescue" their clients from a range of biopsychosocial issues.

Teaching clinical practice courses and supervising students and workers from a relational perspective often also requires that instructors shift their framework from a modernist to a postmodernist perspective. Generally, this change entails a shift to a more equitable and/or feminist approach to the teaching relationship. When influenced by relational theory thinking, classroom teachers and supervisors see the teaching relationship as a fluid interaction in which each part of the dyad has some sense of authority and knowledge. Although relational supervisors recognize that supervisees need knowledge and skills, they do not presume that the learning process is one based upon their authority, but upon mutual respect and collegiality. The power inherent in any learning situation is shared, and the instructor does not hold a monopoly on expertise or knowledge.

Utilizing principles of relational theory in the classroom affords the student and teacher the opportunity to interact in a learning environment that is growth promoting for all, on different levels. Relational-based teaching has a great deal in common with teaching strategies framed in a feminist perspective. This chapter describes the interface of these two pedagogical frameworks and demonstrates the process of teaching and learning in the relational classroom. It discusses the characteristics of the supervisory relationship when utilizing relational theory.

THE CLASSROOM PROCESS

The principle of mutual respect between students and teachers characterizes the learning environment that is influenced by relational thinking. Moreover, the learning environment rests on the view that students and teachers alike will benefit from the teaching and learning class experience. Interactions within the student–teacher relationship become an important sources of learning. Mishna and Rasmussen (2001:288) suggest that "the purposeful and reflective use of this relationship enables the instructor to conceptualize interactions with students in ways that advance the students' understanding of social work practice." Edwards, Bryant, and Clark (2008) suggest that the learning process is enhanced when students appreciate the benefit of mutual engagement processes, mutual empathy processes, and mutual empowerment processes as being fundamental attitudes to carry to our clinical work with clients. For example, the use of the Stone Center's relational cultural model, which honors the relationship process in teaching, can be a powerful tool (Walker and Rosen 2004).

Teaching from a relational perspective insures that all voices in the classroom are heard. This is particularly important as our social work classrooms are increasingly diverse—the voices of women, gay/lesbian students, students of color, and disabled individuals, as examples, all have value and relevance in the relationally based social work classroom.

In discussing a framework for black feminist epistemology and teaching, Cozart and Price (2005) present an interesting description of black culture that fits nicely with relational theory. They discuss the concept of call-response that is rooted in African oral traditions. They note the prevalence of call-response in the traditional black church in which the congregation "talks back" to the preacher—emphasizing the relationship between the speaker and audience. They quote Smitherman (1977:104) when he suggests that this tradition offers "an organizing principle of Black American culture generally, for it enables traditional Black folk to achieve the unified state of balance or harmony which is fundamental to the traditional African world view." Their article entitled "Black Women, Identity and Schooling: Reclaiming Our Work in Shifting Contexts" offers insight and explanation that parallels the principles of relational theory and feminist ideology and pedagogy.

Operating from a relational teaching model does not imply that the teacher is "completely" equal to the students. Certainly the teacher has a body of knowledge that comprises the content of the course; however, the pedagogical style of the relational teacher is one in which the learning process is cocreated by students and instructor. In other words, the environment of the classroom is purposefully shaped to encourage and maximize student self-directed learning while integrating the content of the course. As such, the power of the instructor is shared with the students in such a way that the students develop a sense of agency and mastery, while feeling respected as a colleague of the teacher. The relational teacher does maintain the function of evaluation of students, and the principles of evaluation are openly discussed and clearly identified at the outset of the course. At times, a relational teacher may enlist student ideas about types of assignments and ways of evaluation. Certainly, there is some component of student self-evaluation that is considered by the relational teacher.

Historically, clinical social work courses have reflected an understanding of the importance of the clinical relationship as a key component to the helping process (Bogo 1993; Ganzer and Ornstein 1999; Mothersole 1999). In addition, there is abundant literature that addresses the importance of the social worker's "use of self" in the clinical work. These two concepts are compatible with relational theory principles. Teaching from a relational perspective, however, expands upon these ideas. Students learn that they do not have to assume the "expert" role as they shape their working relationships with clients. Rather, students are encouraged to think of their clients as experts of their own experience and that the student-clinician and client will each share in the creation of the treatment relationship. Students are encouraged to approach clinical work with a stance of reflexivity; this necessitates an ongoing and open evaluation of the student's affective responses to the client (Miehls and Moffatt 2000). In other words, relational teaching principles suggest that the student needs to be very aware of responses to his or her client and to continuously reflect on how his or her responses are affecting the clinical relationship.

In the classroom, the teacher models the principles of mutuality and shared power by adopting a "not-knowing" stance in classroom process. In other words, instructors demonstrate the value of encouraging shared dialogue in contrast to behaving as if they had the "definite truth" about any situation. The relational teacher will make specific links to the classroom interaction and invite students to brainstorm about the ways that can create parallel situations in their clinical relationships. Ringel (2007) articulates the idea that students need to understand and appreciate the unconscious aspects of any communication between individuals. In addition to understanding that clients and clinicians share metacommunications with each other on an unconscious basis, Ringel suggests that classroom learning is also enhanced when student learners understand the complexity and layered nature of their interactions with each other.

Miehls (2001:230) suggests that classrooms comprised of students from diverse backgrounds offer opportunities to use relational tension to contribute to potential learning. He says, "In those instances where the classroom composition has been fortunate enough to be inclusive of learners from diverse backgrounds, identity-laden tensions often arise among students who have decidedly different experiences of the world in which we live." Often, learning is enhanced when there is difficulty in classroom interactions, and when the students and teacher can work through the issues in a productive manner. If there is a particular rupture or enactment in the classroom, the ability of the instructor to lead a nondefensive dialogue that results in resolution enriches the learning process on a number of levels. Deconstructing the interactions that led to conflict (between either students themselves or students and teacher) and bringing the interactions to some resolution offers an opportunity for students to practice how to handle these sort of ruptures with clients. The classroom teacher emphasizes that ruptures or enactments are an inevitable part of the classroom environment and the clinical relationship and in so doing, normalizes the experience. Mishna and Rasmussen (2001:393) also emphasize the need to process interpersonal conflict that arises in the classroom and suggest that "failure to address these ruptures in the learning process often results, at the very least, in missed opportunities to model the effective use of a helping relationship to work through such impasses." It is clear that instructors influenced by relational theory underscore that this sort of rupture serves as a therapeutic opportunity in the clinical process. These classroom experiences can be studied as inevitable, challenging, and of great learning value.

Relational teachers can also model a judicious use of self-disclosure in the classroom. When appropriate, the instructor can share her or his dilemmas, feelings, or struggles with issues as a way of illustrating the appropriate use of self-disclosure. The aspect of self-disclosure is a particularly difficult concept for beginning clinicians to learn. Many instructors hesitate to encourage beginning clinicians to disclose their affective responses to clients as they fear that students will run rampant with their disclosures. This is a realistic concern, but here, too, thorough discussion in the classroom and modeling from the classroom teacher is highly instructive (Ringel and Mishna 2007). The relational teacher understands that each student and client will have multiple aspects to their identities, and that some intersection of these complex identities may necessitate some disclosure by the student. Again, the student needs to learn the appropriate timing of such disclosures and also to learn that one needs to be reflective about one's intentions when sharing personal information or feelings with clients. Students need to be encouraged to use supervision or consultation wisely when they are uncertain about how and when to use self-disclosure, and what to disclose, in the relationship with her client. Chapter 6 more fully discusses the use of self-disclosure in the therapeutic relationship.

Mishna and Rasmussen (2001:396) give an excellent example of how an instructor's disclosure of her own feelings of incompetence helped when she could not assist her students to feel "safe" with each other while studying group treatment principles. Recognizing that the students were uncomfortable, the instructor encouraged the students by saying that she hoped they could continue to learn in spite of the discomfort they experienced. She noted that the discomfort could be used as a cue for each to establish an attitude that it would be "in the service of the commitment to make room for everyone's views, and to avoid blame." One of the authors (D.M.), experienced a similar sense of incompetence and anxiety a few years ago when he was teaching a foundation practice course to a particularly diverse class of students in a master's of social work program. He was teaching this class while there was considerable tension in the school community that had initially been precipitated by a classroom rupture in a course taught by a white male professor. The student body had galvanized around the event and had staged a number of "protest" activities to alert the school's administration that they expected some action of the administration to deal with what they perceived as an extremely "privileged and bigoted" attitude on the part of a particular instructor.

Coincidentally, many student leaders attended the instructor's practice class. As the events were unfolding on campus, he was aware of increasing anxiety and self-consciousness. He often slept restlessly before he taught this class, which met two times a week. He somatized some of his anxiety and was experiencing headaches before having to teach the 8:30 a.m. class. He was aware that his anxiety was severely compromising his usual teaching style, a mixture of setting high academic expectations for students' preparation and assignments and creating an environment in which students could "playfully" and appropriately critique ideas. He was somewhat stilted and rigid in his interactions with the students and was self-conscious about his "privilege" as a white male instructor. He felt somewhat immobilized and hesitant to appropriately utilize his authority in the classroom when it was necessary. Several student leaders monopolized the classroom discussions, which increasingly developing a tone of being "politically correct" as opposed to utilizing useful "critical analysis" of the theories being studied.

Some of the students approached the instructor outside of class to comment that they were experiencing the class dynamic as difficult and that they witnessed that he was having a hard time "setting limits" with their peers who seemed to be monopolizing conversation. In addition, these students had taken previous classes with the instructor and commented that he didn't seem to be creating the opportunity to "play" with the material. The instructor knew their assessment of the class was accurate. He was aware of avoiding any sort of conflict and was consciously aware that particularly vocal students were indeed "controlling" the classroom atmosphere. The learning process was at an impasse.

The instructor consulted with some colleagues to process his own feelings and to develop a strategy for dealing with the situation. He was aware that he needed to be careful about confronting and labeling the behavior of the student leaders in the class, a strategy he thought would lead to further rigidity and polarizations in the classroom. In keeping with relational principles in teaching, he decided to use self-disclosure of his feelings in an attempt to alter the dynamic in the class. He started a particular class by saying that he wanted to discuss the classroom process, indicating that he recognized the tension in the class. He shared that he was becoming increasingly anxious about coming to class, was so worried that he was having trouble sleeping, and he was having dreams about the class (there had been many discussions in this class about the countertransference meanings of dreaming about clients). He told the class that he was trying to understand why he was becoming more and more derailed despite his theoretical and practice knowledge. He accepted responsibility for this state of affairs but also invited the students to consider how each might be contributing to the classroom tension.

Much to his relief, many students identified that they also felt incredible tension and anxiety in the room. One student started to cry and said that she was also having a really hard time coming to the class—she felt anxious and afraid. Another student said that he felt he was not learning as much as he could be learning, as he also was worried about being "attacked." One of the more outspoken and provocative of the female students asked if the male student was afraid of her. Before he could respond, the instructor jumped into the dialogue, saying that he was aware of being afraid of her responses at times, carefully emphasizing the difference between her responses and who she was, as a person. The instructor acknowledged that he and the others needed to be responsible for their part of the interaction with her but also cautiously asked her to consider what she might be contributing to the classroom atmosphere. With some hesitation, she did say that she knew she had been really "angry" in class at times, and she had wondered why the instructor was not taking charge of the classroom dynamic. She went on to say that she was enraged by the action of the other professor, but she had felt some disappointment that the instructor was getting so derailed. She commented that this was a really important class and knew that the students needed to know this "stuff" before they returned to the field.

The instructor thanked her for her honesty. Other students also suggested that they wanted to revisit the learning contract that had been set out at the outset of the class. The instructor shared with them that he was feeling less anxious already and apologized for not carrying out his role as facilitator in a more assertive way. He revealed that he thought that his own family of origin issues were contributing to his reactions. He further told them that he was the youngest of seven siblings and had to learn to "run fast" when his older siblings were in a teasing or angry mood. This disclosure brought some chuckles from everyone and one student commented that the instructor must be "running fast" in his own head when he had been coming into the classroom. The instructor agreed, saying he had considered wearing running shoes to the class. This exchange considerably eased the tension in the room.

The instructor then went onto to say that the class would have some readings in the near future on self-disclosure in the clinical situation. He said that he felt okay about sharing some personal feelings and experiences, but that he was uncertain how the disclosure affected the class. He purposefully mentioned that he had thought about this a great deal and had consulted with colleagues about the potential benefits and risks of sharing his anxiety with the class. He again thanked the students for being able to discuss the classroom interaction. When the class discussed self-disclosure the following week, many students commented on the experience of the instructor having modeled the use of self-disclosure to them. To be sure, the process that took place was not "magical," and moments of difficulty in the class reoccurred, but the tension lessened considerably for the rest of the semester.

In summary, the relational-based teacher endeavors to create a learning atmosphere in which students are encouraged to cocreate their learning process. Consistent with feminist pedagogy, the relational teacher shares the power and authority in the classroom and does not assume a modernist stance of expert. Rather, relational teachers utilize their knowledge and experience to lead the students to a process of mutual discovery so as to master course content. Classroom disruptions are expected as part of the learning process, and the management of these disruptions becomes a model for the management of enactments or ruptures in the clinical relationship. Students are encouraged to practice with a reflective stance, implying a continuous monitoring of their affective responses. In addition, the judicious use of self-disclosure by teacher and students alike can also echo the clinical process.

THE SUPERVISORY PROCESS

Although relational theory has had a dramatic impact on clinical practice, it is only in the last five years that the supervision literature has considered the influence of relational thinking on the supervisory process. For example, Ganzer and Ornstein (2004) suggest that even though clinical work has moved to a two-person modality, the supervision literature has not kept pace. Gail Frawley-O'Dea (2003:357) concurs when she says that "psychoanalytic supervision may just now be starting to be reformulated to fit better the great changes in psychoanalytic culture that have occurred over the past 15 years or so." Schamess (2006b:428) agrees by noting that "as contemporary treatment has evolved, ideas about therapeutic action have increasingly emphasized intersubjective and relational processes. However, most supervisory literature has not yet integrated those changes."

Some theorists, however, have critiqued the traditional literature that speaks of parallel processes as being the cornerstone of supervision from a relational perspective. The parallel process literature suggests that supervisees tend to enact dynamic processes with their supervisors that are reflective of similar processes that their clients are enacting with them. There has been a wide acceptance in the clinical field that understanding parallel process in supervision is a cornerstone of the learning process for beginning and advanced clinicians. Relational theorists critique the privileging of the concept of parallel process since it positions the supervisor in an authoritative position and places the "blame" for certain types of interactions in supervision on the supervisee. Stimmel (1995), cited in Miller and Twomey (1999:564), suggests that "attributing supervisory dynamics to a parallel process may be a resistance to the awareness of the supervisor's own transferences to the supervisee." Lesser (1983) takes the argument further, suggesting that the concept of parallel process is actually illusory and that "its use within the supervisory situation may suggest that important relational difficulties between the supervisor and supervisee are being avoided and displaced onto the therapy" (cited in Miller & Twomey 1999:563). Baudry (1993:611) argues that the supervisors may suggest a parallel process experience if they are resistant to identifying their own transference responses to the supervisee, independent of the particular case being presented.

Thus, relational theorists like Miller and Twomey (1999:566) suggest we need to question the occurrence and significance of parallel process "for not adequately taking into account the intersubjective field and the larger relational dynamics that influence all of the participants. An examination from a relational perspective of parallels that can occur in a supervisory situation may provide a deeper appreciation of the complexities involved in any clinical encounter, and thus serve as a caution in applying overarching theory to unwieldy facts."

What are the key components of supervisory relationships, when framed in relational theory? The supervisor does not assume that he or she has objective knowledge that is conveyed to the supervisee in a didactic manner; rather, relationally based supervisors recognize that they occupy a sanctioned position within the clinical community, but the power and authority inherent in the position continuously evolves, in negotiation with the supervisee. Frawley-O'Dea (2003:359) notes that the relationship is asymmetrical in that supervisors do acknowledge their advanced skill and experience. Nevertheless, they also acknowledge the special talents and skills of the supervisee. The relational supervisor is "conscious of the necessary and ever present tension between assumed and authorized power that infuses the work of the supervisory pair." A relational supervisor will be cautious in allowing a supervisee's ide-alization of the supervisor to go unchecked and will also invite dialogue if the supervisee radically shifts her or his views of a client in order to match the supervisor's views. In other words, the supervisor needs to be aware of the potential of false self-behavior of the supervisee that may be motivated by the supervisee's wish for approval of the authority figure. In addition to recognizing these potential dynamics in the supervisory relationship, it also is advisable for relational supervisors to invite supervisees to reflect on what is occurring in the supervisory relationship. Likewise, Bennett (2008) encour-ages supervisors to be aware that students will operationalize their attachment styles in the supervision relationship. Bennett and Saks (2006:99) propose that "supervision is an interactive process influenced by the attachment styles of both persons in the supervisory dyad." They suggest that a successful (se-cure) supervisor–supervisee relationship is partially based on the ability of the supervisor to read the attachment needs of the supervisee and to offer sensitive care and encouragement in the supervisory relationship.

Relational supervisors have a wider acceptance of personal data of the su-pervisee being discussed in the supervision. Rather than a rigid demarcation of supervision and personal therapy (the teach-or-treat dilemma), the rela-tional supervisor will encourage the supervisee to bring herself or himself more personally and authentically into the clinical work and in the supervi-sion relationship. Relational supervisors recognize that there is no easy way to "teach" someone to practice intersubjective theory and technique, but some suggest that the supervisory relationship is a natural place to model an intersubjective approach. Frawley-O'Dea (2003:360) suggests that "the more fully and freely supervisor and supervisee represent the intricacies of their own relationship, in particular clarifying aspects of it centrally related to the supervised treatment, the more completely and effectively the supervisee can engage with the patient in identifying and speaking about the relational paradigms operating within the treatment." Supervision can be particularly helpful when the supervisory dyad engages in dialogue that explores rup-tures and/or mutual transferences that occur during supervision. Schamess (2006a:424) also suggests that "listening attentively for transference enact-ments in supervision enriches supervisory conversations and communicates empathetic interest in the manifest and latent content of what supervis-ees communicate." He also says that "clinical supervision can and should be designed to achieve both educational and therapeutic goals" and "the boundaries between cognitive and affective learning and those between professional development, personal growth, and personality change are permeable in ways the traditional supervisory literature has been reluctant to acknowledge" (428). Likewise, Tosone (1997:30) says that "there is a general consensus that selective disclosure of (supervisor) counter-transference to the supervisee can have a beneficial effect on the supervisee's treatment relationship with the patient." Relational supervisors need to teach by example. The supervisor needs the capacity "to tolerate and acknowledge his or her own anxieties and conflicts as they enter the supervisory relationship, rather than projecting them onto or into the supervisee" (Sarnat 1992:401).

Relational supervisors acknowledge that some regression in both supervisee and supervisor is expected when conducting clinical work, and it is ideal when affectively intense or cognitively primitive material can be discussed openly during supervision. Frawley-O'Dea (2003:360) suggests that the relational supervisor is "open to considering primary-process material delivered into the supervision by dreams, somatic states, fantasies, and dissociative experiences." Supervisees are well advised to be conscious of their bodily sensations, affect, and transitory mental images when engaged with their clients, and that this material is important to bring to the supervisory discussion. Relational thinkers would consider supervision as more than a cognitive process that relies on exclusively sound secondary-process and abstract thinking. In a recent supervision that one of the authors (DM) was conducting, his supervisee reluctantly disclosed that he was feeling very anxious when working with a particular client. He said that he was "almost" experiencing panic attacks and had fantasized about having to leave the office. The supervisee related that he felt nauseous and light-headed and was perspiring at times. The supervisor asked him about the client's demeanor when this was going on — he quickly said that his client seemed to be calmed and composed. The supervisee was quick to realize that he was holding the anxiety of the client through projective identification. In this instance, it was important for the supervisee to share his anxiety experiences as a way of understanding the clinical process. Had he been hesitant to do so, it might not have been possible to understand the client's use of projective identification in a number of interactions with the clinician and others.

Relational supervisors do not necessarily assume that neurotic or characterological aspects of the supervisee would be only discussed in one's own therapy. Rather, relational supervisors have a more open stance to considering some personal data in the supervisory relationship. A relational supervisor recognizes that supervision is enriched when supervisor–supervisee dyads try to understand the enactments of the treatment and the enactments in the supervision. To gain clarity about the dynamic issues, a supervisor cannot ignore the supervisee's or the supervisor's own reactions, personality style, or transferences if he or she hopes to understand the complexity of the enactments that are crucial to the work. Frawley-O'Dea (2003) suggests that personal transactions be pursued only when the needs of the client and the treatment are primarily in focus. Though the boundaries and limits of the supervision are coconstructed by the participants, the supervisee needs to retain the authority and decision making about the extent of the personal issues that are open for scrutiny in the supervision. Frawley-O'Dea encourages a cautious approach if the supervisee has not had his or her own treatment. Therapists who are aware of the therapy process from a personal perspective will likely be less frightened of primitive content when it emerges in the supervision. Citing Bromberg (1998), Ganzer and Ornstein (2004:446) suggest that the "supervisor does need to be respectful of the supervisee's need for privacy, and, as noted, to control the degree of exploration." However, they also say that "each participant needs to be able to walk the tightrope, not knowing whether the process will lead to clarification and insight or to increased complexity and even temporary confusion, but be willing to go either way." Recently a supervisee disclosed that she had begun the process of enquiry about adoption of an international child. A child therapist, she was struggling with her knowledge of the benefits of secure attachments for children. She was cautious to maintain balanced relationships with her child clients (as opposed to rescuing relationships), and she felt it was important that her supervisor knew that she was considering adoption. The supervisor concurred that this was important personal data for him to know about her. It also opened up an opportunity to discuss their respective views about attachment styles, dysfunction, and resiliency.

In summary, relational supervisors expect that there will be enactments between themselves and their supervisees. Rather than attempting to suppress the feelings associated with these interactions, relational supervisors argue for an exploratory approach to better understand the clinical process of the client that is being discussed between the two. The supervisee maintains some control over the data to be discussed, but certainly the supervisor respects the competence of the supervisee and presumes that the relationship will have mutual benefits. Legitimizing some relational principles in supervision permits a more expansive interaction between supervisee and supervisor, especially in the area of working through relationship issues in the supervisory dyad. While not individual therapy, supervision does offer an opportunity for psychological growth for both supervisee and supervisor.

EPILOGUE

As we put the finishing touches on this book, we think we have accomplished the number of goals that we had at the outset of the project. An important goal for us was to articulate how relational theory is specifically practiced by social workers in social work settings. To underscore the compatibility of relational theory and social work practice, we once again remind our readers that social work is truly relational at its core in both practice and theory. As noted in the introduction, social workers have historically been relational practitioners since the inception of the profession. As we review the content of the preceding eleven chapters, we trust that we have made transparent the place of social work theory in the broad field of relational theory. In our introduction we noted that social workers have not often been given credit for the views held dear in the heart of the social work profession. Horowitz (1998:378) commented that social workers have not known (realized) or have been unaware, perhaps, of their leadership in developing ideas that are "relational, postmodern, and cutting-edge." We hope to have countered our profession's reluctance to claim the full impact of our contributions to mental health literature by specifically highlighting the importance of relationally based social work practice and theory in a range of contemporary practice modalities.

We publish this text at a time in the social work profession's history when not only the basics but the nuances of sound clinical practice are only superficially taught in many schools of social work across the country. There is certainly a paucity of psychodynamic theory found in the curriculum of many practice courses in social work schools; there are often practice courses that are increasingly atheoretical at worst and technique-driven at best. Many graduates of schools of social work complete their bachelor's or master's degree training without fully appreciating the complexity of the human condition. Some do not understand how the unconscious world affects the behavior and feelings of their clients. Without this understanding, social work practitioners are at a distinct disadvantage in terms of being able to offer sound, theoretically informed practice. In addition, there is an alarming movement in the mental health field that actively challenges and undermines the tenets upon which this book is founded—that is, that relationships (clinical and otherwise) are healing and restorative. We recognize that healing relationships take time to form and to become instrumental in affecting any change process. Social work practitioners can have an impact on their clients' lives even when mandated to have very brief contact with our most needy clients. However, we suggest that healing relationships take time to work, and that as social workers we need to be challenging the stronghold of managed care companies that dictate that only the briefest of mental health interventions are necessary for the increasingly complex and difficult circumstances and experiences in which our clients live.

We also hope that this text will whet the appetite of social work students, recent social work graduates, and also experienced clinicians to become more familiar with the complexity of practicing from a relational theory perspective. An oversimplification of the theory could potentially give students and practitioners alike a "license" to misuse the tenets of mutuality and equality in clinical relationships. While we certainly suggest that practicing from a relational perspective can facilitate growth for both client and clinician, we also emphasize that the focus of the growth process needs to be squarely centered on the client's needs. As social work academics, we fully recognize the responsibility of the core values and ethics of our profession, and we take seriously the idea that students certainly need to learn that practicing from a relational theory perspective does not mean that we are self-indulgent. For example, self-disclosure of our thoughts and feelings with our clients at every opportunity counters sound treatment principles of relational theory. Perhaps this goes without saying, but we clearly demarcate a relationally based treatment relationship from that of an interpersonal "friendship" with our clients. To this end, we have articulated clear guidelines about the indications and contraindications of self-disclosure and the process of working through enactments in the clinical relationship.

As noted above, we trust that this text will encourage recent social work graduates and experienced practitioners to seek out further opportunities to learn and practice relational principles, responsibly. We included a chapter on learning relational theory (in the classroom and in supervision) as we wanted to underscore that supervision is a vital aspect of our profession's vitality. Even though there has been a movement away from clinical supervision in agencies, we do suggest that supervision and consultation (whether peer or otherwise) are important components of our ongoing professional development. Relational theory will also increasingly influence the "learning" of social work.

Relational theory has captured the attention of many psychodynamic theorists as they conduct their clinical skills in advocacy, counseling, and psychotherapy. We imagine (we cannot predict, of course) that relational theory will continue to have a profound influence in the overall field of mental health. As we noted, we have already experienced a paradigm shift in the field; many clinicians have moved away from a classical "drive" theory position to a one-person and then to a two-person psychology understanding of the clinical process.

We also are excited to imagine that contemporary attachment theory and contemporary neurobiological theory will be synthesized with the tenets of contemporary relational theory. This is a time of great advances in the understanding of brain functioning and how our brains are fundamentally shaped in interactions with others. Again, we imagine an interface of relational theories with the burgeoning field of neurobiology that also suggests that even the most intricate of brain functions and growth *only* happen in relationship with others (Cozolino 2006). The reader is encouraged to explore the work of those authors who are furthering our understanding of how relationships shape our minds; in addition, we know more and more about how treatment relationships can change brain neuronal development that contributes to plasticity across the life cycle (Applegate and Shapiro 2005; Badenoch 2008; Cacioppo and White 2008; Cozolino 2006; Schore and Schore 2008; Siegel 2008). These authors and many others are furthering our understanding of the crucial importance of relationships in our development. We hope this book has furthered your understanding of relational theory principles in your clinical practices, and. as noted, we imagine much more synthesis and progress now and in the future. It is an interesting and challenging time to be a clinical social worker; we hope that you enjoy the excitement of this vibrant time in our field, and that you continue to value your social work roots and traditions.

REFERENCES

Ackerman, D. 2004 *An Alchemy of Mind*. New York: Scribner's.

Adams, A. 2004. The five good things in cross-cultural therapy. In M. Walker and W. Rosen, eds., *How Connections Heal: Stories from Relational-Cultural Therapy*, pp. 151–173. New York: Guilford Press.

Adler, G. 1985. *Borderline Psychopathology and Its Treatment*. New York: Jason Aronson.

Ainsworth, M.D.S. 1963. The development of infant-mother interaction among the Ganda. In B. M. Foss, ed., *Determinants of Infant Behavior*, pp. 67–104. New York: Wiley.

——. 1967. *Infancy in Uganda*. Baltimore: John Hopkins University Press.

——. 1973. The development of mother-infant attachment. In B. Caldwell and H. Ricciuti, eds., *Review of Child Development Research*, 3:1–94. Chicago: University of Chicago Press.

——. 1982. Attachment: Retrospect and prospect. In C.M. Parkes and J. Stevenson-Hinde, eds., *The Place of Attachment in Human Behavior*, pp. 3–30. New York: Basic Books.

Ainsworth, M.D.S., and S. Bell. 1970. Attachment exploration and separation: Illustrated by the behavior of one year olds in a strange situation. *Child Development* 41:49–67.

Ainsworth, M.D.S., M. C. Blehar, E. Waters, and W. Wall. 1978. *Patterns of Attachment*. Hillsdale, N.J.: Erlbaum.

Alexander, F., and M. French. 1946. *Psychoanalytic Therapy*. New York: Ronald Press.

——. 1963. *Fundamentals of Psychoanalysis*. New York: Norton.

Altman, N. 1995. *The Analyst in the Inner City: Race, Class and Culture Through a Psychoanalytic Lens*. Hillsdale, N.J.: Analytic Press.

——. 2000. Black and white thinking. *Psychoanalytic Dialogues* 10:589–605.

Applegate, J., and J. M. Bonovitz. 1995. *The Facilitating Partnership*. Hillsdale, N.J.: Jason Aronson.

Applegate, J., and J. Shapiro. 2005. *Neurobiology for Clinical Social Work: Theory and Practice*. New York: Norton.

Arbona, C., and T. Power. 2003. Parental attachment, self-esteem and antisocial behavior among African American, European American, and Mexican American adolescents. *Journal of Counseling Psychology* 501:40–51.

Aron, L. 1990. One-person and two-person psychologies and the method of psychoanalysis. *Psychoanalytic Psychology* 7:475–485.

——. 1991. The patient's experience of the analyst's subjectivity. *Psychoanalytic Dialogues* 1:29–51.

——. 1992. Interpretation as expression of the analyst's subjectivity. *Psychoanalytic Dialogues* 1:29–51.

——. 1996. *A Meeting of Minds: Mutuality in Psychoanalysis*. Hillsdale, N.J.: Analytic Press.

Aron, L., and A. Harris. 1993. *The Legacy of Sandor Ferenczi*. Hillsdale, N.J.: Analytic Press.

——. 2005. Introduction. In L. Aron and A. Harris, eds., *Relational Psychoanalysis*, 2: xiii–xxi Hillsdale, N.J.: Analytic Press.

Austin, L. 1948. Evolution of our case-work concepts. *Proceedings of the National Conference of Social Work*. Chicago: University of Chicago Press.

Badenoch, B. 2008. *Being a Brain-Wise Therapist: A Practical Guide to Interpersonal Neurobiology*. New York: Norton.

Bader, E., and P. Pearson. 1988. *In Quest of the Mythical Mate: A Developmental Diagnosis and Treatment in Couples Therapy*. New York: Brunner/Mazel.

Bandler, L. 1963. Some aspects of ego growth through sublimation. In H. J. Parad and R. Miller, eds., *Ego-oriented Casework*, pp. 27–44. New York: Family Service Association of America.

Barber, J., M. Connoly, P. Crits-Christoph, L. Gladis, and L. Siqueland. 2000. Alliance predicts patients' outcome beyond in-treatment change in symptoms. *Journal of Consulting and Clinical Psychology* 68:1027–1032.

Barnett, D., S. Kidwell, and K. Leung. 1998. Parenting and preschooler attachment among low-income urban African American families. *Child Development* 696:1657–1671.

Basham, K., and D. Miehls. 2004. *Transforming the Legacy: Couple Therapy with Survivors of Childhood Trauma*. New York: Columbia University Press.

Baudry, F. 1993. The personal dimension and management of the supervisory situation with a special note on the parallel process. *Psychoanalytic Quarterly* 62:588–614.

Beck, A. T., J. Rush, B. Shaw, and G.. Emery. 1979. *Cognitive Therapy of Depression*. New York: Guilford Press.

Beebe, B., and F. Jaffe. 1997. Mother-infant interaction structures and pre-symbolic self and object representations. *Psychoanalytic Dialogues* 7:133–182.

Beebe, B., and F. M. Lachmann. 1988a. Mother-infant mutual influence and precursors of psychic structure. In A. Goldberg, ed., *Progress in Self Psychology*, 3:3–25. Hillsdale, N.J.: Analytic Press.

———. 1988b. The contribution of mother-infant mutual influence to the origins of self- and object relationships. *Psychoanalytic Psychology* 5:305–337.

———. 2002. *Infant Research and Adult Treatment: Co-constructing Interactions*. Hillsdale, N.J.: Analytic Press.

Beebe, B., J. Rustin, D. Sorter, and S. Knoublauch. 2003. An expanded view of intersubjectivity in infancy and its application to psychoanalysis. *Psychoanalytic Dialogues* 13, 6:805–841.

Benjamin, J. 1988. *The Bonds of Love: Psychoanalysis, Feminism, and the Problem of Domination*. New York: Pantheon.

———. 1990. An outline of intersubjectivity: The development of recognition. *Psychoanalytic Psychology* 7:33–46.

———. 1995. *Like Subjects: Love Objects*. New Haven: Yale University Press.

———. 2002a. The rhythm of recognition: Comments on the work of Louis Sander. *Psychoanalytic Dialogues* 12, 1:43–53.

———. 2002b. Sameness and difference: An over inclusive view of gender. In M. Dimen and V. Goldner, eds., *Gender in Psychoanalytic Space*, pp. 181–206. New York: Other Press.

Bennett, C. S. 2008. Attachment-informed supervision for social work field education. *Clinical Social Work Journal* 36:97–107.

Bennett, C. S., and L. Saks. 2006. A conceptual application of attachment theory and research to the social work student-field instructor supervisory relationship. *Journal of Social Work Education* 42, 3:157–169.

Bergman, S., and J. Surrey. 1997. The woman-man relationship: Impasses and possibilities. In J. Jordan, ed., *Women's Growth in Diversity: More Writings from the Stone Center*, pp. 260–278. New York: Guilford Press.

Berzoff, J., L. M. Flanagan, and P. Hertz 1996. *Inside Out and Outside In*. Northvale, N.J.: Jason Aronson.

Bibring, G. 1950. Psychiatric principles in casework. In C. Kasius, ed., *Principles and Techniques in Social Casework: Selected Articles 1940–1950*, pp. 370–379. New York: Family Service Association of America.

Billow, R. 2003. Relational levels of the "container-contained" in group therapy. *Group* 24, 4:243–259.

Binder, J., and H. Strupp. 1991. The Vanderbilt approach to time-limited dynamic psychotherapy. In P. Crits-Christoph and J. P. Barber, eds.. *Handbook of Short-Term Psychotherapy*, pp. 137–165. New York: Basic Books.

Bion, A. 1959. *Experiences in Groups*. New York: Basic Books.

———. 1963. *Elements of Psychoanalysis*. London: Heinemann.

Black, M. 2003. Enactment: Analytic musings on energy, language and personal growth. *Psychoanaltytic Dialogues* 13, 5:633–655.

Blanck, G. and R. 1974. *Ego Psychology: Theory and Practice*. New York: Columbia University Press.

——. 1979. *Ego Psychology, II: Psychoanalytic Developmental Psychology*. New York: Columbia University Press.

Bogo, M. 1993. The student/field instructor relationship: The critical factor in field education. *The Clinical Supervisor* 11, 2:23–36.

Bowlby, J. 1958. The nature of the child's tie to his mother. *International Journal of Psychoanalysis* 39:350–373.

——. 1960. Grief and mourning in infancy and early childhood. *Psychoanalytic Study of the Child* 15:3–39.

——. 1969. *Attachment and Loss*, vol. 1: *Attachment*. New York: Basic Books.

——. 1973. *Attachment and Loss*, vol. 2: *Separation: Anxiety and Anger*. New York: Basic Books.

——. 1980. *Attachment and Loss*, vol. 3: *Loss*. London: Hogarth.

——. 1988. *A Secure Base*. New York: Basic Books.

Brandell, J., and S. Ringel. 2007. *Attachment and Dynamic Practice: An Integrative Guide for Social Workers and Other Clinicians*. New York: Columbia University Press.

Bromberg, P. M. 1998. *Standing in the Spaces: Essays on Clinical Process, Trauma and Dissociation*. Hillsdale, N.J.: Analytic Press.

Budman, S., and A. Gurman. 1988. *Theory and Practice of Brief Therapy*. New York: Guilford Press.

Burke, W., and M. Tansey. 1992. Countertransference disclosure and models of therapeutic action. *Contemporary Psychoanalysis* 27:351–384.

Cacioppo, J., and W. White. 2008. *Loneliness, Human Nature and the Need for Social Connection*. New York: Norton.

Chenot, D. K. 1998. Mutual values: Self psychology, intersubjectivity and social work. *Clinical Social Work Journal* 26:297–311.

Chin, J. L., V. De La Cancela, and Y. M. Jenkins. 1993. *Diversity in Psychotherapy: The Politics of Race, Ethnicity, and Gender*. Westport, Conn.: Praeger.

Chodorow, N. 1978. *The Reproduction of Mothering: Psychoanalysis and the Sociology of Gender*. Berkeley: University of California Press.

——. 1999. *The Power of Feelings*. New Haven: Yale University Press.

Chused, J. 2003. The role of enactments. *Psychoanalytic Dialogues* 13:677–687.

Cockerill, E., et al. 1953. *A Conceptual Framework of Social Casework*. Pittsburgh: University of Pittsburgh Press.

Cohen, B., and V. Schermer. 2001. Therapist self disclosure in group psychotherapy from an intersubjective and self psychological standpoint. *Group* 25, 1/2:41–57.

Cooper, S. H., and D. Levit. 2005. Old and new objects in Fairbairnian and American relational theory. In L. Aron and A. Harris, eds., *Relational Psychoanalysis*, 2:51–74. Hillsdale, N.J.: Analytic Press.

Cozart, S., and P. Price. 2005. Black women, identity and schooling: Reclaiming our work in shifting contexts. *Urban Review* 373:173–179.

Cozolino, L. 2006. *The Neuroscience of Human Relationships: Attachment and the Developing Social Brain.* New York: Norton.

Davanloo, H., ed. 1978. *Basic Principles and Techniques in Short-term Dynamic Psychotherapy.* New York: Spectrum.

———. 1980. *Short-term Dynamic Psychotherapy.* New York: Jason Aronson.

Davies, J., and M. G. Frawley. 1994. *Treating the Adult Survivor of Childhood Sexual Abuse: A Psychoanalytic Perspective.* New York: Basic Books.

Dawson, G., H. Panagiotides, L. Grofer Klinger, and D. Hill. 1992. The role of frontal lobe functioning in the development of infant self-regulatory behavior. *Brain and Cognition* 20:152–175.

DeYoung, P. 2003. *Relational Psychotherapy: A Primer.* New York: Brunner-Routledge.

Dies, R. 1973. Group therapist self-disclosure: An evaluation by clients. *Journal of Counseling Psychology* 20, 4:344–348.

Dimen, M. 1991. Deconstructing difference: Gender, splitting, and transitional space. *Psychoanalytic Dialogues* 1:335–352.

Dunlap, K. 1996. Function theory and social work practice. In F. Turner, ed., *Social Work Treatment*, 4th ed., pp. 319–340. New York: Free Press.

Dunlap, K., and V. Goldner. 2002. *Gender in Psychoanalytic Space.* New York: Other Press.

Edwards, J., S. Bryant, and T. Clark. 2008. African American female social work educators in predominantly white schools of social work: Strategies for thriving. *Journal of African American Studies* 12:37–49.

Ehrenberg, D. B. 1992. The intimate edge. New York: Norton.

———. 1995. Self-disclosure: Therapeutic tool or indulgence? *Contemporary Psychoanalysis* 31:213–228.

Elicker, J. M. Englund, and A. Sroufe. 1992. Predicting peer competence and peer relationships in childhood from early parent child relationships. In R. Park and G. Ladd, eds., *Family Peer Relationships: Modes of Linkage*, pp. 77–106. Hillsdale, N.J.: Lawrence Erlbaum.

Elson, M. 1986. *Self Psychology in Clinical Social Work.* New York: Norton.

Fairbairn, W.R.D. 1940. Schizoid factors in the personality. In W.R.D. Fairbairn, *Psychoanalytic Studies of the Personality*, pp. 2–27. London: Routledge.

———. 1941. A revised psychopathology of the psychoses and the psychoneuroses. In W.R.D. Fairbairn, *An Object Relations Theory of the Personality.* New York: Basic Books.

———. 1952. *Psychoanalytic Studies of the Personality.* London: Routledge.

Fedele, N. 2004. Relational movement in group psychotherapy. In M. Walker and W. Rosen, eds., *How Connections Heal: Stories from Relational-Cultural Therapy*, pp. 174–192. New York: Guilford Press.

Ferenczi, S. 1932. *The Clinical Diary of Sandor Ferenczi.* J. Dupont, ed., M. Balint and N. Z. Jackson, trans. Cambridge: Harvard University Press, 1988.

——. 1933. The confusion of tongues between adults and children: The language of tenderencess and of passion. In M. Balint ed., *Final Contributions to the Problems and Methods of Psychoanalysis,* 3:156–167. London: Karnac Books, 1980.

Ferenczi, S., and O. Rank. 1924. *The Development of Psychoanalysis.* Madison, Conn.: International Universities Press, 1986.

Fishbane, M. 2001. Relational narratives of the self. *Family Processes* 40, 3:273–291.

Fonagy, P. 2001. *Attachment Theory and Psychoanalysis.* New York: Other Press.

Fonagy, P., G. Gergely, E. Jurist, and M. Target. 2002. *Affect Regulation, Mentalization and the Development of the Self.* New York: Other Press.

Frawley-O'Dea, G. 2003. Supervision is a relationship too: A contemporary approach to psychoanalytic supervision. *Psychoanalytic Dialogues* 13, 3:355–366.

Freedberg, S. 2007. Re-examining empathy: A relational-feminist point of view. *Social Work* 52:251–260.

Freud, S. 1912. The dynamics of transference. *Standard Edition,*12:99–108. London: Hogarth Press.

Fromm-Reichmann F. 1950. *Principles of Intensive Psychotherapy.* Chicago: University of Chicago Press.

Gagerman, J. 2004. The search for fuller mutuality and self experiences in a women's psychotherapy group. *Clinical Social Work Journal* 32, 3:285–306.

Gambrill, E. 2003. Ethics, science, and helping professions: A conversation with Robyn Dawes. *Journal of Social Work Education* 39:27–40.

Ganzer, C., and E. D. Ornstein. 1999. Beyond parallel process: Relational perspectives on field instruction. *Clinical Social Work Journal* 27, 3:231–246.

——. 2004. Regression, self-disclosure, and the teach or treat dilemma: Implications of a relational approach for social work supervision. *Clinical Social Work Journal* 32, 4:431–449.

Garrett, A. 1958. Modern casework: The contributions of ego psychology. In H. J. Parad, ed., *Ego Psychology and Dynamic Casework,* pp. 38–52. New York: Family Service Association of America.

Gaston, L. 1991. The concept of the alliance and its role in psychotherapy: Theoretical and empirical considerations. *Psychotherapy* 27:143–153.

Gentile, J. 2007. Wrestling with matter: Origins of intersubjectivity. *Psychoanalytic Quarterly* 76, 2:547–582.

Germain, C. B. 1970. Casework and science: An historical encounter. In R. W. Roberts and R. H. Nee, eds. *Theories of Social Casework,* pp. 3–32. Chicago: University of Chicago Press.

——. 1979. *Social Work Practice: People and Environments.* New York: Columbia University Press.

Germain, C. B., and A. Gitterman. 1980. *The Life Model of Social Work Practice.* New York: Columbia University Press.

——. 1986. The life model of social work practice revisited. In F. H. Turner, ed., *Social Work Treatment: Interlocking Theoretical Approaches*, 3rd ed., pp. 618–644. New York: Free Press.

——. 1996. *The Life Model of Social Work Practice*, 2nd ed. New York: Columbia University Press.

Glassgold, J. M., and S. Iasenza, eds. 1995. *Lesbians and Psychoanalysis: Revolutions in Theory and Practice*. New York: Free Press.

Goldner, V. 2002. Toward a critical relational theory of gender. In M. Dimen and V. Goldner, eds., *Gender in Psychoanaltyic Space*, pp. 63–90. New York: Other Press.

Goldstein, E. 1980. The knowledge base of clinical social work. *Social Work* 25:173–178.

——. 1994. Self disclosure in treatment: What therapists do and don't talk about. *Clinical Social Work Journal* 22:417–433.

——. 1995. *Ego Psychology and Social Work Practice*. New York: Free Press.

——. 1996. What is clinical social work? Looking back to move ahead. *Clinical Social Work Journal* 24:89–104.

——. 1997. Countertransference reactions to borderline couples. In M. Solomon and J. Siegel, eds., *Countertransference in Couples Therapy*, pp. 38–71. New York: Norton.

——. 2001. *Object Relations Theory and Self Psychology in Social Work Practice*. New York: Free Press.

——. 2007. Social work education and clinical learning: Yesterday, today, and tomorrow. *Clinical Social Work Journal* 35:15–24.

Gonsiorek, J. C. ed. 1982. *Homosexuality and Psychotherapy: A Practitioner's Handbook of Affirmative Models*. New York: Haworth Press.

Gordon, R. 1991. Intersubjectivity and the efficacy of group psychotherapy. *Group Analysis* 24:41–51.

Greenberg, J., and S. Mitchell 1983. *Object Relations in Psychoanalytic Theory*. Cambridge: Harvard University Press.

Grossmark, R. 2007. From familiar chaos to coherence: Unformulated experience and enactment in group psychotherapy. In M. Suchet, A. Harris, and L. Aron, eds., *Relational Psychoanalysis*, 3:193-208. Mahwah, NJ: Analytic Press.

Gubman, N. 2004. Disorganized attachment. A compass for navigating the confusion of the "difficult-to-treat" patient. *Clinical Social Work Journal* 32:154–170.

Guntrip, H. S. 1969. *Schizoid Phenomena, Object Relations, and the Self*. New York: International Universities Press.

——. 1975. My experience of analysis with Fairbairn and Winnicott. *International Review of Psychoanalysis* 2:145–156.

Hadley, M. 2008. Relational Theory: Inside out, outside in, in between and all around. In J. Berzoff, L. Malano Flanagan, and P. Hertz, eds., *Inside Out and Outside In*, 2nd ed., pp. 205–228. New York: Jason Aronson.

Hamilton, G. 1958. A theory of personality: Freud's contribution to social work. In H. J. Parad, ed., *Ego Psychology and Dynamic Casework*, pp. 11–37. New York: Family Service Association of America.

Hanna, E. A. 1993a. The implications of shifting perspectives in countertransference on the therapeutic action of clinical social work, part 1: The classical and early-totalist position. *Journal of Analytic Social Work* 1:25–52.

——. 1993b. The implications of shifting perspectives in countertransference on the therapeutic action of clinical social work, part 2: The recent-totalist and intersubjective position. *Journal of Analytic Social Work* 1:53–80.

—— 1998. The role of the client's subjectivity using countertransference in psychotherapy. *Journal of Analytic Social Work* 25:1–25.

Harris, A. 1991. Gender as contradiction. *Psychoanalytic Dialogues* 1:197–224.

——. 2002. Gender as contradiction. In M. Dimen and V. Goldner, eds., *Gender in Psychoanalytic Space*, pp. 91–118. New York: Other Press.

——. 2007. The house of difference: Enactment, a play in three scenes. In M. Suchet, A. Harris, and L. Aron, eds., *Relational Psychoanalysis*, vol. 3: *New Voices*, pp. 81–96. Mahwah, N.J.: Analytic Press.

Harwood, R. 1992. The influence of culturally derived values on Anglo and Puerto Rican mothers/ perceptions of attachment behavior. *Child Development* 63:822–839.

Hoffman, I. 1973. *Psychoanalytic Theory, Therapy, and the Self*. New York: Basic Books.

——. 1983. The patient as interpreter of the analyst's experience. *Contemporary Psychoanalysis* 19:389–422.

——. 1996. Intimate and ironic authority of the psychoanalyst's presence. *Psychoanalytic Quarterly* 65, 3:102–135.

——. 2006. The myths of free association and the potentials of the analytic relationship. *International Journal of Psychoanalysis* 87:43–61.

Hollis, F. 1949. The techniques of casework. *Journal of Social Casework* 30:235–244.

——. 1964. *Casework: A Psychosocial Therapy*. New York: Random House.

——. 1972. *Casework: A Psychosocial Therapy*, 2nd ed. New York: Random House.

Hollis, F., and M. Woods. 1981. *Casework: A Psychosocial Therapy*, 3rd ed. New York: Random House.

Holmes, D. 1992. Race and transference in psychoanalysis and psychotherapy. *International Journal of Psychoanalysis* 73, 1:1–11.

Hopkins, L. 2006. *False Self: The Life of Masud Khan*. New York: Other Press.

Horney, K. 1945. *Our Inner Conflicts, a Constructive Theory of Neurosis*. New York: Norton.

Horowitz, J. 1998. Contemporary psychoanalysis and social work theory. *Clinical Social Work Journal* 26:369–383.

Horvath, A., and L. Greenberg. 1989. Development and validation of the working alliance inventory. *Journal of Counseling Psychology* 36:222–233.

Horvath, A., and B. Symonds. 1991. Relation between working alliance an outcome in psychotherapy: A meta analysis. *Journal of Counseling and Psychology* 38:139-149.

Isay, R. 1989. *Being Homosexual: Gay Men and Their Development*. New York: Farrar, Straus and Giroux.

Jackson, L. C., and B. Greene, eds. 2000. *African American Women: Innovations in Psychodynamic Perspectives and Practice*. New York: Guilford Press.

Jacobs, T. 2007. On the adolescent neurosis. *Psychoanalytic Quarterly* 76, 2:487–514.

Jacobson, E. 1964. *The Self and the Object World*. New York: International Universities Press.

Johnson, S. 2002. *Emotionally Focused Couple Therapy with Trauma Survivors: Strengthening Attachment Bonds*. New York: Guilford.

Jordan, J. V. 1995. *Relational Awareness: Transforming Disconnection: Work in Progress, No. 76*. Wellesley, Mass.: Stone Center Working Paper Series.

——. 1997. The meaning of mutuality. In J. V. Jordon, A. Kaplan, J. Baker Miller, I. Stiver, and J. Surrey, eds., *Women's Growth in Connection: Writings from the Stone Center*, pp. 81–96. New York: Guilford Press.

——, ed. 1997. *Women's Growth in Diversity: More Writings from the Stone Center*. New York: Guilford Press.

Jordan, J. V., A. Kaplan, J. Baker Miller, I. Stiver, and J. Surrey. 1991. *Women's Growth in Connection: Writings from the Stone Center*. New York: Guilford.

Kaplan, A., and J. Surrey. 1984. The relational self in women: Development theory and public policy. In I. Walker, ed., *Women and Mental Health Policy*. Beverly Hills, Calif.: Sage Publications.

Karen, R. 1998. *Becoming Attached*. New York: Oxford University Press.

Kernberg, O. 1975. *Borderline Conditions and Pathological Narcissism*. New York: Jason Aronson.

——. 1976. *Object Relations Theory and Clinical Psychoanalysis*. New York: Jason Aronson.

——. 1980. *Internal World and External Reality*. New York: Jason Aronson.

Klein, M. 1932. *The Psychoanalysis of Children*. London: Hogarth Press.

——. 1948. On the theory of anxiety and guilt. In *Envy and Gratitude and Other Works, 1946–1963*. New York: Delacorte Press.

——. 1952. The origins of transference. In *Envy and Gratitude and Other Works*. London: Hogarth Press, 1975.

——. 1957. Envy and gratitude. In *Envy and Gratitude and Other Works, 1946–1963*. New York: Delacorte Press.

Kobak, R., J. Cassidy, and Y. Ziv. 2002. Attachment-related trauma and posttraumatic stress disorder: Implications for adult adaptation. In W. S. Rholes and J. A. Simpson, eds., *Adult Attachment: Theory, Research and Clinical implications*, pp. 388–407. New York: Guilford Press.

Kohut, H. 1971. *The Analysis of the Self*. New York: International Universities Press.

——. 1977. *The Restoration of the Self*. New York: International Universities Press.

——. 1984. *How Does Analysis Cure?* A. Goldberg and P. Stepansky, eds. Chicago: University of Chicago Press.

Kohut, H., and E. S. Wolf. 1978. Disorders of the self and their treatment. *International Journal of Psychoanalysis* 59:412–425.

Lachkar, J. 1992. *The Narcissistic/Borderline Couple: A Psychoanalytic Perspective on Marital Treatment.* New York: Brunner/Mazel.

Leary, K. 1995. Interpreting in the dark. *Psychoanalytic Psychology* 12:127–140.

——. 1997. Race, self disclosure and "forbidden talk": Race and ethnicity in contemporary clinical practice. *Psychoanalytic Quarterly* 66:163–189.

——. 2000. Racial enactments in dynamic treatment. *Psychoanalytic Dialogues* 10:639–653.

Lee, J.A.B. 1996. The empowerment approach to social work Practice. In F. H. Turner, ed., *Social Work Treatment: Interlocking Theoretical Approaches,* 4th ed., pp. 618–644. New York: Free Press.

Lesser, R. 1983. Supervision: Illusions, anxieties, and questions. *Contemporary Psychoanalysis* 19:282–289.

Levenson, E. 1993. Shoot the messenger: Interpersonal aspects of the analyst's interpretations. *Contemporary Psychoanalysis* 29:383–396.

Levenson, H. 1995. *Time-limited dynamic psychotherapy.* New York: Basic Books.

Lichtenberg, J. 2007. Brilliance before its time: A commentary on "instinct and the ego during infancy." *Psychoanalytic Quarterly* 76, 2:433–438.

Lichtenberg, J., F. Lachmann, and J. Fosshage. 2001. *Self and Motivational Systems: Toward a Theory of Psychoanalytic Technique.* Hillsdale, N.J.: Analytic Press.

——. 2002. *A Spirit of Inquiry: Communication in Psychoanalysis.* Hillsdale, N.J.: Analytic Press.

Lide, P. 1966. Dynamic mental representation: An analysis of the empathic process. *Social Casework* 47:146–151.

Liotti, G. 1995. Disorganized/disoriented attachment in the psychotherapy of the dissociative disorders. In S. Goldberg, R. Muir, and J. Kerr, eds., *Attachment Theory: Social Development and Clinical Perspectives,* pp. 343–363. Hillsdale, N.J.: Analytic Press.

Luborsky, L., J. Barber, L. Siqueland, S. Johnson, L. Najavits, A. Frank, and D. Daley. 1985. The revised helping alliance questionnaire HAQ–II: Psychometric properties. *Journal of Psychotherapy Practice Research* 5:260–271.

Luepnitz, D. 1988. *The Family Interpreted: Feminist Theory in Clinical Practice.* New York: Basic Books.

Lyons-Ruth, K., and D. Jacobvitz. 1999. Attachment disorganization: Unresolved loss, relational violence, and lapses in behavioral and attentional strategies. In J. Cassidy and P. Shaver, eds., *Handbook of Attachment: Theory, Research and Clinical Applications,* pp. 520–554. New York: Guilford Press.

Mahler, M., F. Pine, and A. Bergman. 1975. *The Psychological Birth of the Human Infant: Symbiosis and Individuation.* New York: Basic Books.

Main, M., and R. Goldwyn. 1991. Predicting rejection of her infant from mother's representation of her own experience: Implications for the abused-abusing intergenerational cycle. *Child Abuse and Neglect* 8:203–217.

Main, M., R. Goldwyn, and E. Hesse. 2002. *Adult Attachment Scoring and Classification Systems*. Berkeley: Regents of the University of California.

Main, R., and E. Hesse. 1990. Parents' unresolved traumatic experiences are related to infant disorganized attachment status: Is frightened and/or frightening parental behavior the linking mechanism? In M. Greenberg, D. Cicchetti and E. M. Cummings, eds., *Attachment in the Preschool Years: Theory, Research and Intervention*, pp. 161–182. Chicago: University of Chicago Press.

Main, R., and J. Solomon. 1990. Procedures for identifying infants as disorganized/disoriented during the strange situation. In M. Greenberg, D. Cicchetti, and E. M. Cummings, eds., *Attachment in the Preschool Years: Theory, Research and Intervention*, pp. 139–164. Chicago: University of Chicago Press.

Malan, D. H. 1963. *A Study of Brief Psychotherapy*. New York: Plenum.

——. 1976. *The Frontier of Brief Psychotherapy*. New York: Plenum.

Mann, J. 1973. *Time-Limited Psychotherapy*. Cambridge: Harvard University Press.

——. 1991. Time limited psychotherapy. In P. Crits-Christoph and J. Barber, eds., *Handbook of Short-term Dynamic Psychotherapy*, pp. 17–44. New York: Basic Books.

Maroda, K. 1994. *The Power of Countertransference: Innovations in Analytic Technique*. Northvale, N.J.: Aronson.

——. 1999. *Seduction, Surrender, and Transference: Emotional Engagement in the Analytic Process*. Hillsdale, N J · Analytic Press.

Martin, D., J. Garske, and M. Davis. 2000. Relation of the therapeutic alliance with outcome and other variables: A meta-analytic review. *Journal of Consulting Clinical Psychology* 68:438–450.

Masterson, J. 1976. *Psychotherapy of the Borderline Adult: A Developmental Approach*. New York: Brunner/Mazel.

Mattei, L. 1999. A Latina space: Ethnicity as an intersubjective third. *Smith College Studies in Social Work* 69, 2:255–267.

——. 2008. Coloring development. Race and culture in psychodynamic theories. In J. Berzoff, L. Melano Flanagan, and P. Hertz, eds., *Inside Out and Outside In*, 2nd ed., pp.245–270. New York: Jason Aronson.

McCormick, M. J. 1962. The old and the new in casework. In C. Kasiius, ed., *Social Casework in the Fifties: Selected Articles, 1951–1960*, pp. 16–27. New York: Family Association of America.

McLaughlin, J. 1996. Power, authority and influence in the analytic dyad. *Psychoanalytic Quarterly* 65, 3:201–233.

Meltzoff, A. 1990. Foundations for developing a concept of self: The role of imitation in relating self to other and value of social mirroring, social modeling and self practice in infancy. In D. Cicchetti and M. Beeghly, eds., *The Self in Transition: Infancy to Childhood*, pp. 139–164. Chicago: University of Chicago Press.

Mencher, J. 1997. Intimacy in lesbian relationships: A critical reexamination of fusion. In J. Jordan, ed., *Women's Growth in Diversity: More Writings from the Stone Center*, pp. 311–328. New York: Guilford Press.

Messer, S., and C. Warren. 1995. *Models of Brief Psychodynamic Therapy: A Comparative Approach.* New York: Guilford Press.

Meyer, C. H. 1970. *Social Work Practice: A Response to an Urban Crisis.* New York: Free Press.

Miehls, D. 1993. Conjoint treatment with narcissistic couples: Strategies to increase empathic interaction. *Smith College Studies in Social Work* 64, 1:3–17.

——. 1995. Countertransference as an ally in sexual therapy. *Journal of Couples Therapy* 5, 3: 49–59.

——. 1996. Psychosomatic illness considered as a manifestation of triangulation in couples therapy. *Smith College Studies in Social Work* 67, 1:7–19.

——. 1997. Projective identification in sexual abuse survivors and their partners: Couple treatment implications. *Journal of analytic social work* 4, 2:5–22.

——. 1999. Couple therapy: An integration of object relations and intersubjective theory. *Smith College Studies in Social Work* 69, 2:335–355.

——. 2001. The interface of racial identity development with identity complexity in clinical social work student practitioners. *Clinical Social Work Journal* 29, 3:229–244.

Miehls, D., and K. Moffatt. 2000. Constructing social work identity based on the reflexive self. *British Journal of Social Work* 30:339–348.

Mikulincer, M., and P. Shaver. 2004. Security based self-representations in adulthood: Contents and Processes. In W. S. Rholes and J. Simpson, eds., *Adult Attachment: Theory, Research and Clinical Implications*, pp. 159–195. New York: Guilford Press.

Miller, J. B., ed. 1973. *Psychoanalysis and Women: Contributions to New Theory and Therapy.* New York: Brunner/Mazel.

——. 1997. *Towards a New Psychology of Women.* Boston: Beacon Paperback.

Miller, L., and J. Twomey. 1999. A parallel without a process: A relational view of a supervisory experience. *Contemporary Psychoanalysis* 35, 4:557–580.

Mishna, F., and B. Rasmussen. 2001. The learning relationship: Working through disjunctions in the classroom. *Clinical Social Work Journal* 29, 4:387–399.

Mitchell, S. 1988. *Relational Concepts in Psychoanalysis: An Integration.* Cambridge: Harvard University Press.

——. 1993. *Hope and Dread in Psychoanalysis.* New York: Basic Books.

——. 1997. *Influence and Autonomy.* Hillsdale, N.J.: Analytic Press.

——. 2000. *Relationality from Attachment to Intersubjectivity.* Hillsdale, N.J.: Analytic Press.

——. 2003. *Can Love Last?: The Fate of Romance over Time.* New York: Norton.

Mitchell, S., and L. Aron. 1999. *Relational Psychoanbalysis: The Emergence of a Tradition.* Hillsdale, N.J.: Analytic Press.

Mitchell, S., and M. Black. 1995. *Freud and Beyond.* New York: Basic Books.

Modell, A. H. 1984. *Psychoanalysis in a New Context.* New York: International Universities Press.

———. 1991. The therapeutic relationship as a paradoxical experience. *Psychoanalytic Dialogues* 1, 1:13–27.

Mothersole, G. 1999. Parallel process: A review. *The Clinical Supervisor* 18, 2:107–121.

Muran, J. 2002. A relational approach to understanding change: Plurality and contextualism in a psychotherapy research program. *Psychotherapy Research* 12, 2:113–138.

Ogden, T. 1982. *Projective Identification and Psychotherapeutic Technique*. Northvale, N.J.: Aronson.

———. 1997. *Reverie and Interpretation: Sensing Something Human*. Northvale, N.J.: Jason Aronson.

Ornstein, E. D., and C. Ganzer. 1997. Mitchell's relational conflict model: An analysis of its usefulness in clinical social work. *Clinical Social Work Journal* 25:391–406.

———. 2005. Relational social work: A model for the future. *Families in Society* 86, 4:565–572.

Perez-Foster, M. 1963. *Fundamentals of Psychoanalysis*. New York: Norton.

———. 1996. What is a multicultural perspective for psychoanalysis? In R. Perez-Foster, M. Moskowitz, and R.A. Javier, eds., *Reaching Across Boundaries of Culture and Class*, pp. 3–20. Northvale, N.J.: Jason Aronson.

———. 1999. An intersubjective approach to cross-cultural clinical work. *Smith College Studies in Social Work* 69, 3:269–291.

Perez-Foster, M., M. Moskowitz, and R. A. Javier, eds. 1996. *Reaching Across Boundaries of Culture and Class: Widening the Scope of Psychotherapy*. Northvale, N.J.: Jason Aronson.

Perlman, H. H. 1957. *Social Casework: A Problem-solving Process*. Chicago: University of Chicago Press.

———. 1974. The problem-solving model. In F. H. Turner, ed., *Social Work Treatment: Interlocking Theoretical Approaches*, 3rd ed., pp. 245–266. New York: Free Press.

———. 1979. *Relationship: The Heart of Helping People*. New York: Random House.

Piper, W., H. Axim, A. Joyce, and M. McCallum. 1991. Transference interpretations, therapeutic alliance and outcome in short term individual psychotherapy. *Archives of General Psychiatry* 48:946–953.

Pollack, S. D., D. Cicchetti, K. Hornung, and A. Reed. 2000. Recognizing emotion in faces: Developmental effects of child abuse and neglect. *Developmental Psychology* 36:679–688.

Rachman, A. 1990. Judicious self-disclosure in group analysis. *Group* 14, 3:132–144.

———. 1993. Ferenczi and sexuality. In L. Aron and A. Harris, eds., *The Legacy of Sandor Ferenczi*, pp. 81–100. Northvale, N.J.: Analytic Press.

Racker, H. 1957. The meaning and use of countertransference. *Psychoanalytic Quarterly* 26:303–357.

Rank, O. 1924. *The Trauma of Birth*. New York: Harper and Row.

———. 1928. *Will Therapy*. J. J. Taft, trans.. New York: Knopf.

———. 1936. *Truth and Reality*. J. J. Taft, trans. New York: Knopf.

———. 1941. *Beyond Psychology.* Philadelphia: Privately published. Printed by Haddon Craftsmen, Camden, N.J.

———. 1945. *Will Therapy and Truth and Reality.* New York: Knopf.

Reamer, F. J. 1992. The place of empiricism in social work. *Journal of Social Work Education* 28:260–269.

Renik O. 1993. Analytic interaction: conceptualizing technique in light of the analyst's irreducible subjectivity. *Psychoanalytic Quarterly* 62:553–571.

———. 1995.The ideal of the anonymous analyst and the problem of self disclosure. *Psychoanalytic Quarterly* 64:466–495.

Richmond, M. 1917. *Social Diagnosis.* New York: Russell Sage Foundation.

———. 1922. *What Is Social Casework?* New York: Russell Sage Foundation.

Ringel, S. 2000. Close encounters: Exclusion and marginalization as an intersubjective experience. *Smith College Studies in Social Work* 71:51–60.

———. 2001. A reconceptualization of the working alliance in cross-cultural practice with non-Western clients: Integrating relational perspectives and multicultural theories. *Clinical Social Work Journal* 29:53–63.

———. 2002. To disclose or not to disclose: Political conflicts in the countertransference. *Smith College Studies in Social Work* 72:347–358.

———. 2005. Therapeutic dilemmas in cross-cultural practice with Asian American adolescents. *Child and Adolescent Social Work Journal* 29:53–63.

———. 2007.Using the classroom to examine unconscious communication between student and client: A supervisory perspective. *Clinical Supervisor* 26, 1/2:49–59.

Ringel, S., and F. Mishna. 2007. Beyond avoidance and secrecy: Using students' practice to teach ethics. *Journal of Teaching in Social Work* 27, 1/2:251–270.

Ringstrom, P. 1995. Exploring the model scene: Finding the focus in an intersubjective approach to brief psychotherapy. *Psychoanalytic Inquiry* 15:493–513.

Robinson, V. 1930. *A Changing Psychology in Social Casework.* Chapel Hill: University of North Carolina Press.

Roland, A. 1998. *Cultural Pluralism and Psychoanalysis.* New York: Routledge.

Safran, J. 2002. Brief relational psychoanalytic treatment. *Psychoanalytic Dialogues* 12, 2:171–195.

Safran, J., J. Muran, L. Wallner Samstag, and A. Winston. 2005. Evaluating alliance-focused intervention for potential treatment failures: A feasibility study and descriptive analysis. *Psychotherapy: Theory, Research, Practice, Training* 42, 4:512–531.

St. Clair, M. 1996. *Object Relations and Self Psychology: An Introduction,* 2nd ed. New York: Brooks/Cole.

Sander, L. 1977. The regulation of exchange in the infant-caretaker system and some aspects of the context content relationship. In M. Lewis and L. Rosenblum, eds., *Interaction, Conversation and the Development of Language,* pp. 133–156. New York: Wiley.

Sandler, J. 1976. Countertransference and role responsiveness. *International Review of Psychoanalysis* 3:43–47.

Sarnat, J. 1992. Supervision in relationship: Resolving the teach-treat controversy in psychoanalytic supervision. *Psychoanalytic Psychology* 93:387–403.

Schamess, G. 2006a. Transference enactments in clinical supervision. *Clinical Social Work Journal* 34, 1:407–425.

———. 2006b. Therapeutic processes in clinical supervision. *Clinical Social Work Journal* 34, 1:427–455.

Scharff, D., and J. Savege Scharff. 1991. *Object relations couple therapy.* Northvale, N.J.: Jason Aronson.

Schore, A. 2003. Early relational trauma, disorganized attachment, and the development of a predisposition to violence. In M. Solomon and D. Siegel eds., *Healing Trauma: Attachment, Mind, Body, and Brain*, pp. 107–167. New York: Norton.

Schore, J., and A. Schore. 2008. Modern attachment theory: The central role of affect regulation in development and treatment. *Clinical Social Work Journal* 36:9–20.

Schulte, P. 2000. Holding in mind: Intersubjectivity, subject relations and the group. *Group Analysis* 33, 4:531–544.

Schwartzman, G. 1984. Narcissistic transferences: Implications for the treatment of couples. *Dynamic Psychotherapy* 2:5–14.

Seinfeld, J. 1996. *Containing Rage, Terror, and Despair: An Object Relations Approach to Psychotherapy.* Northvale, N.J.: Jason Aronson.

Sharpe, S. 2000. *The Ways We Love: A Developmental Approach to Treating Couples* New York: Guilford Press.

Sheppard, D. 2001. Clinical Social Work 1880–1940 and American Relational Psychoanalysis: An Historical-Integrative Analysis of Relational Concepts in Practice. Ph.D. Dissertation, New York University School of Social Work.

Shilbert, C. T. 2005. Some clinical applications of attachment theory in adult psychotherapy. *Clinical Social Work Journal* 33:55–68.

Siegel, D. 2008. *The Neurobiology of "We": How Relationships, the Mind, and the Brain Interact to Shape Who We Are.* Sounds True Audio Learning Course.

Siegel, J. 1997. Countertransference as a focus of consultation. In M. Solomon and J. Siegel, eds., *Countertransference in Couples Therapy*, pp. 272–282. New York: Norton.

Sifneos, P. 1992. *Short-term Anxiety-provoking Psychotherapy.* New York: Basic Books.

Simpson, C. A., J. C. Williams, and A. B. Segall. 2007. Social work education and clinical learning. *Clinical Social Work Journal* 35:3–14.

Slochower, J. 2005. Holding: Something old and something new. In L. Aron and A. Harris, eds., *Relational Psychoanalysis*, 2:29–50. Hillsdale, N.J.: Analytic Press.

Smitherman, G. 1977. *Talkin and Testifyin: The Language of Black America.* Boston: Houghton Mifflin.

Spitz, R. 1945. Hospitalism: An inquiry into the genesis of psychiatric conditions in early childhood. *Psychoanalytic Study of the Child* 1:53–73.

———. 1959. *A Genetic Field Theory of Ego Formation: Its Implications for Pathology.* New York: International Universities Press.

Sroufe, A., B. Egeland, and T. Kreutzer. 1990. The fate of early experience following developmental change: Longitudinal approaches to understanding adaptation in childhood. *Child Development* 61:1363–1373.

Stamm, I. 1959. Ego psychology in the emerging theoretical base of social work. In A. J. Kahn, ed., *Issues in American Social Work*, pp. 80–109. New York: Columbia University Press.

Stern, D. 1985. *The Interpersonal World of the Infant.* New York: Basic Books.

——. 1989. The representation of relational patterns: Developmental considerations. In A. J. Sameroff and R. N. Emde, eds.. *Relationship Disturbances in Early Childhood*, pp. 52–69. New York: Basic Books.

Stern, D., B. Beebe, J. Jaffee, and S. Bennett. 1975. Vocalizing in unison and alternation: Two modes of communication within the mother-infant dyad. *Annals of the New York Academy of Science* 263:89–100.

——. 1997. The infant's stimulus world during social interaction: A study of caregiver with particular reference to repetition and timing. In H. R. Schaffer, ed., *Studies in Mother–Infant Interaction.* London: Academic Press.

Stern, D., L. Sander, J. Nahum, A. Harrison, K. Lyons-Ruth, A. Morgan, N. Bruschweiler-Stern, and E. Tronick. 1998. Non-interpretive mechanisms in psychoanalytic therapy. The something more than interpretation The Boston Change Process Study Group, Report # 1. *International Journal of Psychoanalysis* 79:903–921.

Stimmel, B. 1995. Resistance to awareness of the supervisor's transferences with special reference to the parallel process. *International Journal of Psychoanalysis* 76:609–618.

Stolorow, R. D., and G. Atwood. 1992. *Contexts of Being: The Intersubjective Foundations of Psychological Life.* Hillsdale, N.J.: Analytic Press.

Stolorow, R. D., B. Brandchaft, and G. Atwood. 1994. *The Intersubjective Perspective.* Northvale, N.J.: Jason Aronson.

Strupp, H., and J. Binder. 1984. *Psychotherapy in a New Key: A Guide to Time-Limited Dynamic Psychotherapy.* New York: Basic Books.

Suchet, M. 2004. A relational encounter with race. *Psychoanalytic Dialogues* 14:423–438.

Sullivan, H. S. 1953. *The Interpersonal Theory of Psychiatry.* New York: Norton.

——. 1954. *The Psychiatric Interview.* New York: Norton.

Surrey, J. 1991. What do you mean by mutuality in therapy? In J. B. Miller, J. V. Jordan, A. G. Kaplan, I. P. Stiver, and J. L. Surrey, eds., *Some Misconceptions and Reconceptions of a Relational Approach.* Work in Progress, No. 85. Wellesley, Mass.: Stone Center Working Paper Series.

Tacon, A., and Y. Cladera. 2001. Attachment and parental correlates in late adolescent Mexican American women. *Hispanic Journal of Behavioral Sciences* 23, 10:71–78.

Taft, J. J. 1933. *The Dynamics of Therapy in a Controlled Relationship.* New York: Macmillan.

Tansey, M., and W. Burke, W. 1989. *Understanding Countertransference.* Hillsdale, N.J.: Analytic Press.

Tantillo, M. 2000. Short-term relational group therapy for women with bulimia nervosa. *Eating Disorders* 8:99–121.

Tatum, B. 1997. Racial identity development and relational theory: The case of black women in white communities. In J. Jordan, ed., *Women's Growth in Diversity: More Writings from the Stone Center*, pp. 91–106. New York: Guilford Press.

Thyer, B. A. 1994. Are theories for practice necessary? No! *Journal of Social Work Education* 30:144–152.

———. 2001. Research on social work practice does not benefit from blurry theory: A response to Tomi Gomory. *Journal of Social Work Education* 37:9–78.

Tolpin, M. 2002. Doing psychoanalysis of normal development: Forward edge transferences. In A. Boldberg, ed., *Postmodern Self Psychology: Progress in Self Psychology*, 18:167–192. Hillsdale, N.J.: Analytic Press.

Tosone, C. 1997. Countertransference and clinical social work supervision: Contributions and considerations. *The Clinical Supervisor* 16, 2:17–32.

Towle, C. 1936. Factors in treatment. In H. H. Perlman, ed., *Helping: Charlotte Towle on Social Work and Social Casework*, pp. 46–58. Chicago: University of Chicago Press, 1969.

———. 1940. Some uses of relationship. In H. H. Perlman, ed., *Helping: Charlotte Towle on Social Work and Social Casework*, pp. 66–72. Chicago: University of Chicago Press, 1969.

———. 1948. *The Emotional Element in Learning in Education for Social Work*. New York: Council on Social Work Education.

Trevarthen, C. 1989. Development of early social interactions and the affective regulation of brain growth. In C. von Euler, J. Frossberg, and H. Lagercrantz, eds., *Neurobiology and Early Infant Behavior*, pp. 191–216. London: Macmillan.

Tronick, E., N. Bruschweiler-Stern, A. Harrison, K. Lyons-Ruth, J. Nahum, L. Sander, and D. Stern. 1998. Dyadically expanded states of consciousness and the process of therapeutic change. *Infant Mental Health Journal* 290–299.

Trop, J. 1997. An intersubjective perspective of countertransference in couples therapy. In M. Solomon and J. Siegel, eds., *Countertransference in Couples Therapy*, pp. 99 109. New York: Norton.

Turner, C. 1997. Psychosocial barriers to black women's career development. In J. Jordan, ed., *Women's Growth in Diversity: More Writings from the Stone Center*, pp. 162–175. New York: Guilford Press.

Turner, F. ed.. 1996. *Social Work Treatment: Interlocking Theoretical Approaches*, 4th ed. New York: Free Press.

Turner, F., and R. M. Jaco. 1996. Problem-solving theory and social work practice. In F. Turner, ed., *Social Work Treatment: Interlocking Theoretical Approaches*, pp. 503–522. New York: Free Press.

Van Ijzendoorn, M., and M. Bakermans-Kraneneberg. 1996. Attachment representations in mothers, fathers, adolescents, and clinical groups: A meta-analytic search for normative data. *Journal of Consulting and Clinical Psychology* 64, 1:8–21.

Wachtel, P. 2008. *Relational Theory and the Practice of Psychotherapy*. New York: Guilford Press.

Walker, M., and W. Rosen, eds., 2004. *How Connections Heal: Stories from Relational-Cultural Therapy*. New York: Guilford Press.

Wallin, D. 2007. *Attachment in Psychotherapy*. New York: Guilford Press.

Walls, C. 2004. Me, them, us: Developing mutuality in a couple's therapy. In M. Walker and W. Rosen, eds., *How Connections Heal: Stories from Relational-Cultural Therapy*, pp. 107–127. New York: Guilford Press.

Walsh, F. 2003. *Normal Family Processes: Growing Diversity and Complexity*. New York: Guilford Press.

Wells, M., and C. Glickauf-Hughes. 1986. Techniques to develop object constancy with borderline clients. *Psychotherapy* 23:460–468.

Whiston, S. C., and T. L. Sexton. 1993. An overview of psychotherapy outcome research: Implications for practice. *Psychotherapy Theory, Research, and Practice* 24:43–51.

Windholtz, M., and G. Silberschatz. 1988. Vanderbilt psychotherapy process scale: A replication with adult out-patients. *Journal of Consulting Clinical Psychology* 56:56–60.

Winnicott, D.W. 1965. *The Maturational Processes and the Facilitating Environment*. Madison, Conn.: International Universities Press.

——. 1971. The use of an object and relating through identifications. In *Playing and Reality*. Harmondsworth, U.K.: Penguin Books.

——. 1975. *From Peaediatrics to Psychoanalysis*. New York: Basic Books.

Wolf, E. S. 1988. *Treating the Self*. New York: Guilford Press.

Woods, M., and F. Hollis. 1990. *Casework: A Psychosocial Therapy*, 4th ed. New York: McGraw Hill.

Yelaja, S. A. 1986. Functional theory for social work practice. In F. H. Turner, ed., *Social Work Treatment: Interlocking Principles*, 3rd ed., pp. 46–67. New York: Free Press.

Zerbe Enns, C. 2004. *Feminist Theories and Feminist Psychotherapies*. New York: Haworth Press.

INDEX

abandonment anxieties, 20, 73
abuse, xii, 13, 21, 73; mirroring interac
   tions and, 67–68; from parents, 183;
   therapeutic case study of survivor, 104;
   verbal and psychological, 49. *See also*
   sexual abuse
acculturation, 11
Ackerman, D., 76
Adams, A., 185
adaptation, 11, 21, 22
Addams, Jane, 2
adolescence/adolescents, 64, 188, 190–91
Adult Attachment Interview, 23–24, 63
adult development, xii, 15, 23–24, 29
affect regulation, 64–66, 102–3, 111, 158, 161
African Americans, 11, 44, 148, 159, 160–61;
   client's subjectivity, 151–52; mixed-race
   couple in therapy, 183–86; teaching of
   relational theory and, 195; therapists
   and clients, 150; white therapist and,
   153–54, 155, 157–58
agency, 47, 56, 64, 195
aggression, 25, 29, 74, 176, 178; affect
   regulation and, 64; bad affective experiences and, 30; borderline personalities
   and, 31; identification with aggressor,

73; paranoid/schizoid position and, 70;
   self psychology view of, 33
Ainsworth, Mary, 23–24, 63
alcohol abuse, 87, 96, 99; clinicians' efforts
   to curb, 117; domestic violence and, 101;
   by parents, 89, 100, 102, 184. *See also*
   substance abuse
Alcoholics Anonymous, 99, 100
Alexander, Franz, 9, 22
alone, capacity to be, 61
alter-ego. *See* twinship (alter-ego)
Altman, N., 150, 152, 155
ambivalent attachment, 23, 63
American Object Relations School. *See*
   object relations theories
American Psychoanalytic Association, 32
anger, 50, 89, 92, 140, 171; in abused wom-
   en, 77; affect regulation and, 74; disruption in treatment and, 137; ethical issues
   in treatment and, 44, 47; in families,
   178, 185–86, family therapy and, 185–86;
   management of, 125, 126; multicultural
   issues and, 153, 157, 159, 160; as parental
   affect, 65, 73; passive-aggressive, 182;
   projective identification and, 59, 142; as
   protection, 133–36; rules

anger (*continued*)
  of treatment and, 117; termination of
  treatment and, 176
annihilation anxieties, 20
anti-libidinal ego/object, 22, 71
anxiety, 26, 69, 77, 165; about aging parents,
  112–15, 120–21; brief relational therapy
  and, 170; in drive theory, 166; holding
  environment and, 109; self-regulatory
  mechanisms and, 74; supervisory process and, 203; traumatic past as source
  of, 80–82
Aron, Lewis, xiii, 37, 43, 46; on children's
  study of parental personalities, 62; on
  drawbacks of therapist self-disclosure,
  147; on therapist self-disclosure, 124
arousal, emotional, 64, 74, 102
Asians, 11, 159
assessment process, xvii, 10, 79; affect
  regulation and mentalization, 102–3;
  countertransference as tool of, 90–93;
  data from clinician–client interaction,
  85–90; data sources, 79–80; focus of,
  93–99; gender/culture/sexual orientation as factors, 105; significance of early
  events, 104
Association for the Advancement of Psychoanalysis in Clinical Social Work,
  xvi
asymmetry, 38
attachment, 13, 20; brain development and,
  191; disorganized, 72–73; internalized
  patterns of, 59–60; metacognition and,
  66; patterns of, 62–63; in supervisory
  process, 202
Attachment-Affiliation Motivational
  System, 56
attachment theory, 14, 23, 36, 38, 167, 207
Atwood, George, xiii, 37
Austin, Lucille, 8, 9
authenticity, 11–13, 38, 39, 40, 191
autism, 29
autonomy (independence), 35, 36, 55;
  balance with intimacy, 60; as ideal of
  Western society, 76, 149; of infants, 56;
  termination of therapy and, 176
Aversive Motivational System, 56
avoidant attachment, 23, 63, 99

bad object, 22, 70–71, 72, 74, 106
Bandler, Louise, 8
Barber, J., 53
Basham, K., 22, 24, 29
Baudry, F., 201
Beck, A. T., 168
Beebe, Beatrice, 38, 47, 48
Benjamin, J., 42, 52, 62, 75
Bennett, C. S., 202
Bergman, S., 182
Berzoff, J., xiii
Beth Israel Medical Center (Boston), 165,
  179
Bibring, Grete, 8
Billow, R., 188–89
Binder, Jeffrey, 166–67, 168
biofeedback, 16
Bion, A., 161
birth trauma, 5
Black, M., 21, 27, 29
"Black Women, Identity and Schooling:
  Reclaiming Our Work in Shifting Con-
  texts" (Cozart and Price), 195
"blaming the victim," 11
Blanck, Gertrude and Rubin, 14
borderline disorders, 14, 30, 31
boundaries, therapeutic, xvii, 43, 44, 107,
  129–30, 186
Bowlby, John, xiii, 14, 23–24; on children
  and separation/loss, 72; on internal
  working models, 59–60
brain imaging studies, 65
Brandchaft, Bernard, xiii, 37
brief adaptive psychotherapy, 168
Brief Relational Therapy, 53
brief relational therapy, 165, 168–79
British Object Relations School. *See* object
  relations theories
Bromberg, P.M., 204
Bryant, S., 194
Budman, Simon, 167–68
bulimia nervosa, 191
Burke, W., 45

California Psychotherapy Alliance Scale
  (CALPAS), 53
Cannon, Ida, 2
caregivers: abusive/neglectful, 74; disorga-

nized attachment and, 72; empathic environment and, 32, 33; holding environment and, 20; idealization of, 33; reciprocal interactions with infants, 47, 48

caretaking environment, xi, 23, 54, 55, 57, 99–102

case studies, therapeutic: affect regulation, 102–3; clinician–client interaction and, 85–90; clinicians' feelings used in, 90–93; couple therapy, 182–86; disruption of transference, 139–41; empathic attunement, 112–16; enactments, 50–51, 144–46; family therapy, 186–87; group therapy, 189–91; multicultural diversity, 151–62; religious differences, 125–26; resistance to selfobject transference, 133–36; self-disclosure of therapist, 46–47, 120–24; sexual addiction, 117–19; short-term treatments, 170–79; therapeutic action, 158–62; third space, 52–53, 157–58; transitional experiences, 109–11, transparency of therapist, 41–42; understanding and coconstructing client's story, 80–85

Casework: A Psychosocial Therapy (Hollis), 10

Caucasians, 148

causality, multiple, 7

central ego, 71

change process, 36, 192

charity work, 2

children/child development, xii, 15, 29; abused children, 21–22; attachment theory and, 23; children as clients, 204; coherent sense of self, 32; mutual recognition and, 191; object relations theories on, 24–25; phases of, 30; self-psychology and, 33; splits in endopsychic structure, 71. See also infants; mother–infant relationship

Chodorow, N., 14, 34

civil rights movement, 10

Clark, T., 194

class, social, 10, 157, 183

clients: agency/choice exercised by, 6, 47; clinicians' self-disclosure and, 120; cultural background, 2; empowerment of, 11; free association of, 43; frustration with termination of therapy, 176; pathologizing of, 39; posttherapy symptoms, 53; problem-solving capacities, 9; reactions to disruptions, 137; subjectivity of, xii, 107, 111, 149, 150–52, 163; transference and, 131; understanding and coconstructing stories of, 80–85

clinician–client interaction, xiv, xvii, 2, 37, 77; assessment process and, 85–90; in brief relational therapy, 170–73; clinician self-disclosure and, 15; collaborative process, 11, 107–8; ego psychology and, 8; e-mail correspondence, 109, 110–11; enactments in, 144; in interpersonal theory, 28; mutual influence of subjectivities, 38–39, 47–49, 124–26; mutuality and asymmetry in, 42–45; in object relations theories, 22, 25–26, 29, 31; psychoanalytic theory and, 3, 4; in self-in-relations theory, 36; in self-psychology, 14, 33, 34; in short-term treatments, 165; supportive and corrective potential, 7–9; therapeutic space, 154–56, 161; transference aspects, 3

clinicians/therapists: assessment process and, xvii; authority of, 107; boundary and ethical issues, 129–30; countertransference as assessment tool, 90–93; in couple therapy, 182–83; disruptions in treatment and, 137–38; empathic attunement employed by, 111–16; narcissistic needs of, 147; as "neutral facilitators," 189; participation in therapeutic interaction, 38–39; professional code of ethics, 44; responsiveness of, 126–27, 130; subjectivity and authenticity of, 70–17, 106. See also self-disclosure, therapists'; social workers

Cockerill, Eleanor, 8

cognitive/behavioral approach, xvi, 1, 16, 168, 169

collaboration, xvii, 11, 15, 80, 107–8

communication, verbal and nonverbal, 43, 48, 52, 64, 149; English-language skill level, 156; memory and, 65; mentalization and, 67

community, 149

concern, capacity for, 61
confidentiality, 10
conflict, 25, 185, 198
constructivism, postmodern, xiv
contact-shunning, 69
containment, 47, 161–62
contingency, 48
corrective experience, 47
countertransference, xii, xvii–xviii, 3, 41,
    107; as assessment tool, 90–93; clients'
    contributions to, 106; complementary
    and concordant, 152; in couple therapy,
    181, 182; enactments and, 141–42, 143; in
    interpersonal theory, 28; multicultural
    diversity and, 150, 151, 154; objective,
    142; in object relations theories, 25, 32;
    projective identification and, 40; self-
    disclosure of therapist and, 120; self-in-
    relations theory and, 36; self-psychology
    view of, 34; in supervisory process, 203;
    teaching of relational theory and, 199;
    therapist's self-disclosure and, 45–46,
    146–47; in traditional psychoanalytic
    theory, 131
couples, xii, xviii, 181–82, 192; power shar-
    ing with clinician, 180; short-term treat-
    ments for, 167; termination of therapy,
    177–79; therapeutic case studies, 182–86
Cozart, S., 195
creativity, 33, 34, 51, 66, 132
crisis approach, 1
culture, xiv, xvii, 125; assessment process
    and, 105; cultural diversity, 54, 76; cul-
    tural subjectivities, xviii; "ethnic third"
    and, 157; in object relations theories, 28;
    psychoanalytic theory and, 149; psycho-
    logical development and, 35; reflective
    functioning and, 160; therapeutic space
    and, 148. See also multicultural diversity
cutting/self-mutilation, 65, 102, 103, 117, 162

Davanloo, Habib, 165–66
Davies, J., 50
day treatment, 108
defense mechanisms, 21, 39; Aversive Moti-
    vational System and, 56; "false self," 68;
    impulse-defense-anxiety triangle, 166;
    projective identification, 59

depression, 72, 77, 94, 121; depressive posi-
    tion, 70; diagnosis of, 49; short-term
    treatments, 165, 170
detachment, 12
developmental theory, xvii
Dewey, John, 5, 9
DeYoung, P., 19, 181, 182
diagnostic (psychosocial) model, 3, 5–7, 9,
    10–11
Dimen, M., 75
disability, persons with, xii, 35, 41, 76, 195
disorganized attachment, 72–73
disruptions, management of, 107
dissociation, 73, 74, 203
domestic violence, 77, 101, 129
drive-structural model, 18, 19, 30
drive theory, 28, 30, 32; resistance in formu-
    lation of, 39; shift away from, 207; short-
    term treatments and, 166; therapist's
    self-disclosure and, 45; Western cultural
    notions and, 148–49
drug abuse, 89, 103, 117, 173, 174

eating disorders, 65, 74, 191
economic conditions, 16, 164
Edwards, J., 194
ego: of abused children, 22; ego ideal, 154;
    ego-relatedness, 60–61; endopsychic
    structure, 71; Fairbairn's view of, 21, 22;
    functioning, 10; libidinal and anti-libidi-
    nal, 71; mastery of, 9; paranoid/schizoid
    position and, 70; schizoid state and, 72
ego psychology, xiii, 14; American Object
    Relations School and, 28; on disrup-
    tions in transference, 136; Freudian
    theory and, 7; resistance in formulation
    of, 39; on structure of adult mind, 21;
    Time Limited Psychotherapy (TLP)
    and, 165; Western cultural notions and,
    148–49
Ehrenberg, D. B., 45–46, 124
elderly people, 67
empathic attunement, xvii, 14, 77, 106, 107;
    case studies in use of, 111–16; child's
    empathy for caretaker, 62; core nuclear
    self and, 55
empathy, 13, 36, 62, 102; anticipatory, 12;
    in couple therapy, 181; failures of, 33,

57; in group therapy, 188, 190; holding environment and, 108; limits on problematic behavior and, 116–19; mirroring interactions and, 66; mutual, 62; self-development and, 32

empowerment approaches, 11

enactments, xvii, 49–51, 53; management of, 107; multicultural diversity and, 155, 156–57; recognizing and managing, 142–47; repetitive transference and, 141–42; in short-term treatments, 170; in supervisory process, 203, 204

endopsychic structure, 22, 71

engagement process, 9, 10

essentialist theory, 75

ethical issues, 107, 129–30

ethnicity, 10, 125; "ethnic third," 157; psychoanalytic theory and, 149; reflective functioning and, 160; socially constructed perception of, 151; therapeutic space and, 148. See also multicultural diversity

evidence-based practice, 16

exciting object, 71

existential theory, 167

experiences: disavowed, 15; drive theory and, 30–31; incorporation of, 12; problematic parenting and, 13

Exploratory-Assertive Motivational System, 56

eye contact, 64

eye movement desensitization, 16

facial expressions, 45, 64, 65, 67–68

Fairbairn, W.R.D., xiii, 19, 21–23, 73; on internalization of bad objects, 70–71; on schizoid state, 72

families, xi, xviii, 1, 181–82, 192; conflict as relational event in, 185–86; "hard-to-reach," 9; nuclear family structure, 149; power sharing with clinician, 180; self in non-Western societies and, 67; short-term treatments for, 167; socioeconomic conditions and, 2; therapeutic case study, 186–87

fantasy: childhood sexual abuse and, 27; of infants in depressive position, 70; object relations theory and, 20; pathological developments, 68, 69; pretend play and,

66; projective identification and, 40; in self- and object representations, 58; supervisory process and, 203; transitional space and, 51

father: abusive behavior by, 104; anger of, 186–87; distant relationship with, 87; dominant and controlling, 115, 116; gender development and, 75; hypercritical, 144, 145

fear, 69, 82, 83, 114, 151, 190; attachment trauma and, 73; countertransference and, 154; defense formation and, 56; disorganized attachment and, 72–73, 74; of intrusion, 77; of isolation, 27; as parental affect, 65; psychic equivalence and, 66; schizoid position and, 70, 72; traumatic past and, 128, 187; of vulnerability, 185, 186, 191

Fedele, N., 188

feminism/feminist theories, xiv, 10, 36, 37; essentialist and social constructionist, 75; multicultural diversity and, 161, 162; teaching strategies and, 194, 195, 200

Ferenczi, Sandor, xiii, xvii, 43; on childhood trauma, 191; on "mutual analysis," 42; origins of brief psychotherapy and, 164; on sexual abuse of children, 27

fight-or-flight response, 76

Flanagan, L. M., xiii

Fonagy, Peter, xiii, 66, 67, 74, 173

Fosshage, James, 37, 56

fragmented self, 69

Frankel, Victor, 154

Frawley, M. G., 50

Frawley-O'Dea, Gail, 200, 201, 202, 203, 204

French, M., 22

French, Thomas M., 9

Freud, Anna, 21

Freud, Sigmund, xiii, 3, 23, 42, 131; British Object Relations School and, 20; on childhood sexuality, 27; on countertransference, 132; drive-structural model, 19, 30, 31; instinctual emphasis, 28; on narcissism, 33; oedipal model of gender development, 75; on personality development, 5

Freudian theory, xiii, 18, 30

Fromm, Erich, 27

Fromm-Reichmann, Frieda, 26, 27
functional model, 5–7

Gagerman, J., 191
Ganzer, C., 200, 204
Garrett, Annette, 8
gay and lesbian liberation movements, 10
gay men, 11, 76, 194; multicultural factors
    in treatment and, 152, 154, 159; stereo-
    types about, 115–16; therapeutic case
    studies with, 88–90, 99–100, 160–61
gender, xii, xvii, 10, 54, 78; assessment
    process and, 105; developmental
    process of, 75–76; multicultural factors
    and, 156–57; postmodern constructiv-
    ist ideas about, xiv; self-disclosure of
    clinician/therapist and, 125, 183; socially
    constructed perception of, 151. See also
    multicultural diversity; transgender
    people
genuineness, xvii, 77, 107, 119, 129; holding
    environment and, 108; self-disclosure
    and, 14
Germain, C. B., 11–12, 13
Gestalt psychology, 7
Gilligan, Carol, 34
Gitterman, A., 11–12, 13
Goldner, V., 75
Goldstein, Eda, 29, 46
Great Depression, 6
Greenberg, J., 18–19
Greenson, Ralph, 21
grief, 23, 72, 74, 89, 113, 188
Grossmark, R., 178
group therapy, xi, xviii, 1, 187–89, 192;
    disruption in transference, 139–40;
    therapeutic case studies, 189–91
growth process, 5, 6
guilt, racial, 150, 155
guilt, survivor, 187
Guntrip, Harry S., xiii, 14
Gurman, Alan, 167–68

Hamilton, Gordon, 2, 7–8
Harris, A., 43, 75, 152
health care system, 16
Helping Alliance Questionnaire (HAQ), 53
helping process, xiv, xviii, 2, 8

"here-and-now" interactions, xii, 143,
    169, 176; group therapy and, 188, 191;
    interpersonal theory and, 28; problem-
    solving model and, 9; transferences
    and, 131, 132
Hertz, P., xiii
Hoffman, Irwin, xiii, 40, 124
holding environment, xvii, 14, 20, 25, 47, 107;
    establishment of, 108–11; maternal, 61;
    multicultural diversity and, 158, 161–62;
    transitional experience and, 109–11
Hollis, Florence, 8, 9–10
Holmes, D., 150, 151
homophobia, 116
Horney, Karen, xiii
Horowitz, J., xiv, 22–23, 205
How Connections Heal: Stories from Rela-
    tional-Cultural Therapy (Walker and
    Rosen, eds.), 34, 35
human potential theory, 167

ideal-hungry pathology, 69
idealization, 14, 33, 130; in clinician–client
    interaction, 41; disruption in treatment
    and, 147; multicultural factors and, 157;
    pathological, 68; as selfobject need, 55;
    selfobject transference and, 132
idealized object, 71
identification, 12, 58; with aggressor, 73;
    complementary, 142, 145; gender differ-
    ence and, 75; multicultural factors and,
    149, 157
identity, 27, 105; formation of, 11; multicul-
    tural diversity and, 152, 162; multiple
    selves in, 153, 162, 169, 197; oppression
    and identity diffusion, 76; teaching/
    learning process and, 196; transgender,
    177, 178
illness, physical, xii
immigrants, nineteenth-century, 2
impasses/disruptions, xvii, 136–41, 155,
    156–57
independence. See autonomy (indepen-
    dence)
individuality, 33, 149
individualization, 13
individuation, 13, 29–30
infants: caretaking environment and, 54;

developmental stages, 55–56; environmental transactions of, xi; motivational systems and, 56–57; pleasure and unpleasure experiences, 28; rage and destructiveness of, 42; reciprocal interactions with caregivers, 47, 48; relatedness and, 12, 20; self- and object representations by, 57–58; self–other relationship and, 54–55; unregulated stress in, 73. *See also* children/child development; mother–infant relationship
infant studies, xvii, 38
interactive repair, 74
internalization, 57, 58, 64, 70–71, 127, 149
internal object relations, 20, 22, 23, 25
interpersonal-developmental existential (I-D-E) domain, 167
Interpersonal School, 19, 26–27, 28, 36
interpersonal theory, 19, 28, 37
interpretation, xvii, 38; of client's free association, 43; of client's resistance, 39; dialogue and, 77; differential use of, 127–29; "experience distant," 175; resistance to transference and, 136
intersubjectivity, xvii, 15, 36, 37; affect regulation and, 64; in couple therapy, 181; in group therapy, 188; intersubjective field, 62; preverbal, 48; self-psychology and, 32. *See also* two-person (intersubjective) psychologies
introjection, 58, 59, 129, 167
intrusion, 77, 108
isolation, 17, 27, 72

Jacobson, Edith, xiii, 21, 28, 30, 59
Jews, 150, 151, 153, 154, 156, 162
Jones, Ernest, 29
Jordan, Judith, 34

Kaplan, Alexandra, 34
Kernberg, Otto, 21, 28, 30–31
Klein, Melanie, xiii, 20–21, 30; on paranoid/schizoid and depressive positions, 70; on projective identification, 31, 40
Kohut, Heinz, xiii, 14, 32–33, 61; on self-disorders, 68, 69; on selfobject transferences, 132, 133; on types of selfobject needs, 55

Lachmann, Frank, 38, 48, 56
Latinos, 11, 148
Leary, K., 150
lesbians, 11, 35, 76, 157–58, 194
Lesser, R., 201
Levenson, Hanna, 167
libidinal drive, 30
libidinal ego, 71
libidinal energy, 20, 21
libidinal object, 22
Lichtenberg, Joseph, xvii, 38, 56
Lide, P., 12
life cycle, 33, 207
life model, 12–13
life situation/experiences, xii, 11, 94, 105
loss, xii, 76, 94, 104; disruption of treatment and, 137; fear of, 68, 73; I-D-E domain and, 167; impact on children, 72–73; multiple losses, 11; September 11 terrorism and, 113; termination of treatment and, 177–79
love object, primary, 29

macrosystems practice, 10, 11
Mahler, Margaret, 21, 28, 29, 30, 35, 55
Main, Mary, 23–24, 63, 65, 72
Malan, David, 165–66
managed care, xvi, 16, 27, 80, 206
Mann, James, 165
Maroda, K., 124, 146
masculinity, 115, 144, 185
Masterson, James, 14
Mattei, L., 52
maturity, 36, 42
McLaughlin, J., 39
Mead, Herbert, 5
meaning, construction of, 42
Meltzoff, A., 48
memory research, 65
men: brain and gender difference, 75–76; needs for connection, 35
Menninger Clinic, 30
mental health, 2, 16, 24, 206; group therapy and, 188; insurance companies and, 27; psychotherapy for mentally ill patients, 27; relationships and, 35; short-term treatments and, 165
mentalization, 66–68, 74, 102–3, 176;

mentalization (*continued*)
   multicultural diversity and, 158, 159–60;
   objective reality and, 66–67; in short-
   term treatments, 173
mentors, 61, 65
merger experiences, 55, 56, 69
Messer, S., 165–66
metacognition, 66
microsystems practice, 11
Miehls, Dennis, 22, 24, 29, 181, 196
Mikulincer, M., 65
Miller, Jean Baker, xiii, 34
Miller, L., 201
mirroring, 14, 33, 74; in clinician–client
   interaction, 40; disruptions in treatment
   and, 147; mirror-hungry pathology, 69;
   neurons of frontal cortex and, 65–66,
   67; as selfobject need, 55; selfobject
   transference and, 132
Mishna, F., 194, 196–97
Mitchell, Stephen, xiii, xvii, 18–19, 29, 37;
   on Kleinians, 21; on relational matrix,
   54; on Thompson, 27
Modell, A. H., 43
mother–infant relationship, 20, 29; affect
   regulation and, 64; attachment patterns,
   62–63; ego-relatedness, 60–61; internalized object relations and, 59; patterns
   of interaction, 52; in pregnancy, 24;
   uniqueness of dyads, 28
mother/mothering, 24, 29; abusive, 109–10;
   child's separateness from, 58; emotionally unavailable, 134; gender development and, 75; good-enough, 55, 60–61;
   as good object, 70; ideal object and, 22;
   infant's rage and, 42, 70; maternal holding environment, 61, 108; separation
   from, 55; subjectivity of, 61–62
motivational patterns/systems, 56–57, 97–98
mourning process, 72
multicultural diversity, xvii, 148, 162–63;
   new and old perspectives on, 148–49;
   subjectivities of client and clinician,
   150–54; therapeutic action and, 158–62,
   163; therapeutic space and, 154–56, 161;
   transitional (third) space and, 157–58.
   See also culture
Muran, J. Christopher, 165, 168, 169, 179

Muslims, 161–62
mutuality, xii, 15, 36, 39, 54, 206; early social work and, 2; life model and, 11–13;
   multicultural diversity and, 162; mutual
   recognition, 42; mutual regulation,
   47–49; therapeutic space and, 154–56;
   therapist's self-disclosure and, 45

narcissism, 30, 33, 34, 139, 181
natural disasters, 76, 114
neglect, 13, 50, 67, 73
neurobiology, xviii, 36, 65–66, 77, 207
neuroscience, xvii, 67, 73, 75–76
New York Psychoanalytic Institute, 27
New York School of Social Work, 3

object experiences, 14, 31–32, 109–11
objectivity, 8, 12, 45
Object Relations in Psychoanalytic Theory
   (Greenberg and Mitchell), 18
object relations theories, xvii, 14; American,
   19, 28–32, 33, 336; British, 19–26, 33,
   36; ideal object, 22, 29; ideal self, 29;
   multicultural diversity and, 161; real
   object, 29; real self, 29; Western cultural
   notions and, 148–49
object representations, 57–58
objects: ego and, 21; libidinal energy and,
   20
obsessive-compulsive disorder (OCD), 49
Ogden, T., 52
one-person psychologies, xiii, 32, 36, 37,
   180, 207; Kleinian, 40; short-term treatments, 165
oppression, 1, 11, 13, 54, 67–77; assessment
   process and, 105; identification with
   oppressor, 163; self-psychology and,
   33; social worker's empathy and, 12;
   therapist's own links to, 153, 154
Ornstein, E. D., 200, 204
overburdened self, 69
overstimulated self, 69

parallel processes, 201
paranoid/schizoid anxieties, 20, 70
parent–child relationship: aging parents,
   112–15; clinician–client interaction
   compared with, 14, 49–50; empathic

attunement in, 55; internalized attachment patterns in, 60; mentalization
and, 67; mutual recognition in, 42
parenting, xii, 13, 14, 60
part-object experiences, 58
past–present relation, xiii–xiv, xvii
peer relationships, 67, 73
Pennsylvania School of Social Work, 5
Perlman, Helen Harris, 9
personality, 13, 14, 23, 60; of clinician/thera-
pist, 85, 120, 124, 132, 147; endopsychic
structure and, 71; interpersonal relationships and, 26–27; motivational systems
and, 57; parental, 62; reorganization of,
28; shaped by relationships, 19
personality disorders, 165, 168
person-in-situation perspective, xvi, 1, 7,
10, 165
pharmacological treatments, 27
physiological requirements, regulation of,
56
Piaget, Jean, 9
political conditions, 2, 11, 16
Post-Traumatic Stress Disorder, 73–74
poverty, xviii, 3, 11, 153, 161, 162
power dynamics, 155, 180, 196
"power-over" negotiating model, 185, 186
pregnancy, 24, 60, 83, 133
prejudices, overcoming, 8
present time, 28, 172–73, 174
pretend play, 66–67, 74
Price, P., 195
problem-solving model, 9, 117, 190
projection, 20, 59, 173
projective identification, 21, 31, 32; countertransference and, 40; as early defense
mechanism, 59; enactments and, 143,
144, 145; objective countertransference
and, 142; supervisory process and, 203
psyche, 20, 26
psychiatry, xv, 26
psychic equivalence, 66, 74
psychoanalytic theory, xi, xiii, xv, 59; on disruptions in transference, 136; feminist,
75; Freudian, 3; humanistic, 27; Interpersonal School and, 26; Kohut and, 32;
multicultural factors and, 149; object
relations theories and, 19, 30; shift to

relational thought and, 18–19; transference and countertransference in, 131
psychodynamic theory, xiii, xv, 1, 12, 206;
multicultural diversity and, 148, 149;
shift to relational thinking, 36; short-
term treatment and, 164; teaching of,
xvi; therapist's detachment/restraint in,
38, 130; treatment outcomes and, 53
psycho-educational approach, 187, 188,
189
The Psychological Birth of the Infant
(Mahler et al.), 29–30
psychology, xv
psychopathology, 4, 13, 57, 74–75, 127;
depressive position, 70; disorganized
attachment, 72–73; dissociation, 74; internalization of bad/persecutory objects,
70–71; paranoid/schizoid position, 70;
schizoid state or problem, 72; separation
and loss, 72; trauma, 73–74; vulnerability in self, 68–69
psychosis/psychotic anxieties, 20, 21, 68
psychosocial model. See diagnostic (psychosocial) model
psychotherapy, 12, 27, 44, 207
Psychotherapy in a New Key: A Guide to
Time-Limited Psychotherapy (Strupp
and Binder), 166

quantitative research paradigm, 17

race, xiii, xiv, 10, 125; "ethnic third" and,
157; mixed-race couple in therapy,
183–86; psychoanalytic theory and, 149;
racial identity development, 35; reflective functioning and, 160; socially constructed perception of, 151; therapeutic
space and, 148. See also multicultural
diversity
Rachman, A., 190
racism, 150, 151, 152, 153, 184
Rank, Otto, xiii, 5, 164
Rasmussen, B., 194, 196–97
Reamer, F. J., 17
reciprocity, 12
reflective functioning, 160
regressed ego, 72
rejecting object, 71

rejection, 50, 51, 63, 69, 83, 94; defense against, 160; disruption in treatment and, 137, 140–41; early experiences with, 105; fear of, 99

relatedness, 12, 20, 22, 60–61, 176

relational-cultural model, 185, 189, 191

relational theory, 106, 205–7; on asymmetrical roles, 43; couples/families/groups and, 180–82, 192; defined, xi–xiv; empirical basis for, 53; evolution of, xvii; multicultural factors and, 148; psychoanalysis and, xiii; shift to, 18–19; synthesis with other theories, xviii; teaching of, 193–204; time (past–present relation) and, xiii–xiv; treatment impasses and, 31

religion, 10, 125–26, 161

Renik, O., 38, 40, 46, 124

repetitive transference, 131, 141–42

reprocessing, 16

resistance, xii, 6, 9; lower-level defenses, 32; nature of, 38, 39; reconceptualizing and overcoming, 133–36; in short-term treatments, 172

resistant attachment, 63

responsibility, individual, 7

reverberation, 12

Reynolds, Bertha, 2

Richmond, Mary, 2–3

Ringel, Shoshanna, 196

Robinson, Virginia, 5, 6

Roland, A., 150, 159

Rosen, Wendy, 34, 35

Safran, Jeremy D., 53, 164, 165, 168, 177, 179; on present moment in brief therapy, 172, 174; principles of brief therapy, 169–70; on termination of therapy, 176

St. Clair, M., 23, 30

Saks, L., 202

Samstag, L. Wallner, 168

Sandler, J., 52, 152

Schames, G., 200, 202–3

schizoid state/problem, 72

schizophrenia, 26, 27, 72

Schore, A., 66, 73

Searles, Harold, 27

secure attachment, 23, 62–63

security, earned, 65

self: core nuclear self, 55, 56; cultural difference and, 76; emergent, 56; "false self," 24–25, 68, 176, 202; infant's developmental stages and, 56; innate sense of, 32, 33; internalization and, 57; multiple selves, 58–59; mutuality as goal, 180; perspectives on, 54–55; subjective, 56; true self, 55, 68; vulnerability in, 68–69

The Self and Object World (Jacobson), 29

self-concept, 13, 34, 96, 105

self-destructive behaviors (self-harm), 65, 74

self-determination, 5, 7, 10

self-disclosure, therapists', 14–15, 36, 38, 45–47, 107; boundary issues concerning, 130; case studies in, 120–24; in couple therapy, 181, 183–86; in group therapy, 181, 188, 189, 190–91; guidelines for, 206; multicultural diversity and, 158–59, 163; negative aspects of, 121–22, 147; as retaliation for client aggression, 178–79; in short-term treatments, 170; teaching of relational theory and, 197, 199–200; types of, 119–20

self-esteem, 11, 13, 34, 77; attachment styles and, 73; blows to, 69; regulation of, 55, 68, 96

self-history, 56

self-in-relations theory, xvii, 19, 34–35, 36

self-integration, 56

selfobject, 14, 33; clinician as, 127; failures of, 68; infant's selfobject needs, 55; selfobject environment, 61; strengthening of self and, 106; transference and, 131, 132, 136; transmuting internalization and, 57

self–other relationship: affect regulation, 64–66; attachment patterns, 62–63; intersubjective field, 62; metacognition and mentalization, 66–68; multicultural factors and, 149; mutuality in, xii, 62; relational matrix, 54

self-psychology, xvii, 14, 19, 32–33, 36, 66; clinician as selfobject, 127; intersubjective theorists and, 37; treatment process in, 34, 40

self-regulation, 64, 102, 103

self-representations, 57–58, 59, 65
Sensual-Sexual Motivational System, 57
separation experiences, 5, 13; "Strange
    Situation" and, 62; tragic impact of, 23;
    young children and, 72, 73
separation-individuation process, 29, 31, 35
settlement workers, 2
sex/sexual impulses, 75, 83, 102; affect regu-
    lation and, 64; excitement/relaxation,
    57; gender differentiated from sex, 134;
    sexual identity, xiii
sexual abuse, xii, 52, 77, 104, 187; enact-
    ments and, 50; "mutual analysis" and,
    42; sexual addiction arising from, 118;
    trauma resulting from, 27
sexual addiction, 65, 74, 117–19
Sexual and Love Addicts Anonymous
    (SLAA), 118, 119
sexual orientation, 10, 13, 105, 125, 151, 152
shame, 69, 82–85, 120, 185; abuse and, 110,
    187; group therapy and, 189; of parents,
    178
Shaver, P., 65
Short Term Anxiety-Provoking Psychothera-
    py (Sifneos), 166
short-term dynamic psychotherapy
    (STDP), 168, 169
short-term treatments, xviii, 1, 27, 164–68
Sifneos, Peter, 165–66
silence, 45
Slochower, J., 124
Smitherman, G., 195
Smith School of Social Work, 3
social constructionist theory, 37, 73
social science theory, 1
"Social Work Education and Clinical
    Learning" (Simpson, Williams, Segall),
    15
social workers, xiv, 10, 205; authenticity of,
    9; couple therapy and, 181; empathy
    of, 12; in Great Depression period, 6;
    group therapy and, 187–88, 189; as role
    models, 8, 10; self-knowledge of, 8;
    subjectivities of, 15. See also clinicians/
    therapists
social work practice, xi, xiv–xv, 1–2, 11, 148;
    assessment, 79; diversity of approaches,
    16; evolution of, 2–3; as humanistic pro-

fession, xiv, 2, 7, 12, 17, 169; psychoana-
    lytic theory and, 3–4; relational thinking
    and, xvii; short-term treatments, 169;
    teaching/learning process and, 193
sociology, 2
Solomon, J., 72
space, third (transitional), 51–53, 61, 157–
    58
spiritual models, 16
Spitz, Renee, xiii, 23, 72
spontaneity, xvii, 106–7, 119, 124, 129
Sroufe, Allan, 73
Stamm, Isabel, 8
stereotypes, of race/culture/gender, 52, 76,
    115–16, 149, 185
Stern, Daniel, 38, 47, 48, 55–56
Stimmel, B., 201
Stiver, Irene, 34
Stolorow, Robert, xiii, 37, 60, 62
Stone Center for Developmental Services
    and Studies, xiii, xvii, 34–35, 185, 191,
    194
"Strange Situation Experiments," 23, 62
stress management, 73, 76
Strupp, Hans, 166–67, 168
subjectivity: of clients, xii, 107, 111, 149,
    150–52, 163; of clinicians/therapists, 38,
    106, 107, 149, 150, 152–53; maternal,
    61–62; therapist's self-disclosure and,
    45
substance abuse, xii, 77, 94, 102, 103;
    disorganized attachment and, 65; as
    self-regulatory mechanism, 74. See also
    alcohol abuse; drug abuse
Suchet, M., 152
Sullivan, Harry Stack, xiii, xvii, 19, 76–77
supervisory process, 200, 204, 207
Surrey, Janet, 34, 182
symbiosis, 29, 55

Taft, Jessie, 5, 6
Tansey, M., 45
Tantillo, M., 191
teach-or-treat dilemma, 202
"tend-and-befriend" response, 76
terrorism, anxiety and, 113
Theory and Practice of Social Casework
    (Hamilton), 7

therapeutic process, xiv, 37; experience and, 5; holding environment, xvii, 14; termination of, 175–79; time as motivating force, 5

Thompson, Clara, 26, 27

Time Limited Dynamic Psychotherapy (Levenson), 167

Time Limited Psychotherapy (TLP), 165, 166, 167

time limits, 5

toddlers, 56, 73

Tolpin, M., 132

torture, victims of, 77, 156

Tosone, C., 203

Towle, Charlotte, 8, 9

transference, xii, xvii, 107; disruptions in, 136–41; eroticized, 123; Freud's view of, 3, 4; in interpersonal theory, 28; multicultural diversity and, 151, 156–57; projective identification and, 31; in psychodynamic theories, 38; repetitive, 131, 141–42; self-in-relations theory and, 36; selfobject, 131, 132, 136; self-psychology view of, 33; in short-term treatments, 166–67, 168; supervisory process and, 201, 202; in traditional psychoanalytic theory, 131

transgender people, 156–57, 159, 177–78

transmuting internalization, 57, 68

trauma, xii, xviii, 11, 13, 73–74; couple therapy with survivors of, 181; need for authentic interaction and, 191; from political and natural disasters, 76–77; right brain development and, 66; self-regulation compromised by, 48; shame dynamics and, 189

treatment process: developmental process and, 77–78; impasses in, 31; interpersonal theory and, 28; object relations theories and, 25–26, 31–32; self-in-relations theory and, 36; in self-psychology, 34

Trevarthen, C., 48

trust, 13, 43, 48, 51, 101, 176

twelve-step programs, 102, 108, 118, 184

twinship (alter-ego), 14, 33, 55, 68–69, 132

Twomey, J., 201

two-person (intersubjective) psychologies, xiii–xiv, 32, 36, 37, 180, 207; short-term treatments, 179; supervisory process and, 200; third space and, 52. *See also* intersubjectivity

unconscious (Freudian concept), 28

understimulated self, 69

uniqueness, 61

visitors, friendly, 2

vocalizations, 65

voice, tone of, 45

Wachtel, P., 180

Walker, Maureen, 34, 35

Warren, C., 165–66

Washington School of Psychiatry, 27

William Alanson White Institute, 27

Winnicott, Donald W., xiii, 14, 24–25, 42, 66; on good-enough mother, 60–61; holding concept, 61, 161; on maternal failure and "false self," 68; on objective countertransference, 142; on sense of self, 55; on transitional space, 51

Winston, A., 168

Wolf, E.S., 69, 132

women, 191, 194; brain and gender difference, 75–76; essentialist views of, 75; "pathologizing" of behavior of, 11; rape and sexual abuse of, 77; self-esteem of, 35; social constructionist views of, 75

Women's Growth in Connection (Stone Center), 34

Women's Growth in Diversity (Stone Center), 34

Working Alliance Inventory (WAI), 53

work issues, xii

Yelaja, S.A., 5